COOKING FOR MEN ONLY

Caroline Kriz

**Illustrations by
Veronica di Rosa**

**101 Productions
San Francisco**

To Daddy, whose loving encouragement and
insatiable appetite prompted this book,
and to Mother, whose marvelous from-scratch
cooking has always been my inspiration.

Published by 101 Productions
834 Mission Street, San Francisco, California 94103.
Distributed to the book trade in the United States
by The Scribner Book Companies, New York.

Library of Congress Cataloging in Publication Data

Kriz, Caroline.
  Cooking for men only.

  Includes index.
  1. Cookery.   I. Title.
TX652.K64 1984   641.5   84-5179
ISBN 0-89286-227-0
ISBN 0-89286-230-0 (pbk.)

CONTENTS

ACKNOWLEDGMENTS

Cookbook authors may not suffer like great novelists, but they do nonetheless suffer. If they are very lucky, they will have friends and supporters who understand their wild cooking schedules, incessant pleas for tasters, midnight-oil typing sessions and generally bizarre behavior while the volume is conceived and incubates. When the book is finally given birth, it is only fair that these kind souls be given their due. And so my special thanks go out to Simone Beck, my beloved Simca, who once advised me to "Be a good teacher, Caroline"; to Chicago photographer Peter Basdeka and his wife Charlotte, for their generous offering of time and talent; to food consultant Judy Vance, a good friend and trusted professional; to Lee Flaherty and Allyn Miller of Flair Communications, for their confidence and patience over the long months; to Lindsey and T. J. Kesman, who quite remarkably put up with a lot of "sorry, I can't" rhetoric from Auntie Kikine; and to all the terrific men who shared their recipes and kitchen experiences with me. But most of all my thanks go to Ronnie, for his insight into the subject matter, strong support, gentle manner and understanding love.

INTRODUCTION

Current societal thinking would have us all believe that men and women are so equal as to share the same tastebuds. It simply isn't the case.

Backed up by information gathered from teaching my customized "Cooking for Men Only" classes and from extensive research into the culinary likes and dislikes of males from coast to coast, I proclaim with unbridled confidence that men have an eating style all their own.

What is gastronomically alluring to women is not necessarily the same as what appeals to men. And what logically follows is that man's cooking-method preferences and talents are different from woman's. That is *different*, not necessarily *better*.

While men may point to the proliferation of male chefs as proof of man's superiority in the kitchen, it is a false standard of excellence. Social roles and physical strength have much more to do with man's success in the professional kitchen than does his raw talent. Men and women have always shared the culinary chores of the world—men as the professionals in restaurants and other institutional kitchens, women as family cooks.

In recent years, this pattern has shifted dramatically. More and more women are making their marks as chefs and other highly regarded food professionals, while at the same time more men have become the chief cooks and bottle washers of their families. According to 1981 Bureau of Census statistics, 1,994,555 men head motherless households with children and/or other adults. In addition, consider the 32,960,822 men who are single, separated, divorced or widowed as another category of males who must fend for themselves. Add to those the married men who willingly share cooking responsibilities with their spouses and what results is an awesome number of men who need to know how to cook.

And yet, traditionally cookbooks have been written for women who grew up at their mother's knees sifting flour, chopping onions, rolling out pie dough and learning almost by osmosis the basics and the nuances of cooking. Books, for the most part, have assumed basic culinary knowledge on the part of their readers, which excluded most men who, as society would have it, spent their youths outside the kitchen rather than endure the embarrassment of being tagged a mama's boy by their peers.

What finally broke these rigid kitchen roles was the coming of the "Great Gourmet Age" in the 1970s. This highly energetic movement with its food magazines, gourmet shops, cooking lessons, equipment catalogs, specialty-food lines, epicurean dining clubs and products for everyone from the chocoholic to the fitness fanatic piqued the interests and talents of more men than were ever before interested in cookery. Food as a topic of conversation is now more than just socially acceptable—it is fashionable. In many circles, a man who does not appreciate the finer points of food as a dining pleasure and health regulator is not considered up-to-date or worldly.

What we have, in brief, is a great many men who either need to or want to know how to cook but have had minimal training, and a great many cookbooks that assume their readers have watched every PBS cooking show ever produced, taken classes with every teaching chef who ever hit the road, and shopped in a myriad of markets. It is a blatant disparity.

And it is precisely to this disparity that *Cooking for Men Only* speaks. This book is designed to bridge the gap between what a man wants to do in the kitchen and what he is capable of doing at the moment. Cooking is, after all, even at its most grandiose, only a series of simple procedures, strung together so that they in the end may appear more complex than they actually are.

WHO IS THIS MAN WHO COOKS?

As a result of constant research since originating my "Cooking for Men Only" classes in 1977, I have come up with a profile of the American male's cooking habits. This composite of culinary preferences is based on interviews with and on questionnaires sent to the men in my classes, those who attended the in-store demonstrations I conducted for my previous book, *Convection Cookery*, and just about any man I encountered who had some measure of food in-terest, from an all-consuming passion to only a passing fancy.

This is not to say that all men who cook fit this profile, but it does reflect what I have learned in general about the tastes and talents of men in the kitchen. And it is to this profile that the recipes in this book are tailored. My years of steady research produced the following findings.
• Regardless of cuisine minceur, nouvelle cuisine and other culinary fads, men still, for the most part, characterize themselves as "meat-and-potatoes" types and as diners who eat for the sensuous and aesthetic pleasures it brings. One significant trend is that men are more likely to include fish and poultry in that meat-and-potatoes category, which fits nicely since . . .
• Most men who watch their diets do so to keep weight down. More specifically but in lesser numbers, they try to restrict fat (cholesterol) intake and salt consumption. Hardly any of them worry about sugar consumption, which follows because . . .
• Men are not generally interested in sweets. This is not a revelation to those who have cooked for men. Their interest in baking revolves around bread and rolls.
• Men voiced a resounding yes when asked if they feel a need to know more about food terms and techniques.
• Man's favorite cooking styles are broiling and barbecuing, followed by a desire to use any style that is fast. They ranked stir frying high and braising low in preferred styles. But they put braised dishes, e.g., stews and ragouts, second only to broiled and roasted meats in their list of types of recipes they are most interested in using. This contradicts the cooking-style findings, perhaps indicating a lack of understanding of braising. Fish and seafood, then poultry followed meats in recipe preference.
• There is a certain desire to learn potato, vegetable and salad recipes, but only as an adjunct to meat, seafood and poultry dishes.
• From-scratch recipes are about twice as desirable as those utilizing convenience foods.
• Men who have an interest in food tend to exercise regularly and are concerned about their health.
• Men like following recipes and "winging it" equally well.

• While men do cook for themselves, they are much more interested in cooking for family and friends.

• And last, and possibly most telling, about two-thirds of the men screened think of cooking as therapeutic, a way to ease tension. The rest obviously attach a certain amount of tension to cooking, which indicates they take it seriously and may have familial cooking obligations.

Over and above these preferences of today's cooking male, this research reaffirmed two cogent traits I discovered when I first began teaching. Call them male personality traits, culinary quirks or sexist drivel if you like, but I contend that the following male approach to the culinary arts has significance beyond this volume and may be a valid explanation for why men do make great chefs: they approach cooking with an adventurous spirit, and they have very definitive palates.

In simpler terms, men like to experiment with recipes. They are more likely to lend their own interpretation to a dish than to follow the recipe letter for letter. As for their palates, have you ever heard a man give a wishy-washy opinion of a dish he has eaten? When it comes to a flavor, a foodstuff or a recipe, a man will either love it or hate it. There is no middle ground. In cooking, this is very good, as it helps the cook establish gustatory guidelines that can lead to extremely satisfying eating.

So with the thoughts of adventurous cooking and definitive tastebuds freshly implanted, let us begin our epicurean journey into that gap between acquired skill and desired skill in the kitchen. Let's get cookin'!

—Caroline Kriz

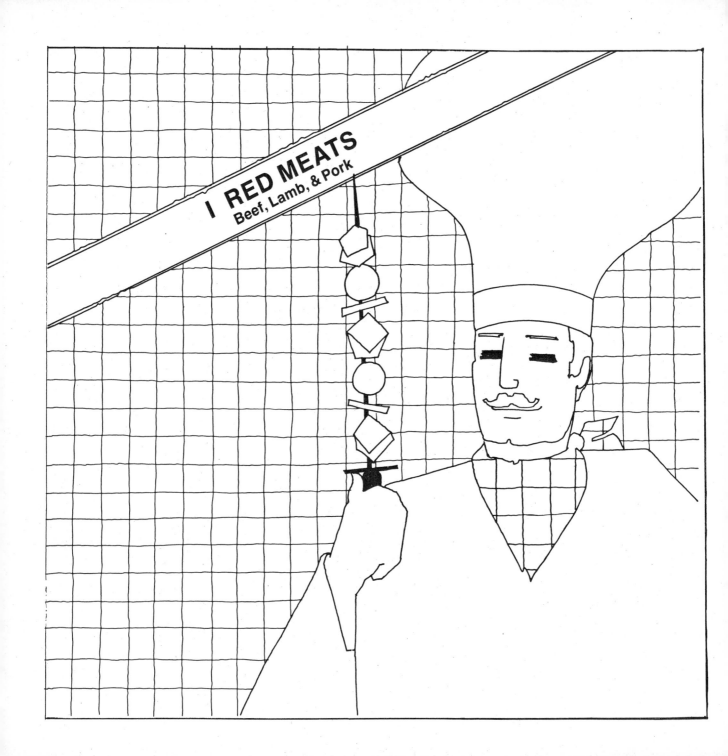

Despite cholesterol warnings, heightened fitness awareness, and the popularity of nouvelle cuisine, the expression "meat-and-potatoes man" is still very much a part of the American vocabulary. Those items most frequently identified with the male diet—prime rib, grilled steak, barbecued ribs—are all red meats, foods that are both simple to prepare and easy to ruin. A perfectly cooked steak or roast is only minutes away from being irretrievably beyond perfection.

Red-meat purists believe these favorite foods are at their best when broiled, barbecued, roasted or stir fried. Those are the cooking techniques on which this chapter concentrates. There are also recipes for sautéed and fried meats, and a smashing version of steak tartare for those who like their meat raw.

BROILING AND GRILLING

Broiling is cooking foods by direct high heat. This broad definition includes outdoor grilling, as well as broiling in standard gas or electric ranges and in convection ovens. The factors crucial to successful broiling are those that determine the cooking time: (1) temperature of the heat source (gas flame, electric heating element, charcoal or lava briquets); (2) distance of the foodstuff from the heat source; and (3) the degree of doneness desired. Lack of success results from cooking foods too long, placing delicate items like chicken and fish too close to the heat source, and selecting a food that is not suitable for broiling.

Broiled foods need to be turned at least once during cooking, except in portable convection ovens where the elevated foods are hit by heat from all sides.

TIPS ON BROILING, INDOORS AND OUT

• Select only tender cuts of red meats for broiling, unless you use a mechanical meat tenderizer (see Equipping the Kitchen). Steaks and chops are generally good candidates, but be careful when selecting steaks. The word "steak" on a meat product does not guarantee sufficient tenderness for broiling. For example, round steak, a very flavorful but less tender cut, cannot usually be broiled successfully. (For the exception to this rule, see Wise Man's Steak, page 13.)

The best steaks for broiling or grilling include rib, porterhouse, T-bone, rib eye or Delmonico, sirloin and New York strip.* Chuck and round steaks, along with some cuts of sirloin, are better if braised. Flank steak, classically used for London broil, can be broiled very briefly and served rare if thinly sliced across the grain.
• Buy steaks for broiling by thickness, not weight. A two-pound steak that's 1/2 inch thick will not be as satisfactory as a two-pound steak that's 1-1/2 inches thick.
• Allow 1/2 pound boneless steak per serving for ordinary eaters. Big beef eaters will need 3/4 to 1 pound per serving. If the steak has bone, allow 3/4 to 1 pound for ordinary eaters, 1-1/2 pounds for big eaters.
• Foods that tend to dry out in broiling, like pork chops, chicken

*To order steaks, including succulent New York strip steaks usually reserved for restaurant use, see Prime Time Beef listing in Mail-Order Sources.

and fish, should be broiled farther from the heat source than well-marbled beef cuts. Broiling these delicate items in a convection oven or covered barbecue grill is a gentler style of broiling and yields superior results.

• When selecting red meats for broiling (or any style of cooking), look for fresh red color and small streaks of fat, called marbling. Remember that fat is flavor in meat and that what makes a cut of meat "prime" is the amount and distribution of fat.

• Broilers and outdoor grills should always be preheated before adding foods.

• Marinate meats for flavor. Marinades can add flavor and reduce cooking times of broiled meats, though they will not necessarily make meat more tender.

• When turning meats, use tongs. A fork will pierce the meat and release natural juices.

• Use an instant-read thermometer to test for doneness of broiled meats one inch thick or thicker. Insert the thermometer horizontally into the steak or chop so the probe sits in the middle of the meat's thickness, not touching bone.

Look for the following readings and remember that the internal temperature will continue to rise another five to ten degrees after the item is removed from the broiler. Thick cuts (over two inches) can be allowed to "rest" on a platter or meat board five to ten minutes before slicing and serving. Thin cuts should be served immediately to keep them from cooling too much.

	BEEF & LAMB	PORK*
Rare	135°F	—
Medium rare	140°F	—
Medium	150°F	150°F
Well done	160°F	160°F

*See note on pork on page 18.

SPECIAL TIPS FOR OUTDOOR COOKING

• When selecting a grill, look for one with a domed or high cover, which lends versatility to your outdoor cooking. Covered grills, especially the kettle style, allow you to roast large items like rib roasts, turkeys and other whole birds.

• Be sure to read the grill manufacturer's care-and-use booklet

and follow the specified directions. Remember that recommended cooking times are approximates and can be altered to your liking.

• When cooking with charcoal, always allow enough time for the fire to get started properly, at least thirty minutes. Use a reputable brand of charcoal and store it indoors in a dry place.

• Avoid using liquid chemical charcoal starters, as they can impart an unpleasant taste to foods. Invest in an electric starter, available at hardware stores.

• When cooking in a kettle-style grill, always lift the lid off to one side rather than straight up. The latter may create enough suction to draw ashes up onto the food.

FLAVORING THE BARBECUE WITH WOOD

For years, Texans, long famous for barbecued meats, have been using wood chips, including the highly prized mesquite, to give a sweet smoky flavor to meats. Southeastern barbecue restaurants traditionally use hickory to flavor their incomparable ribs. Now wood flavoring agents, including mesquite, hickory and oak, are available commercially in chips, and sometimes chunks, at hardware stores and supermarkets. These woods add special character to grilled meats, poultry and fish, with mesquite imparting the most delicate smoky flavor.

Chips are more convenient to use and chunks smoke longer. To use wood on your outdoor grill, soak chips in water for about one hour, chunks several hours or overnight. Drain off water and sprinkle a handful or more of chips over hot coals. If using chunks, place three to five pieces on the coals with long-handled barbecue tongs. Put grill in place over coals, and cook the foods in the usual manner. The soaked wood will smoke rather than flame.

Covering the grill will result in the most intense smoky flavor, but foods can be cooked on an open grill and still absorb some of the wood's characteristics. If your grill has no cover, use a wok lid to cover foods during cooking.

To use wood on a gas or electric grill, place soaked chips or chunks on a cast-iron griddle or cornbread pan and set on top of the rocks. The cast iron conducts heat so well, the wood will smoke and heat

is not lost. When cooking is finished, put water on the wood to put it out and save it to use another day.

BROILED OR GRILLED STEAKS

Rib, rib eye, New York strip, porterhouse, fillet or other tender beef steaks, 1-1/2–2 inches thick
Kosher salt
Freshly ground black pepper
Bourbon Butter or Jerry G.
  Bishop's Showstopper Steak
  Sauce (following)

Preheat broiler, positioning broiler pan so steak surface will be 3–4 inches from heat source. Or prepare outdoor grill so coals are white hot and grill is 3–5 inches from coals, the distance depending on how charred you like your steak. Place serving platter and plates in a 200°F oven to keep them warm until serving time. Trim excess fat from steaks, leaving no more than 1/2 inch along the edge. Slash fat along edge at 1-inch intervals to prevent curling.

Just prior to cooking, pat steaks dry and rub all surfaces with a moderate amount of salt and as much pepper as desired. Immediately place steaks in broiler or on grill. (If a salted steak sits, the salt can draw moisture out of the meat and to the surface.) Sear first on one side, then on the other. Cook a total of 4–5 minutes per side for rare, 5–7 minutes per side for medium rare.

Test for doneness by inserting an instant-read thermometer. Allow steak to rest a minute or so before cutting. This is about the time it takes to get a steak from broiler to table. Top each steak with a dollop of Bourbon Butter or Jerry G. Bishop's Showstopper Steak Sauce. For faster cooking, bring steaks to room temperature, or use George Garrett's Steak Tip (following).

BARBECUED STEAK To season a steak on the grill with barbecue sauce or any high-sugar sauce with a catsup or chili-sauce base, brush onto steak during last 2–3 minutes of cooking. The intense heat will burn the sauce if it is added earlier.

BOURBON BUTTER

The trick to serving seasoned butters over broiled steaks is to have the butter at room temperature so it will melt easily without cooling down the steak.

Makes about 1/2 cup
1/4 pound (1 stick) unsalted butter, at room temperature
1 tablespoon minced fresh parsley
1 tablespoon minced green onion
1 tablespoon bourbon
1 tablespoon fresh minced tarragon, or 2 teaspoons dried tarragon, crushed
1/4 teaspoon dry mustard
1/8 teaspoon kosher salt
1/8 teaspoon white pepper powder

With a spoon, beat butter in small bowl to lighten. Beat in remaining ingredients. (For a finer texture, use food processor to combine ingredients.) Serve immediately by spooning a dollop on each hot steak. Or make ahead, refrigerate and allow to stand at room temperature 1 hour before serving.

JERRY G. BISHOP'S SHOWSTOPPER STEAK SAUCE

Jerry is a television talk-show host in San Diego, and food is one of his abiding interests. In addition to owning a Greek restaurant, Jerry likes to take to the grill and cook for friends and family. He serves this sauce, redolent with mushrooms, with steak, for an off-camera stellar performance.

Makes 2 cups
1/4 pound (1 stick) unsalted butter, cut into 4 equal pieces
2 medium onions, peeled and chopped (about 2 cups)
2–3 garlic cloves, peeled and minced
1 sweet green pepper, seeded and chopped
1/2 pound fresh mushrooms, sliced
2 teaspoons minced fresh rosemary leaves, or 1/2 teaspoon dried rosemary, crushed
1/3 cup bottled diable sauce*
1/4 cup burgundy or other dry red wine

Melt butter in a heavy 10-inch frypan. Add onion and garlic and sauté over medium heat until onion is transparent, about 3 minutes. Add green pepper, mushrooms and rosemary. Continue to sauté until vegetables are very tender, about 20 minutes, stirring occasionally. Stir in diable sauce and wine and simmer until most of the liquid has evaporated, about 10 minutes.

*Available in gourmet shops and some supermarkets.

GEORGE GARRETT'S STEAK TIP

As a radio news director in Seattle, Washington, George has a busy schedule, but still cooks for his family about once a week. He offers this tip for grilling steaks outdoors to his ideal medium rare.

Meat should be at room temperature or warmer before placing on the grill. Cold steaks from the refrigerator can be terrible—raw in the middle and burned on the surface. For steaks that are seared on the outside and medium rare throughout the inside, heat them in a warm (150°F) oven about 30 minutes, or until they just begin to turn color. Then "burn 'em quick over hot coals. Yum!"

WISE MAN'S STEAK

It is a wise man who can eat well for less and save time in the bargain. Here an inexpensive, tasty cut that is usually too tough for quick cooking becomes tender enough to broil successfully. The answer to broiling less tender cuts lies with the mechanical meat tenderizer. To locate this hard-to-find item, see Mail-Order Sources.

Makes 2 servings
1–1-1/4 pounds boneless round steak, 1–1-1/2 inches thick, or 1–1-1/2-inch steaks cut from a round tip roast
Worcestershire sauce or bottled teriyaki sauce
Healthful Seasoned Salt (page 99), or purchased seasoned salt (optional)
Freshly ground black pepper

Preheat broiler or convection oven or prepare outdoor grill. Treat steak with mechanical meat tenderizer on both sides. Sprinkle with Worcestershire sauce and rub into surface. Sprinkle with seasoned salt and pepper. Broil 2–3 inches from heat source for 2–4 minutes per side, or a total of 5–8 minutes in a convection oven. The shorter times will result in a rare steak, the longer ones, a medium-rare one. Let rest in a warm place 3–5 minutes before serving.

KEN FILEWICZ'S POT ROAST ON THE GRILL

A busy systems analyst for Chicago's First Federal Savings and Loan, Ken finds cooking a relaxing pastime. For the past decade, he has been preparing this family favorite year-round on his covered outdoor gas grill.

Makes 6 servings
One 7-bone or chuck arm pot roast (about 3–3-1/2 pounds)
Down-Home Barbecue Sauce (page 54), or bottled barbecue sauce

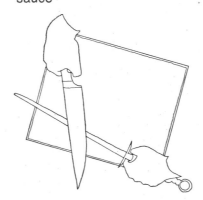

MARINADE
1/4 cup fresh lemon juice
1/4 cup soy sauce
1/4 cup dry red wine
1/4 cup catsup
2 tablespoons firmly packed brown sugar
2 tablespoons vegetable oil
1 tablespoon Worcestershire sauce
1 teaspoon kosher salt
1/2 teaspoon freshly ground black pepper
Pinch of garlic powder

In a mixing bowl, whisk together all marinade ingredients. Puncture beef with a fork repeatedly so marinade penetrates. Place beef in a shallow glass baking dish, pour marinade over beef, cover with plastic wrap and refrigerate 24 to 72 hours, turning occasionally.

Prepare outdoor grill. Drain meat, place meat on grill 4–5 inches from heat source and cook, covered, over medium-hot (red) coals about 1 hour for medium, basting with barbecue sauce during last 30 minutes. Cut into serving-size pieces or slice thinly across the grain.

THE DETROIT BURGER

This burger was inspired by the one served at Detroit's renowned London Chop House, a must-stop for meat lovers visiting the Motor City. Serve plain, or top with Bourbon Butter (page 12).

Makes 4 servings
3 tablespoons vegetable oil
2 small onions, peeled and minced
2 garlic cloves, peeled and crushed
2 pounds lean ground beef
1 large egg, lightly beaten
1/2 teaspoon kosher salt
1/4 teaspoon freshly ground black pepper
1 tablespoon minced fresh parsley
4 pieces roquefort or blue cheese (about 1 by 1 by 1/4 inch *each*)

In a 9-inch frypan, heat oil, add onion and cook over medium heat until transparent. Add garlic and cook and stir 2 minutes. Pour into a mixing bowl, add remaining ingredients except roquefort and blend well with a spoon or your hands. Divide meat mixture into 4 equal portions and form each portion into a patty with a well in the center. Put a piece of roquefort in each well and carefully enclose cheese in burgers by pressing meat mixture over top of cheese to cover completely. Each patty should be about 1 inch thick. Broil about 3 inches from heat source to rare or medium rare (about 3 minutes per side for rare).

BEEF KABOBS FOR THE FAMILY

This is a great dish for a summertime family get-together. The marinade can be made one to two days in advance and the kabobs can be assembled before guests arrive. The actual cooking goes quickly. Steamed rice is a good side dish.

Makes 8 servings
4 pounds boneless beef, such as arm chuck roast or sirloin, cut into 1-1/2-inch chunks*
8 or more small onions, peeled
2 sweet green peppers, seeded and cut into 1-1/2-inch pieces
1/2 pound fresh medium mushrooms

MARINADE
1 cup catsup
1 cup water
1/2 cup red wine or cider vinegar
1/2 cup vegetable oil
1 envelope dry onion soup mix
3 tablespoons sugar
2 tablespoons prepared yellow mustard
1/2 teaspoon kosher salt
Pinch of cayenne pepper

In a medium saucepan, whisk together all marinade ingredients. Bring to a boil, reduce heat and simmer, uncovered, about 35 minutes. Pour into a large bowl and cool to room temperature. Add beef chunks, stir to coat and refrigerate overnight, or up to 48 hours.

To precook vegetables, steam or boil onions 5–8 minutes or until crisp tender, green pepper pieces 4–5 minutes, and whole mushrooms about 4 minutes. Transfer vegetables to a large bowl of ice water to stop further cooking. When vegetables are completely cool, drain. Preheat broiler or prepare outdoor grill. Drain marinade from meat into a saucepan.

Thread meat and vegetables alternately on 8 skewers, pushing pieces close together. Brush vegetables lightly with marinade. Broil 4–5 inches from heat source (coals should be medium-red hot) 10–20 minutes, turning often and brushing with marinade during last 5 minutes. If kabobs are browning too quickly, move farther away from heat source. To test for doneness, remove a kabob to a platter and slit a beef chunk with a paring knife; the center should be a rosy pink. To serve, heat marinade and pass as a sauce.

*If desired treat meat with mechanical meat tenderizer before cutting into chunks. Watch for faster cooking time.

BRAD WEST'S BEER-BRAISED BARBECUED RIBS

Brad, a young man from Sauk Village, Illinois, manages a gas station and loves to cook, especially on weekends. Here he shares one of his specialties—ribs flavored and tenderized by marinating and braising in beer before barbecuing.

Makes 2–4 servings
2 slabs pork loin ribs or country ribs (about 3 pounds total)*
1-1/2–2 bottles (12 ounces *each*) dark beer
Down-Home Barbecue Sauce (page 54), or bottled barbecue sauce

Place ribs in shallow glass dish, overlapping if necessary. Pour beer over ribs to cover. Cover dish with plastic wrap and refrigerate overnight. Remove ribs from beer marinade, reserving marinade, and cut into 4- to 5-rib pieces. Place ribs in a large (5-quart or larger) saucepan and add reserved marinade and enough water to cover ribs completely. Bring to a boil, reduce heat and boil gently about 1 hour or until fork tender.
   Prepare outdoor grill or preheat broiler. Remove ribs from saucepan and brush with barbecue sauce. Cook on grill or in broiler 4–5 inches from heat source about 5 minutes; turn and cook another 5 minutes, basting with additional sauce if desired.
   To roast these ribs in the oven, place boiled ribs on a jelly-roll pan bone side up, brush with barbecue sauce and roast in a preheated

350°F oven 15 minutes. Turn, baste and roast another 15 minutes, brushing with sauce as desired. To broil in a convection oven, preheat at "broil," brush with barbecue sauce and broil 5–10 minutes.

*If you find the chewy membrane on the back of spareribs and back ribs annoying, remove as follows: Place ribs on board, bone side up. From the small end of the slab, slide the tines of a fork under the slick membrane between the second and third ribs. Pull up to loosen, remove fork, grip membrane with hand and pull off in a single piece.

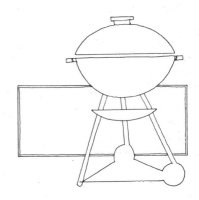

CYNTHIA'S VEAL CHOPS WITH PECAN BUTTER

Veal chops are a delicious but infrequently used cut for broiling. This delightful recipe, originated by Cynthia's Restaurant in Chicago, is elegant enough for company cooking.

Makes 4 servings
4 veal rib chops, 3/4–1 inch thick
Kosher salt and freshly ground
   black pepper to taste
4 tablespoons unsalted butter,
   melted in a shallow pan

PECAN BUTTER
1/4 cup hot water
1/4 teaspoon beef base
6 tablespoons pecan pieces or
   halves
1/4 pound (1 stick) unsalted butter
1 teaspoon minced garlic
1/8 teaspoon kosher salt

To prepare Pecan Butter, stir together water and beef base until beef base dissolves; cool to room temperature. In a food processor, process pecans with on-off pulsing until very finely chopped, or finely chop by hand. With an electric mixer, beat butter and cooled stock until light. Beat in garlic, salt and pecans. Transfer to a small bowl and refrigerate at least 20 minutes before serving. If storing Pecan Butter in refrigerator more than 30 minutes, bring to room temperature before using on chops.

Preheat broiler or prepare outdoor grill. If desired, sprinkle a handful of mesquite wood chips over hot coals. Trim excess fat from veal chops. Stir salt and pepper into melted butter. Dip each chop in melted butter and broil or grill to rare or medium rare. Test for doneness by inserting instant-read thermometer. Remove chops to warm serving plates and immediately top each with a generous dollop of Pecan Butter.

MEDITERRANEAN ANCHOVIED LAMB CHOPS

Lamb chops are best when served medium rare. Here they are seasoned with Mediterranean herbs and anchovies. Note that no salt is used, as the anchovies provide enough.

Makes 2 servings*
4 rib lamb chops, 1–1-1/2 inches
   thick
Olive oil
Freshly ground black pepper
1/2 lemon

ANCHOVY SEASONING
4 anchovy fillets, drained, or 1 tablespoon anchovy paste**
2 tablespoons olive oil
1 garlic clove, peeled and crushed
1 teaspoon dried oregano,
   crushed
1 teaspoon ground sage
1/2 teaspoon dried thyme,
   crushed
1/2 teaspoon freshly ground black
   pepper

Preheat broiler or convection oven set on "broil." To prepare Anchovy Seasoning, mash anchovies in a small bowl with a fork. Stir in all remaining seasoning ingredients. Mixture should be pasty. Set aside.

Trim lamb chops of excess fat; slash fat along edge at 1/2-inch intervals. Brush 1 side of each chop lightly with olive oil and sprinkle with pepper. Broil, oil side up, 4 inches from heat source for 4–5 minutes. Turn chops, spread each generously with the Anchovy Seasoning and continue to broil 4–5 minutes. In a convection oven, broil 12–15 minutes total, applying Anchovy Seasoning halfway through cooking time. Remove chops to warm plates and immediately squeeze the lemon over them. Serve at once.

*Halve this recipe for a simple meal for one.

**Anchovy paste is a convenient product that has the flavor and color of anchovies but no bones! It is available in a tube in gourmet shops and specialty-food sections of supermarkets.

ROASTING

If you want to start an argument among cooks, bring up the topic of roasting. Everyone has his own idea on the best technique, with most opinions falling into three schools of thought: The Sear-First School, The Cook-Slow-and-Even School and The Convection Is Perfection School.

SEAR FIRST advocates recommend placing the roast (beef, pork, poultry) into an intensely hot oven (450°F or higher) for ten to twenty minutes, depending upon roast size, then reducing heat to 325°F and roasting at that temperature nine to eleven minutes per pound.

COOK-SLOW-AND-EVEN aficionados say nay to searing. They claim cooking a roast at 325° for the full duration is the way to go for the most succulent result.

CONVECTION IS PERFECTION devotees say nothing beats the constant searing action of a convection (circulating hot air) oven, where roasts are cooked at 325° or 350°F. Natural juices are sealed in and cooking time is saved.

It is each at-home cook's responsibility to experiment with these techniques and select his favorite. As for the recipes that follow, each includes at least one of the first two methods *and* convection instructions, except for Monique's Filet de Porc Grandmère, which is "roasted" on the range top. Remember, a kettle-style outdoor grill becomes a convection oven when covered.

BASIC ROASTING

Place meat rack in shallow roasting pan; set seasoned roast on rack to elevate it and to allow hot air to penetrate from all sides. Place in oven and roast at temperature and time designated in recipe. A good-quality cut for roasting does not need basting; it will have enough internal and surface fat to keep it moist.

ROASTING TIPS

• As in broiling, only the tender beef, pork and lamb cuts are appropriate for roasting. Prime or choice rib roasts, pork loin roast, and rack, saddle and leg of lamb are excellent selections. Some cuts labeled "roast" actually do not have the fat content and muscle tenderness to make for good roasting, for example sirloin tip roast and rump roast. These cuts are better braised.
• Use a roasting rack that is strong and elevates the meat so it doesn't sit in the juices that accumulate in the pan. If it does, it is apt to have a braised rather than roasted flavor. A nonstick rack in a stationary V-shape makes for sturdiness, and easy roast re-

moval and cleanup. Use the shallowest roasting pan you can find, or set the rack on a heavy-gauge jelly-roll pan, and if drippings rise too high during cooking, remove excess from pan with a large spoon or a ball baster.

• Don't let the liquid in the roasting pan dry up, as roast drippings may scorch and burn on the pan bottom. Since this is only a danger near the beginning of the roasting time, pour a thin film of water into the pan before placing it in the oven. If the liquid dries up, add another film of water. This water will act as a carrier of the meat juices that can be used in sauces and gravies, or for a simple au jus presentation.

• Always let a roast "rest" out of the oven in a warm place for ten to twenty minutes before carving. This allows internal juices to become evenly distributed throughout the meat.

• Use an instant-read thermometer to test for doneness. Estimate roasting time, then take a reading about ten to twenty minutes before that time is up by inserting thermometer probe into center of roast, being sure it is not touching bone or resting in fat. If roast is not done, return it to oven and test

again. Look for these times on the thermometer and remember that internal temperatures rise five to ten degrees while roast is resting.

	BEEF	*PORK	LAMB
Rare	135°F	—	135°F
Medium rare	140°F	—	140°F
Medium	150°F	150°F	150°F
Well done	160°F	160°F	—

*Much of the American populace is still cooking pork to death due to a fear of trichinosis, a disease caused by the presence of trichinae. This parasite, however, is rarely, if ever, present in American pork today, so this deliberate overcooking is unnecessary. This book does not advocate cooking pork to an internal temperature of 170° or 180°F as so many other references do. Since any trichinae that *may* have been present die at 138°F, an internal temperature of 150° to 160°F is more than sufficient to rid the pork of potential danger. Cooking pork to these lower temperatures retains natural juiciness and flavor. Don't be shocked to discover that pork roasts can be tender and moist.

MONIQUE'S FILET DE PORC GRANDMERE

Chef-proprietor Monique Hooker of Chicago's fashionable Monique's Cafe calls this one of her favorite recipes. It is a perfect example of why a large, double-handled saucepan is called a dutch oven. The roast is cooked in the pot on the range top, but the result is as if it were cooked in the oven.

Makes 4–6 servings
3 garlic cloves, peeled
One 3-pound rolled pork loin roast
2 tablespoons unsalted butter
1 tablespoon vegetable oil
3 carrots, peeled and thinly sliced
2 medium onions, peeled and thinly sliced
4 shallots, peeled and quartered
2 bay leaves
1/4–1/2 teaspoon dried thyme, crushed
2 sprigs parsley, with stems
20 pitted prunes
1/4 cup water

Cut each garlic clove in half lengthwise. With a paring knife, make 6 well-spaced, deep narrow slits in the roast; insert a garlic sliver in each slit. Melt butter with oil over medium heat in a heavy-gauge 5-quart dutch oven. When foam on butter subsides, add pork and brown on all sides. Use tongs or two large spoons to turn meat; do not puncture the surface. Reduce heat to low, cover and simmer about 15 minutes. Add all remaining ingredients except prunes and water, cover and cook 20 minutes. Sprinkle prunes over pork and vegetables and cook another 10 minutes, or until instant-read thermometer inserted in center of roast reads 150°–160°F. Remove roast to a warm platter. Lift out vegetables and prunes with a slotted spoon and arrange around roast. Let roast rest in a warm (150°F) oven 5–10 minutes.

To make sauce, add water to dutch oven and bring to a boil, stirring constantly; continuing to stir, boil 1–2 minutes, scraping up all the brown bits from bottom of pot. Pour into small serving bowl. To carve pork, slice to desired thickness. Pass sauce.

JAMAICAN ROAST PORK

A piquant sweet glaze gives this roast a distinctive Caribbean flavor.

Makes 4–6 servings
One 4-pound center-cut pork loin
  roast
1 tablespoon kosher salt
1/2 teaspoon cayenne pepper
1 cup chicken stock

SUGAR GLAZE
3 garlic cloves, peeled and minced
1 teaspoon ground ginger
1/2 teaspoon ground cloves
1 bay leaf, crumbled
1/8 teaspoon cayenne pepper
1/2 cup firmly packed light brown
  sugar
1 tablespoon dark rum
1/2 lime

Preheat standard oven to 350°F, or convection oven to 325°F. With

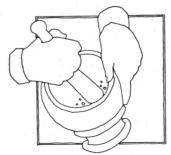

a knife, score fat side of roast diagonally to form diamond pattern. Rub all sides of roast with salt and cayenne pepper. Place fat side up on rack in roasting pan. Add chicken stock to roasting pan to collect pork drippings. Roast pork in preheated oven 40–45 minutes.

While meat is roasting, make Sugar Glaze. Mash together garlic, ginger, cloves, bay leaf and cayenne pepper in mortar with pestle or in bowl with back of spoon. Add brown sugar and stir in rum.

When roast has cooked 40–45 minutes, remove from oven and, with a metal spatula, spread Sugar Glaze over scored portion of roast. Return roast to oven and continue to cook 40–45 minutes, or until glaze is crusty and instant-read thermometer registers 155°–160°F. Remove roast to warm platter, cover with aluminum foil and let rest in warm place 10–12 minutes. Pour contents of roasting pan into a small saucepan and heat to serving temperature. (If desired, boil to reduce, but adjust seasonings once drippings are concentrated.) To serve, squeeze lime juice over roast and slice the roast. Pass the sauce.

STANDING RIB ROAST WITH HORSERADISH SAUCE

For that very special dinner in honor of a meat-lover's birthday or promotion, nothing tops the natural tenderness of a rib roast. Select either a prime or choice cut and make sure it is from the "small end," the most tender portion. Ask the butcher to remove the chine bone, feather bones and back strap, or carving will be a problem.

Roasting a standing rib successfully is a matter of timing, so make sure you have an instant-read thermometer before cooking this tasty, expensive cut. For estimating amount needed, buy one rib for each two servings and add one rib for good measure.

Makes 8 servings
One 5-rib standing rib roast,
   trimmed as described above
Kosher salt
Freshly ground black pepper
1 cup Quick Beef Stock (page 99),
   or other beef stock (optional)
Horseradish Sauce (following)

Position oven rack so roast will sit in the center of the oven. Preheat oven to 325°F. Rub salt sparingly over roast; rub with pepper to taste. Place roast bone side down on roasting rack in shallow roasting pan. Add water to roasting pan so a 1/8-inch film covers the bottom. Roast meat 18–24 minutes per pound (15–20 minutes per pound in a convection oven), checking internal temperature with an instant-read thermometer. When roast reaches desired degree of doneness (135°F for rare, 140°F for medium rare, 150°F for medium), remove to a platter, cover with aluminum foil and let rest in a warm place 15–20 minutes.

To make an au jus (optional), pour drippings from pan into large glass measuring cup. Pour off and discard the yellow fatty drippings and reserve the dark-brown meaty ones. Combine these drippings with beef stock in a small saucepan; taste and correct seasonings. To concentrate flavor, simmer 5–10 minutes to reduce.

Serve au jus and Horseradish Sauce in separate bowls. To carve roast, turn it on its larger side for stability, then cut downward along bones about 2 inches into roast. Slice horizontally to desired thickness and lift slices with carving fork and knife to serving plate. Top with a spoonful of au jus and pass Horseradish Sauce.

HORSERADISH SAUCE

Makes about 2 cups
1 cup sour cream
1/2 cup whipping cream, whipped*
   to soft peaks
1/3 cup prepared horseradish,
   drained
1 tablespoon snipped fresh dill, or
   1 teaspoon dried dill, crushed
1 teaspoon kosher salt
1/4 teaspoon freshly ground white
   pepper

In a small mixing bowl, stir sour cream to lighten slightly. Stir in remaining ingredients, cover and refrigerate about 3 hours to blend flavors. Let sit 30 minutes at room temperature before serving.

*For best results when beating whipping cream, use a stainless-steel bowl and hand-held electric mixer. Refrigerate bowl and beaters until just before beating cream. Whip the cream on high speed, moving the beater in a circular motion.

FRENCH LEG OF LAMB BORDEAUX

This preparation is based on one taught at La Varenne Ecole de Cuisine, France's famous bilingual cooking school. Marinating the lamb for an extended period in a fine red wine gives it a wonderful flavor. Boiled potatoes make a good side dish.

Makes 6–8 servings
One 5- to 6-pound leg of lamb
  (prime or choice only)
3 tablespoons unsalted butter
3 tablespoons olive or vegetable
  oil
2 teaspoons beef base

MARINADE
1 bottle (750 ml) good-quality red
  Bordeaux wine
2 onions, peeled and thinly sliced
2 carrots, peeled and thinly sliced
4 shallots, peeled and sliced
2–3 bay leaves
3 large sprigs parsley, with stems
1 sprig thyme, or 1 teaspoon dried
  thyme, crushed
2 tablespoons red wine vinegar
2 garlic cloves, peeled
2 tablespoons olive or vegetable
  oil
Pinch of kosher salt
4–5 juniper berries
1/2 pound lean beef scraps or
  bones (optional)

In a mixing bowl, stir together all marinade ingredients. Place leg of lamb in large glass bowl or other nonaluminum container so it fits snugly. Pour marinade over lamb, cover with plastic wrap and refrigerate 3 days, turning 3–4 times.

Preheat standard or convection oven to 400°F. Remove lamb from marinade and pat dry with paper toweling. Strain the marinade into a saucepan, reserving liquid and vegetables separately. Melt butter and olive oil in a heavy roasting pan over medium-high heat. Brown lamb in pan, turning it frequently (with tongs or 2 spoons) to brown evenly. Remove from heat, lift lamb by bone (shank) end and spread reserved vegetables over bottom of pan. Set lamb on top of vegetables and roast in preheated oven 12 minutes per pound for rare, 15 minutes per pound for medium. (A shorter roasting time than usual is appropriate here, as the lamb has already started to "cook" in the marinade. If using a convection oven, times may need to be reduced further.)

While lamb is roasting, reduce reserved marinade liquid by boiling about 45 minutes. When roast is done, remove to a warm platter, cover loosely with foil and let rest in a warm place. Place roasting pan with meat juices over medium-high heat and reduce until juices thicken and begin to brown (caramelize). With a large spoon, skim off excess fat. Add reserved marinade and beef base, stir to scrape up any brown bits on bottom of pan and reduce until the sauce is glossy, 10–15 minutes, skimming off fat if needed. Taste and correct seasonings. If sauce is too concentrated, add water by spoonfuls until thinned as desired. Strain sauce into a serving bowl.

To carve the French way, wrap an impeccably clean linen napkin around shank end of roast, grasp lamb by shank, and lift shank so roast is sitting at a 45-degree angle. Beginning near shank end and slicing down to wide end of roast, thinly slice lamb parallel to the bone, flipping slices onto serving plates with the carving knife as you finish each one. Pass the sauce separately.

SPINACH-STUFFED HAM

This interesting and simple treatment for ham takes it out of the ordinary and into the fancy. With this recipe in your repertoire, you can volunteer to make Easter dinner for the family.

Makes 8–10 servings
4 large bunches spinach, washed and stems removed, or 2 packages (10 ounces *each*) frozen chopped spinach, thawed and drained
1 pound ricotta cheese
6 green onions, minced
2 tablespoons Dijon-style mustard
1/4 teaspoon freshly ground black pepper
1/4 teaspoon hot pepper sauce
Kosher salt (optional)
1 whole boneless ham or shank portion ham (7–8 pounds)
1/2 cup dry white wine or dry vermouth
1/2 pound shredded natural swiss cheese

Preheat standard oven to 325°F, or a convection oven to 300°F. Place fresh spinach in a 5-quart saucepan with the washing water that clings to the leaves. Cover and cook over high heat just until leaves wilt, stirring occasionally, about 5 minutes. Rinse in cold water and squeeze out all moisture with your hands. Chop coarsely. If using frozen spinach, simply squeeze out as much moisture as possible from thawed spinach. Stir together spinach, ricotta, onions, mustard, pepper and hot pepper sauce. Taste and add salt, if desired; remember that ham is salt-cured and will impart saltiness to the other ingredients.

With a large knife, slice halfway down into ham at 1-inch intervals. Pack spinach mixture between ham slices. Place ham on rack in a roasting pan and pour wine into pan. Cover by gently pressing aluminum foil over ham and around edge of pan. Bake in the preheated oven 1-1/4–1-1/2 hours (50–60 minutes in a convection oven). Uncover, press swiss cheese over top of ham and return to oven. Cook uncovered for about 15 minutes or until cheese melts.

STIR FRYING

Learning to stir fry delicious Chinese dishes is enough to turn a regular restaurant goer into an at-home Chinese cook. While stir frying can be done in a frypan with a pancake turner, it is most successfully executed with the proper equipment, including a wok with lid and ring, and a Chinese spatula.

Shop for these items in Chinese markets for the best price, or in gourmet shops. Steel woks are preferred. Never even consider an electric wok; its thermostat will not allow it to maintain the constant high heat needed for this type of cookery. If your merchant seasons woks, have him do it for you. Otherwise do it yourself as follows. (For more information on woks, see Adding for Style section of Equipping the Kitchen.)

SEASONING A WOK

Wash the wok in hot soapy water with a plastic pad to remove any oil or grit. Set wok on its ring over high heat to dry. With wok still on burner, wad up a paper towel, pour vegetable oil onto it and rub the entire inside surface of the hot wok with the oil. Replenish the oil and keep rubbing over high heat to burn the oil into the wok's surface, thereby sealing it. After the wok has turned black in the center, start moving the wok around so the rest of the inside surface heats and blackens, continually rubbing with oil and replenishing the oil as needed. Keep kitchen ventilation fan on, as the burned oil will create an odor. When entire surface (or as much as possible) has blackened, the wok is ready to be used for cooking.

COOKING IN A WOK

Heat dry wok over high heat two to three minutes, then pour amount of oil specified in recipe in a thin stream around inside rim of wok near top edge. The oil will run down to the bottom, coating most of the surface as it flows. At this point the oil should be very hot but not smoking. Immediately add foods as directed in recipe. If food does not give off a loud sizzle as it hits the wok, the pan was not hot enough. Stir ingredients with a Chinese spatula.

CLEANING A WOK

After cooking, always immediately remove all food to a bowl, platter or individual plates. Do not turn off heat. Place dirty wok in empty sink at once, run hot tap water into pan and gently scour with a plastic pad or Chinese bamboo whisk to clean away excess oil, gravy, etc. *Do not use soap or metal pads, as they can wash away the seasoning*. Rinse wok and spill off water. Place wet wok on ring over hot burner to dry pooled water, then turn burner down to medium-low and sit down to eat. *Do not dry wok with towel or any other material. Always dry it with heat*.

This cleaning procedure takes less than a minute and the wok can dry completely while you eat. This also allows any oil clinging to the surface to burn on and become part of the seasoning. You may have to rub the hot wok briefly with oil after the first several times you use it to build up the seasoning further. Store wok on hanging pot rack or in a cupboard. Be careful not to damage seasoning by nesting heavy pots in it.

SHOPPING FOR STIR-FRY INGREDIENTS

To assure authenticity in your stir-fry cooking, shop at well-stocked food markets in Asian neighborhoods. These establishments, which are fascinating to visit, offer the freshest Oriental vegetables due to high turnover, and stock the best assortment of specialty dried and canned ingredients.

You will see bean sprouts, pea pods, bok choy, winter melon and lotus root, to name just a few of the fresh items. Dry ingredients, such as Chinese black mushrooms, bean thread noodles, rice sticks and lily flowers, are found on the often tightly packed shelves. Products like canned bamboo shoots can be found unsliced, leaving the cutting to the cook, which yields superior flavor and texture.

There are no American counterparts to these types of ingredients that will do justice to your stir-fry efforts, and trips to these markets can be an enjoyable way to shop and a rewarding way to break the supermarket routine.

NOTE For Oriental ingredients, see Mail-Order Sources.

STIR-FRYING TIPS

• Stir-fry recipes are easily doubled, halved or cut to single servings by increasing or reducing all ingredients equally.
• Always have all the meat and vegetables cut up and seasoning mixtures combined before beginning to cook. Stir frying is so fast that a dish can overcook if you stop in the middle to prepare an ingredient.
• The soaking of dry ingredients and chopping of fresh and canned ingredients can be done a few hours ahead of cooking time. Cover chopped vegetables with plastic wrap until ready to use. Do not marinate meats in soy-based marinades longer than recipe specifies or the meat might become too salty.
• Since ingredients are added to the wok separately, organize your work area by placing each ingredient in a separate bowl and lining up the bowls near the range for easy access during cooking.
• Time the rice so it is done with or shortly before the stir-fry dish, which should always be served immediately upon completion. If frying rice sticks, prepare them in advance of stir frying.

• Keep the burner temperature hot and constant for proper searing action.
• Plan Chinese menus that include only one stir-fried dish for cooking ease. Other dishes can include a soup cooked in a saucepan, a dish prepared in a steamer, and a roasted or broiled item.
• When planning a Chinese menu, a mixture of fresh orange sections and pineapple chunks makes a cool, refreshing dessert. Top with a scoop of lemon sherbet or a bit of shredded coconut, if you like.

BEEF WITH PEA PODS

A classic Cantonese dish.

Makes 4 servings
1-1/2 pounds flank steak or 1-inch-thick boneless round steak
1/2 pound fresh pea pods
4 ounces peeled whole water chestnuts, drained
1 small sweet red pepper
3 tablespoons peanut or vegetable oil
1 teaspoon light soy sauce
1/4 cup water
2 tablespoons oyster sauce, at room temperature

MARINADE
1 garlic clove, peeled and finely chopped
1/2 teaspoon finely chopped fresh ginger root
1 tablespoon dark soy sauce
1 tablespoon cornstarch
1/4 teaspoon salt
1/8 teaspoon freshly ground black pepper
1/2 teaspoon Oriental sesame oil
1 teaspoon sugar

GRAVY SOLUTION
1 tablespoon cornstarch
3 tablespoons cold water
1/8 teaspoon monosodium glutamate (optional)

Preparation: With a sharp knife, score steak diagonally to a depth of 1/8 inch at 1-inch intervals in both directions on both sides (or treat with a mechanical meat tenderizer). Cut steak into 1-1/2-inch-wide strips along its length. Cut strips into 1/4-inch-wide slices on a diagonal. Remove stems and strings from pea pods. Slice water chestnuts 1/8 inch thick; seed red pepper and cut into short strips about 1/2 inch wide. Place meat in mixing bowl and add all marinade ingredients. Mix with hand and allow to marinate at least 15 minutes, but no more than 30 minutes. While meat is marinating, mix together Gravy Solution ingredients in a small bowl. Assemble all ingredients and wok lid next to range.

To cook: Preheat wok over high heat 2–3 minutes. Add 2 tablespoons oil to wok, add beef, then light soy sauce and stir fry 3–4 minutes. Beef should be almost done. Dish out onto plate and set aside. Add remaining tablespoon oil to wok; add water chestnuts, red pepper and pea pods, stirring between additions. Cook about 1 minute, then add water, cover and cook about 2 minutes or until pea pods turn bright green. Return beef to wok, stir, cover and cook 1 minute. Stir Gravy Solution, add to pan and stir until sauce thickens and coats the ingredients. Sprinkle with oyster sauce, stir and serve immediately.

STEAK WITH GREEN PEPPER

Fermented black beans, always used in small quantities, give this dish its unique flavor.

Makes 4 servings
1-1/2 pounds flank steak or 1-inch-thick boneless round steak
1-1/2 teaspoons fermented black beans
3 sweet green peppers
1 large tomato
4 tablespoons vegetable or peanut oil
1/4 teaspoon salt
1/4 cup water

MARINADE
2 teaspoons dark soy sauce
2 teaspoons cornstarch
1/2 teaspoon Oriental sesame oil

GRAVY SOLUTION
1 tablespoon cornstarch
1/4 cup cold water
1 tablespoon dark soy sauce
1/4 teaspoon freshly ground black pepper
1/8 teaspoon monosodium glutamate (optional)

Preparation: With a sharp knife, score steak diagonally to a depth of 1/8 inch at 1-inch intervals in both directions on both sides (or treat with a mechanical meat tenderizer). Cut steak into 1-1/2-inch-wide strips along its length. Cut strips into 1/4-inch-thick slices on a diagonal. Place meat in mixing bowl and add all marinade ingredients. Mix with hand and allow to marinate at least 15 minutes, but no more than 30 minutes. While meat is marinating, place black beans in a small bowl, cover with water and let stand 5–10 minutes. Lift beans from water and chop finely. Seed green peppers and cut into strips about 1/2 by 1-1/2 inches. Core tomato and cut into wedges. Mix together Gravy Solution ingredients in a small bowl. Assemble all ingredients and wok lid next to range.

To cook: Preheat wok over high heat 2–3 minutes. Add 2 tablespoons oil to wok, add beef and stir fry 3–4 minutes. Beef should be almost done. Dish out onto plate and set aside. Add remaining 2 tablespoons oil to wok, add salt and fermented black beans, stir briefly, and add green peppers. Stir fry about 30 seconds, add water, cover and cook about 3 minutes, lifting lid to stir once. Return beef to wok, cover and cook about 1 minute. Add tomato wedges, stir Gravy Solution and add, and then stir to combine until sauce thickens and coats the ingredients. Serve immediately.

HUNAN PORK WITH RICE STICKS

This "dry" stir fry, a favorite of Chicago cooking teacher Chu Yen Luke, gets its "kick" from chili paste with garlic, a bottled blend found in Oriental markets. Its non-saucy consistency insures the rice sticks stay crispy. While the presentation is particularly pretty with rice sticks, steamed rice can be substituted.

Makes 2 or 3 servings
2 ounces rice sticks
2 cups peanut or vegetable oil
1 can (15 ounces) straw mushrooms, drained
4 ounces peeled whole water chestnuts, drained
1/4 pound pea pods
1 pound boneless pork shoulder or pork tenderloin
1 tablespoon chili paste with garlic

MARINADE
2 garlic cloves, peeled and minced
2 teaspoons light soy sauce
2 teaspoons cooking rice wine
1/2 teaspoon sugar
1 teaspoon Oriental sesame oil
2 teaspoons cornstarch

Preparation: Line a jelly-roll pan with paper toweling. Break rice sticks into 3-inch lengths and arrange loosely on a plate. Heat oil in wok. It is ready when a small piece of rice stick puffs up when dropped into the oil. Since rice sticks need room for expansion, you will need to fry them in 2–3 batches. Slide rice sticks from plate into hot oil. As soon as they puff up, turn the airy mass over with a Chinese spatula and slotted spoon, fry 15–30 seconds more (do not let them color) and remove to lined jelly-roll pan. Turn off heat and allow wok to cool while finishing preparation. Put well-drained mushrooms in a bowl. Cut each water chestnut into 3 or 4 slices. Remove stems and strings from pea pods. If using boneless pork shoulder, first cut in 2- by 2-inch strips and then into slices 2 by 1 by 1/4 inch. If using pork tenderloin, cut in half lengthwise and then in slices as above.* Place meat in bowl, add all marinade in-gredients and mix with hand. Set aside for at least 15 minutes, but no more than 30 minutes. Divide rice sticks equally among 2 or 3 plates. Arrange ingredients and wok lid near range. Pour off all but about 2 tablespoons of oil from wok.

To cook: Heat wok (with oil) over high heat 2–3 minutes. Add pork and stir fry about 3 minutes or until pork loses its pink color. Add water chestnuts, mushrooms and pea pods, stirring after each addition. Stir fry another 1–2 minutes, add chili paste, stir to blend thoroughly and divide equally among the rice-stick-lined plates. Serve immediately.

*To insure tender pork, use mechanical meat tenderizer on meat before slicing.

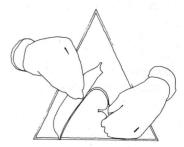

Remove stems from pea pods.

WOOLLY LAMB

This dish gets its woolly name from the white, airy bean threads that top it.

Makes 4 servings
2 cups vegetable or peanut oil
2 ounces bean thread noodles or rice sticks
1 ounce dried Chinese black mushrooms (about 3/4 cup)*
1-1/4 pounds boneless lamb, slightly frozen
1 medium onion
4 ounces peeled whole water chestnuts, drained
4 ounces bamboo shoots, drained
1/4 pound pea pods, strings removed

FLAVORING SAUCE
1 tablespoon dark soy sauce
1 tablespoon cooking rice wine
1 teaspoon sugar
1/2 teaspoon salt

THICKENING SOLUTION
1 tablespoon cornstarch
3 tablespoons cold water

Preparation: Heat oil in wok and fry bean thread noodles or rice sticks as described in Hunan Pork with Rice Sticks (preceding). Remove to a jelly-roll pan lined with paper toweling. Turn off heat and allow wok to cool while finishing preparation. To soften mushrooms, place in a bowl, cover with cold water and top with another bowl to keep them submerged. Soak about 20–30 minutes or until soft; drain, pressing out excess moisture, then cut out hard stems and shred caps. Cut lamb into thin slices; stack a few slices at a time and shred by cutting into matchstick strips. Peel onion, cut in half and slice thinly. Thinly slice water chestnuts and shred bamboo shoots. Remove stems and strings from pea pods; shred the pods by laying them out in a parallel row and cutting them into thin lengthwise strips. In a small bowl, stir together Flavoring Sauce ingredients; in another bowl, stir together Thickening Solution. Assemble all ingredients and wok lid near range. Pour off all but 2–3 tablespoons oil from wok.

To cook: Heat wok (with oil) over high heat 2–3 minutes. Add onion and stir fry until transparent but still firm. Add lamb** and stir until pink color is gone, about 3–5 minutes. Stir Flavoring Sauce and add to wok; then add water chestnuts, bamboo shoots and pea pods, stirring briefly after each addition. Cover and cook about 1 minute. Stir Thickening Solution, add to wok and stir until sauce thickens and coats the ingredients. With a spatula remove to platter and top with fried bean threads.

*Dried Chinese black mushrooms can be purchased whole or shredded. If you have purchased shredded ones, they can be soaked in the same manner as described for the whole ones.

**To make this a Wild and Woolly Lamb, add 1 or more whole "red devils" (dried Chinese hot red peppers) when adding lamb. Whew!

SAUTEING AND FRYING RECIPES

In the following recipes, the meats are sautéed or fried. Look to Chapter 2 for information on these cooking methods.

DAVID RICKE'S BEER-FRIED PORK TENDERS

David Ricke is a handsome mountain of a man who lives in Greensburg, Indiana, with his wife Susan and four daughters. In his travels throughout the Midwest and South as a soil and animal-nutrition consultant, David samples many a down-home dish in roadside eateries. Here's one of his favorites.

Makes 4 servings
1 pork tenderloin (about 1-1/2 pounds)
·1 cup milk
1/2 cup beer
1/2 cup unbleached flour
1/2 teaspoon Healthful Seasoned Salt (page 99), or purchased seasoned salt
Peanut oil
Milk Gravy (following; optional)

Cut pork tenderloin into 1-inch-thick slices. Pound each slice thin with a meat pounder or fist, or use a mechanical meat tenderizer to pound and tenderize all at once. In a shallow glass baking dish, stir together milk and beer. Add meat slices and marinate overnight (or at least 6 hours). In a shallow bowl, stir together flour and seasoned salt. Pour peanut oil into high-sided saucepan or deep-fat fryer to a depth of 1-1/2 inches. Heat until a small piece of bread sizzles upon hitting the oil. Lift pork slice from marinade, letting excess liquid drip off; coat slice with flour mixture, shake off excess and add to hot oil. Repeat with all slices. (Reserve marinade for making gravy.) Fry slices until they float to top of oil and turn golden brown, about 5 minutes. Lift out with slotted utensil and drain on paper toweling. Serve as is or with Milk Gravy.

MILK GRAVY

Makes about 1-1/4 cups
4 slices bacon, cut into 1/4-inch pieces
2 tablespoons unbleached flour
1-1/4 cups reserved milk-beer marinade from David Ricke's Beer-fried Pork Tenders (preceding)
Salt and freshly ground black pepper to taste

Cook and stir bacon in small saucepan over medium heat until bacon renders its fat and pieces begin to brown, about 5 minutes. With slotted spoon, remove bacon from pan; set aside. You should have 2 tablespoons drippings. Add flour to drippings and whisk to combine; cook, stirring, 2 minutes. Add reserved marinade all at once and whisk vigorously to combine. Stir over medium heat until gravy thickens, about 3 minutes. Taste and adjust seasoning with salt and pepper. Continue to simmer over low heat 2–3 minutes. To serve, pour gravy over meat and, if serving, potatoes; sprinkle with reserved bacon pieces.

P.Q.'s SIMPLE STEAK AU POIVRE

P.Q. is a lady who loves to entertain but has little time for cooking. Here's a recipe the men in her life really like.

Makes 4 servings*
4 rib-eye steaks, cut or pounded 1/2 inch thick
2 teaspoons coarsely ground white or black pepper
1–2 tablespoons unsalted butter
1/2–1 tablespoon olive oil
Kosher salt to taste
1/2 cup dry vermouth**
1 cup whipping cream
About 1/2 teaspoon dried tarragon, crushed

Pat steaks dry. Firmly press pepper into both sides of steaks and let stand about 15 minutes. Heat butter and oil in a nonstick 12-inch frypan until sizzling. Add steaks and cook over medium-high heat about 3 minutes per side or to desired doneness. Remove to warm platter, sprinkle with salt, and keep warm in a 150°F oven.

To make sauce, add vermouth to drippings in pan. Bring to a boil and boil until reduced by half. Stir in whipping cream and tarragon; boil 3–4 minutes to thicken slightly. Spoon sauce over steaks. Serve immediately.

*This recipe can be easily halved or quartered.

**Dry vermouth can be substituted for dry white wine in cooking, and once opened has a much longer shelf life.

BRANDIED STEAK FOR TWO

A sauté of tender steaks with a blackberry brandy sauce.

Makes 2 servings*
2 tablespoons unsalted butter
1/2 tablespoon olive oil
2 New York strip steaks,* 3/4–1 inch thick
Kosher salt
Freshly ground black pepper
2 tablespoons minced shallots or green onions
1/2 cup blackberry brandy
2 teaspoons Dijon-style mustard
2 teaspoons Worcestershire sauce
1/2 cup Quick Beef Stock (page 99), or other beef stock
1/8 teaspoon dried thyme, crushed

Melt butter with oil in a 10-inch frypan. Season steaks with salt and pepper. When foam subsides, add steaks and cook over high heat about 2 minutes per side. Reduce heat to medium and cook 2–3 minutes more per side or to desired doneness. (Test by inserting an instant-read thermometer horizontally or by making a small incision in the steak.) Remove to warm platter and put in 150°F oven.

To make sauce, add shallots to pan and cook about 1 minute. Whisk in blackberry brandy, mustard and Worcestershire sauce; boil about 2 minutes, scraping up brown bits from bottom of pan. Add beef stock and thyme and boil until reduced by half. Spoon sauce over steaks and serve immediately.

*To order by mail, see Prime Time Beef listing in Mail-Order Sources.

SHERRIED LIVER WITH ONIONS

If you've given up on liver because you've never found a recipe you like, try this one flavored with a full-bodied *oloroso* sherry. For tender, moist liver, always cook it over low to moderate heat; high heat will quickly toughen it.

Makes 2 servings*
2–3 tablespoons bacon drippings
1 large onion, peeled and thickly sliced
1 tablespoon unsalted butter
3 tablespoons unbleached flour
1/8 teaspoon Healthful Seasoned Salt (page 99), or purchased seasoned salt
2 slices calf or beef liver (about 6 ounces *each*)

SHERRY SAUCE
1/4 cup *oloroso* sherry
1/4 teaspoon Dijon-style mustard
3/4 cup Quick Beef Stock (page 99), or other beef stock
1 teaspoon cornstarch
1 tablespoon cold water

Melt bacon drippings in a 9- or 10-inch frypan over medium-low heat, add onion and sauté until tender, stirring often. With a slotted spoon, remove onion to a heat-proof platter or jelly-roll pan and place in a 150°F oven. Add butter to drippings in frypan. Stir together flour and seasoned salt; coat liver slices with flour mixture and shake off excess. Cook liver in frypan over medium-low heat until lightly browned on the outside and pale pink on the inside, 3–4 minutes per side. To test for doneness, make a small incision in 1 slice. Remove liver to platter with onion and place in warm oven.

To make sauce, pour off all but 2 tablespoons of drippings from pan, add sherry and boil over high heat until syrupy, about 2–3 minutes. Stir in mustard and beef stock and continue to boil about 3 minutes. Stir together cornstarch and water and add to pan, stirring constantly. Bring to a boil, spoon over liver and onion and serve immediately.

*This recipe can be easily doubled or halved.

OTHER MEAT RECIPES

TRIM AND TASTY STEAK TARTARE

This recipe is dedicated to the very fit Mr. Lee Flaherty, founder of Flair Communications, the country's premiere sales promotion firm, and America's Marathon/Chicago. Like Lee, his recipe has no visible fat.

Makes 2 luncheon portions, or 6–8 appetizer servings
1 pound lean top round, trimmed of all fat
2–4 green onions, cut in pieces
1 egg yolk
1 tablespoon Worcestershire sauce
About 1/4 teaspoon kosher salt
Freshly ground black pepper to taste
Cocktail rye bread
Capers, caviar and/or chopped hard-cooked egg

Cut meat into 1-inch chunks. In a food processor fitted with a steel blade, process meat using on-off pulsing until it is chopped to a fine consistency. Transfer meat to mixing bowl. Mince green onions in food processor by dropping them down food tube while machine is running. Add onions to meat with egg yolk, Worcestershire sauce, salt and pepper. Mix thoroughly with a spoon. Taste and correct seasonings. To serve, form into a mound on a platter and surround with cocktail rye. Garnish top of mound with capers, caviar and/or hard-cooked egg, or pass separately in small bowls.

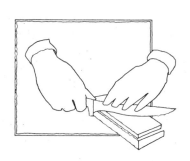

THE PUP PRIMER

There are days in every cook's life when schedules or tastebuds say "It's time for a hot dog!" Here are the basics of hot dog cookery. To give hot dogs a gourmet touch, serve them with exotic mustards like cream or German wholegrain.

BOILED HOT DOGS Bring at least 2 inches water to a boil, add hot dog(s), return to a boil and cook 5 minutes.

STEAMED HOT DOGS Bring water to a boil in a saucepan with steaming basket in place. Add hot dog(s), cover and steam about 5 minutes.

HOT DOGS BRAISED IN BEER Cover hot dog(s) in saucepan with a half beer and half water solution. Bring to simmer and cook 5–7 minutes.

BROILED/GRILLED HOT DOGS Preheat broiler or outdoor grill. Broil hot dog(s) 3–4 inches from heat, turning once or more, for about 5 minutes or until well browned.

II THE MEAT ALTERNATIVES
Fish, Shellfish, & Poultry

Fish and poultry are rising in popularity as alternatives to meat for two basic reasons: (1) they are perceived by those concerned about fitness as healthier than red meats, and (2) it has become easier in recent years to serve a delicious *fresh* fish or poultry meal because of the increased availability of these products.

Frying has long been a favorite method of cooking both fish and poultry. Who doesn't salivate at the mention of fried chicken or shrimp tempura? Poaching, up until recently more of a *haute cuisine* restaurant technique than part of an at-home cook's repertoire, is becoming more widely used because it yields moist, flavorful results and is a low-fat cooking method.

SHALLOW FRYING AND DEEP FRYING

Fried foods, if correctly prepared, are not greasy. The temperature of the oil is the most crucial factor determining success; it should be 325° to 375°F to properly sear the foods as soon as they are added to it.

Frying can be done with a small amount of vegetable or peanut oil, hydrogenated shortening (such as Crisco), lard, or a combination of oil and butter. Peanut or vegetable oil is preferred, however, because these oils have the highest smoking points (that temperature at which an oil or fat smokes and breaks down; in short, the point at which it burns).

SHALLOW-FRYING GUIDELINES

A frypan and oil to a depth of 1/8 to 1/2 inch are commonly used for shallow frying. Heat the oil over high heat. Watch for a hazy pattern to form in the oil; when that pattern has subsided, the oil should be hot enough. Test the temperature by dropping a small piece of onion, celery or bread in the oil; if it sizzles and bubbles, the oil is ready. After frying, discard the oil, or save it as described in the Deep-frying Guidelines that follow.

DEEP-FRYING GUIDELINES

Deep frying, which produces some of America's favorite foods, is a bit trickier than shallow frying and can be messy. Follow these guidelines for best results.
• Use a heavy-gauge, deep, well-balanced pot or a wok. A deep-fat fryer is not necessary but can be useful if you cook fried foods often.
• Use a deep-fat thermometer to gauge the temperature of the oil, or drop a bit of celery, onion or bread into the oil and watch for it to sizzle and float immediately. If the temperature is too low, the food will sink to the bottom and get oil-logged. If it is too high, the outside will burn before the inside is done. Never heat oil over 400°F.
• Select either peanut or vegetable oil. Peanut has the highest smoking point (475°F) and stands up better to repeated use. It also imparts a distinct but subtle flavor to foods and is expensive as oils go. Vegetable oil, which smokes at 425° to 450°F depending on the type (soybean, sunflower, safflower, corn), is less expensive but does not hold up to repeated use as well.

• Fill the pot with oil deep enough to cover food, but leave at least three inches between top of oil and top of pot. When food is added, it will bubble up.
• Foods to be fried should be dry to avoid splattering.
• Do not crowd foods in the pot. They need room to bubble and turn.
• Use a slotted spoon or Chinese skimmer (available at Oriental markets and wherever woks are sold) to remove cooked foods from oil. (The skimmer is also great for removing foods from boiling liquids.)
• Drain fried foods in a single layer on a jelly-roll pan lined with two or three layers of paper toweling. If foods are stacked, they become soggy. Fried foods should be served immediately; if they cannot, keep them warm for a short time by placing jelly-roll pan in a 250°F oven.
• To strain oil after use, let pot cool to handling temperature. Place a clean jar or the oil bottle in a *dry* sink. (If the bottle is touching cold water, it may crack when hot oil is added.) Line a funnel with a coffee filter, two or three layers of cheesecloth (available at gourmet shops) or paper toweling; set fun-nel in jar and pour oil through funnel. Let oil cool completely before covering, then wipe jar, label with item cooked in oil and store in the refrigerator. Oil that has been used for cooking fish should be reused only for fish. Peanut oil can be used a total of three or four times. Discard any oil that turns dark or has an unpleasant odor; it has gone rancid.

POACHING

Poaching is cooking foods in very gently simmering water or stock. In fish and seafood cookery, the poaching liquid is often a court bouillon made by adding onion or shallot, clam juice or fish stock and spices to water. Because the simmer is gentle, poaching does not toughen the tender flesh of fish, shellfish or chicken. Usually the food is added to the already hot poaching liquid. The liquid should cover the food and cooked food should be lifted out with a slotted spoon or Chinese skimmer. Poaching whole fish requires a special long narrow pan known as a fish poacher. The word poach can also refer to cooking foods very gently in butter or butter mixed with liquid.

FISH AND SHELLFISH

BUYING AND HANDLING FISH AND SHELLFISH

There is only one thing you need to know when buying fish and shellfish, and that's your fish market. Is it highly respected and crowded? Yes, crowded! Never complain about standing in line at the fish market; it is a sign of fast turnover, which insures freshness. Supermarket fish departments, while often well planned and well intentioned, just as often do not have the high turnover necessary for optimum quality. Fish is highly perishable. The longer out of the water, the less fresh tasting and moist it will be. Here are some tips for selection.
• Seek out a reputable fish retailer, preferably one who also supplies restaurants. He or she is likely to have better turnover, variety and pricing.
• Buy fresh fish and shellfish whenever possible. While the flash-freezing techniques of the 1980s have come a long way, there is nothing quite so delicious as fresh seafood.

• If you have any doubts about your selection's freshness, plant your nose right near it and take a good whiff. Your nose will tell you in a second: fresh fish have a clean, fresh smell; off-odors indicate lengthy time out of the water or poor handling.

• When purchasing whole fish, look at the eyes. They should be clear as opposed to cloudy, bulging as opposed to sunken.

• "Dressed" is the term that means a fish has been scaled and eviscerated (gutted); you'll want to order whole fish dressed to avoid doing the job yourself.

• Frozen fish may be cooked while still frozen (except for grilling or broiling), but will need extra time. Thaw frozen fish in refrigerator. Never refreeze thawed fish.

• Keep fish in coldest part of refrigerator or meat keeper and cook as soon as possible after purchase.

• Fresh oysters and clams should be alive when opened, and live oysters and clams usually keep their shells closed. To test a partially opened oyster or clam, tap on its shell with a spoon or knife. If it closes, the mollusk is alive. If it doesn't, the critter is dead; discard.

GRILLING FISH

Fish and outdoor grilling are a match made in culinary heaven. Not only are the results delicious, but they are also generally low in fat and calorie count. There are three basic ways to cook fish on the grill:

1. Whole fish or fish fillets can be wrapped in aluminum foil with seasonings and steamed on the grill. This method is best for lean fish like sole, cod and pollock.

2. Fish can be placed in a well-oiled hinged wire basket that is set on the hot grill. This method works weli for whole fish or any fish you will be basting with a sauce.

3. Whole fish or fillets can be placed directly on the hot grill surface. This method and the wire-basket one are good for fattier fish like salmon, swordfish and bluefish.

GRILLING TIPS

• Always try to use fresh fish on the grill. If you must use frozen, thaw it completely before grilling so it cooks evenly.

• When cooking fish directly on the grill, dip the fish in vegetable oil first. When using a basket, generously oil either the fish or the basket to prevent sticking. *Do not* use butter as it will burn.

• Make sure the coals are white and the grill is hot before adding fish. Putting fish on a cold grill could cause sticking.

• Whole fish are sturdier for grilling than fillets.

• Add flavor to grilled fish by sprinkling a handful of water-soaked hickory or mesquite chips over the hot coals before cooking.

• You can also sprinkle a handful of fresh or dried herbs over the hot coals. The resulting smoke will flavor foods.

• For a light smoky flavor, grill fish on an open grill. For a heavier flavor, cover the grill, but be careful not to overcook the fish.

• Weather conditions will affect outdoor cooking times. For example, cooking will probably take longer on a windy day than on a sunny day. Your eyes will tell you when the fish is done: watch for it to become firm and tighten up and look for the bones to *begin* to pop up from the surface. Once these cues are sighted, remove the fish from the grill immediately to prevent it from drying out.

A WORD ABOUT OYSTERS

Let's get right down to it. Are oysters the food of virility as is commonly thought? "Not exactly," says oyster-shucking expert Bob Langley of Burhop's Fish and Seafood Wholesalers. He explains that there are traces of arsenic, a human body element, in all shellfish including oysters, and that if you ate oysters frequently over a period of several months, fertility would likely increase. That's *fertility*, gentlemen, not *virility*. There *is* a difference.

For oyster lovers, however, the question of fertility versus virility does not matter because they are after the taste, texture and delightful "sea freshness" of an oyster newly shucked. Currently, the oyster variety most commonly available around the country is a Long Island–farmed type known simply as a "half shell oyster." People who think bluepoints are the only oysters for raw consumption should be advised that the term refers to a specific geographic area, not to a type of oyster. According to fish retailers, that area simply cannot produce sufficient quantities to satisfy the national oyster demand, so farming oys-

ters in their native waters is now practiced. This development both increases supply and yields a more consistent product.

A true oyster connoisseur would not even bother with a fork when eating these tender mollusks on the half shell. He would pick up the shells one by one and slide the oysters into his mouth, with nary a sauce except for a few drops of red wine vinegar and some minced shallot.

Whether you like your oysters raw or cooked, you'll want to shuck them yourself for freshest flavor. Check your fish market for the proper oyster knife, which is not to be confused with a clam knife. It should have a rubberized handle and strong stainless-steel blade with slightly curved edges and tip.

HOW TO SHUCK AN OYSTER
Shucking oysters does not depend on strength, but rather on technique. It is a matter of leverage and patience. Once you master it, which will not take long, you will amaze yourself and your friends with your proficiency and speed.

1. Rinse oysters under cold running water, scrubbing gently with a stiff-bristle vegetable brush to remove any grit and loose pieces of shell.
2. Place oyster round side down on a folded towel. Wrap second towel around your left hand (if you are right-handed) for protection from the sharp shell edges. Locate the small gap next to the oyster's hinge. Insert tip of oyster knife (with curve facing up) into gap and work blade in by wiggling it from side to side while firmly pushing point into oyster at the same time.
3. Apply pressure until you feel the blade become firmly imbedded. Twist knife in one direction and lift up tip at the same time to "pop" hinge.
4. Wipe knife blade on towel to cleanse it of any shell fragments.

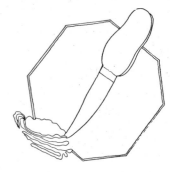

Insert tip of oyster knife into gap.

Slide blade between top and bottom shells near hinge so it goes all the way across and sticks out the other side.

5. Twist the blade to separate the shells, then grasp top shell with free hand and pull it up to open. If oyster is still attached to top shell, slide knife blade along shell to sever the connection. Include the round, tough muscle, if you like, or cut around it. Discard top shell.

6. To disconnect oyster from shell for easy eating, slide knife blade under meat. Serve on the shell or use in your favorite recipes.

HOW TO PEEL AND DEVEIN SHRIMP

1. Starting at underside (leg side) of shrimp, peel away the shell. Leave the last joint next to the tail in place when recipe calls for it. To peel completely, pull open and gently pull off shell tail section.

2. With paring knife, cut shallow slit the length of shrimp along the rounded edge.

3. Pull out vein, which ranges in color from black to clear, depending on the shrimp and what it last ate.

Pull out vein from shrimp.

4. To butterfly the shrimp, cut along slit (from which vein was removed) down through shrimp almost to underside. The shrimp will fan out and cooking time will be shorter due to reduced thickness.

GRILLED SALMON OR BASS

Grilled whole fish is among the most impressive presentations for guests. It's also a delicious, light meal—and very chic! For added panache, try the flaming sauce.

Makes 4–6 servings
1 whole salmon, striped bass or
    sea bass, dressed (3-1/2–4
    pounds)
Kosher salt and freshly ground
    black pepper to taste
About 1/2 teaspoon fennel seeds
About 6 strips lemon rind (yellow
    portion only)
Peanut oil

Flaming Cognac Sauce (following), or Tartare Sauce
(page 41)

Prepare outdoor grill, using mesquite chips for added flavor, if desired. (See Flavoring the Barbecue with Wood in Chapter 1.) Pat fish dry inside and out with paper toweling. Sprinkle salt, pepper, fennel seeds and lemon strips in fish cavity. Brush peanut oil generously over outside of fish.

Enclose fish in basket or place directly on preheated grill 4–5 inches from heat source. Cook 10 minutes for each inch of thickness, turning over halfway through cooking time. (Fish can also be roasted on a jelly-roll pan in a preheated 400°F oven 20–30 minutes.) To test for doneness, look inside cavity to backbone; no pink or red color should remain but cavity should still look moist. Remove fish to platter and top with cognac sauce or accompany with tartare sauce. To serve, slit with serving spoon along backbone; use 2 serving spoons to lift off skin. Cut flesh at intervals down to bones and lift from bones. When all flesh has been removed, turn fish over and repeat procedure on second side.

FLAMING COGNAC SAUCE

1/2 cup cognac
1/2 teaspoon fennel seeds

Heat cognac and fennel seeds in a heavy 9- or 10-inch frypan on range or outdoor grill. When hot but not boiling, remove from heat and immediately touch a match to the cognac to ignite. Let burn about 30 seconds, then pour over fish while still flaming. If you wish to extinguish flames before pouring over fish, either let them die out naturally or cover pan with lid to close off air.

GREEK-STYLE SWORDFISH KABOBS

Makes 4 servings
1-1/2 pounds swordfish steaks (1 inch thick)
1/2 cup olive oil
1/4 cup fresh lemon juice (about 1 lemon)
1 teaspoon dried oregano, crushed
1/2 teaspoon dried rosemary, crushed
1/2 teaspoon kosher salt
1/4 teaspoon freshly ground black pepper

1 large sweet red pepper, seeded and cut into 1-inch chunks
1 medium red onion, peeled, cut into wedges, and wedges halved
1/2 lemon, cut into 4 wedges
12 small bay leaves

Cut swordfish into 1-inch pieces and place pieces in a shallow glass baking dish. Combine oil, lemon juice, oregano, rosemary, salt and pepper and pour over fish. Cover with plastic wrap and refrigerate 2–3 hours.

Preheat broiler or outdoor grill; use mesquite or hickory chips over coals for added flavor, if desired. (See Flavoring the Barbecue with Wood in Chapter 1.) Alternately thread pieces of fish, red pepper, onion and bay leaves onto 4 metal skewers. Add a lemon wedge to the end of each kabob. Reserve fish marinade. Broil kabobs 4 inches from heat source about 10 minutes, turning skewers to brown evenly. Baste occasionally with reserved marinade.

SOLE WITH VEGETABLES

Food stylist Judy Vance recommends this recipe for busy men who like to cook. It can be put together in advance, then cooked quickly.

*Makes 4 servings**
Seasoned Butter (following)
Vegetable oil
Kosher salt and freshly ground black pepper to taste
8 sole fillets (3–4 ounces *each*), or 4 scrod fillets (6–7 ounces *each* and 1/2 inch thick)
1 celery stalk, thinly sliced
1 large carrot, peeled and thinly sliced
3 green onions, thinly sliced

Prepare Seasoned Butter and refrigerate until ready to use. Tear off 4 sheets of heavy-duty aluminum foil 12 inches square. With a pastry brush, lightly oil lower half of each sheet. Sprinkle oiled portions of foil with salt and pepper. For each packet, place 2 sole fillets, one on top of the other, or one scrod fillet over seasonings. Sprinkle celery, carrot and onion over fillets, dividing equally. Top with a generous tablespoon of Seasoned Butter. To seal packets, fold foil over fillets so foil edges are even. Seal by folding edges upward 1/2 inch on all three open edges. Press to make sharp creases, then fold all around once again. Cook immediately or refrigerate no more than 12 hours.

Preheat oven to 500°F. Place heavy jelly-roll pan in oven and heat until hot, about 2 minutes. Arrange packets, butter side down, in single layer 1 inch apart on pan. Bake 4 minutes, turn packets over, bake another 4 minutes. Remove from oven and place packets on individual serving plates. Cut an X in the top of each packet and fold back foil.

*This recipe can be easily halved or quartered.

CHICKEN IN FOIL Substitute skinned boneless chicken breasts for fish fillets.

SEASONED BUTTER

1/4 pound (1 stick) unsalted butter, softened
1/4 cup snipped fresh parsley
2 tablespoons dry sherry
1/4–1/2 teaspoon kosher salt
1/2 teaspoon freshly ground black pepper

2 tablespoons snipped fresh dill, or 2 teaspoons dried dill
2 teaspoons snipped fresh chives

With a spoon, beat together all ingredients until well mixed. Cover and refrigerate until ready to use, or store up to 2 weeks.

TOM SLOUGH'S TABASCO-FRIED CATFISH WITH HUSH PUPPIES

Tom Slough (rhymes with wow) is the South's premiere catfish cook and supporter. This is the recipe he cooked for President Reagan's 1983 international economic summit in Williamsburg. When he's not cookin' up his spicy catfish, Tom chairs the annual National Farm-Raised Catfish Cooking Contest in Jackson, Mississippi, where he's also in the concrete business on the side.

Makes 4 servings
About 1-1/2 pounds farm-raised catfish fillets (3–5 ounces *each*)
Tabasco sauce
2 quarts peanut oil (no substitutions)
Kosher salt and freshly ground black pepper to taste

Self-rising cornmeal mix (available in the South), or purchased cornmeal-and-flour vegetable coating
Hush Puppies (following)
Additional Tabasco sauce, or Homemade Tartare Sauce (page 41)

Sprinkle both sides of catfish fillets liberally with Tabasco sauce and rub it in. Place fillets in a shallow glass baking dish and let stand about 1 hour. Heat oil in a heavy-gauge deep saucepan or deep-fat fryer until it registers 375°F on a deep-fat thermometer. Line a jelly-roll pan with paper toweling; preheat oven to 250°F. Combine cornmeal mix and salt and pepper. Pat fish with paper toweling to blot up excess Tabasco. Season fillets lightly with salt, dredge in cornmeal mix and fry 2–3 fillets (about 1/2 pound) at a time in the hot oil until golden, about 5 minutes. Strive to never let oil drop below 365°F. It if does, let it heat up between batches. Lift fillets out with a slotted utensil, set on lined jelly-roll pan and place in warm oven until all frying is done. Serve with Hush Puppies and more Tabasco sauce or with tartare sauce.

HUSH PUPPIES

Make batter two hours before cooking time, and fry Hush Puppies in oil separately from the catfish. It's a good idea to have a friend fry the Hush Puppies for you at the same time as you fry the fish, then everything is ready at the same time.

Makes 4 servings
1/2 cup unbleached flour
1/4 cup yellow or white cornmeal
1-1/2 teaspoons baking powder
3/4 teaspoon kosher salt
3/4 teaspoon freshly ground black
   pepper
1/4 teaspoon baking soda
1/4 teaspoon ground sage
Pinch of garlic powder
1/3 cup chopped onion
1/4 cup chopped sweet green
   pepper
1 large egg, lightly beaten
1/2 cup buttermilk
2 tablespoons minced fried catfish
   or cooked shrimp (optional)
4 cups peanut oil

Place all dry ingredients and chopped vegetables in a large mixing bowl, add egg and 1/2 cup buttermilk and stir together well.

Cover and let stand 2 hours. Stir in catfish.
   Line a jelly-roll pan with paper toweling. Heat oil in a heavy-gauge deep saucepan until it registers 350°F on a deep-fat thermometer. Drop batter into oil by tablespoonfuls and fry until deep golden brown, about 5 minutes. Do not crowd the pan. Lift out with a slotted utensil, set on lined jelly-roll pan and keep warm with catfish in 250°F oven until frying is done. Serve immediately.

OYSTERS ON THE HALF SHELL

Makes 2 servings
12 freshly shucked oysters
Crushed ice or rock salt
Lemon wedges
Cocktail Sauce (page 41)
Prepared horseradish

Use two specially designed plates that have indentations for holding the oysters, or line 2 shallow plates with crushed ice and nestle the oysters in the ice. Garnish each plate with lemon wedges and a small bowl of Cocktail Sauce. Serve horseradish on the side.

FRIED OYSTERS

The proper texture of cooked oysters is tender, not rubbery.

Makes 4 servings
24 freshly shucked oysters
2 eggs
2 tablespoons water
1/4 teaspoon kosher salt
1/8 teaspoon freshly ground black
   pepper
1 cup bread crumbs
2–3 tablespoons unsalted butter
2–3 tablespoons peanut or vegetable oil
Lemon wedges
Cocktail Sauce or Tartare Sauce
   (following)

Drain oysters. Beat eggs with water, salt and pepper. Dip oysters, one at a time, into the egg mixture, then into the bread crumbs, patting crumbs with fingertips so they cling. Place breaded oysters on plate in a single layer and let stand 5 minutes or refrigerate up to 1 hour before frying.
   Melt butter with oil in a 10-inch frypan (preferably nonstick) over medium heat until butter foam subsides. Add breaded oysters to fill pan without crowding and fry

about 2 minutes. Use 2 spoons to gently turn oysters over and cook another 2 minutes, or until lightly brown but still tender. Drain on paper toweling. Serve with lemon wedges and one of the suggested sauces.

DEEP-FRIED OYSTERS Bread oysters as above. In a deep saucepan, cook oysters 3–5 minutes in 2–2-1/2 inches peanut oil heated to 360°F. Remove with slotted spoon and drain on paper toweling. Serve immediately.

NOTE Peeled and deveined raw shrimp may be fried or deep fried in the same manner as oysters.

COCKTAIL SAUCE

Makes 1-1/2 cups
1 bottle (12 ounces) chili sauce
3–4 tablespoons fresh lemon
   juice
2 tablespoons prepared
   horseradish
2–3 tablespoons Worcestershire
   sauce

Combine all ingredients and stir well. Store in refrigerator in an air-tight container up to 4 weeks.

QUICK THOUSAND ISLAND SALAD DRESSING Stir mayonnaise and pickle relish into leftover Cocktail Sauce to taste. Thin with water, if desired.

TARTARE SAUCE

The secrets to making an outstanding tartare sauce are top-quality mayonnaise and dill pickles. Pickle relish just won't do.

Makes 1 cup
1 cup mayonnaise (preferably
   homemade, page 100)
2 tablespoons minced onion
2 tablespoons minced dill pickle
1/4 cup minced fresh parsley
1–2 tablespoons fresh lemon juice

Combine all ingredients and stir well. Refrigerate at least 1 hour to blend flavors before serving. Store in refrigerator in an air-tight container up to 1 week.

POACHED SHRIMP

If shrimp are to be eaten cold in salads and seafood cocktails, poach them as soon as you get them home. They will keep better in the refrigerator cooked than raw. Medium white shrimp are ideal for poaching, but larger shrimp can be used. In any case, do not overcook them or they will be rubbery.

2-1/2–3 quarts water
1 lemon wedge
1 celery top (leafy portion)
1 small onion or shallot, peeled
2 bay leaves
6 black peppercorns
1/2 tablespoon pickling spice
1 pound fresh raw shrimp, peeled
   and deveined

Combine all ingredients except shrimp in a large saucepan, bring to a boil, reduce heat and simmer 10 minutes. Reduce heat so water is barely simmering, add shrimp, remove pan from heat and let stand 2–3 minutes. With a slotted spoon, remove shrimp to bowl of ice water to stop the cooking. (If you are unsure if the shrimp are cooked, remove just one and taste for doneness.) Replenish ice water as needed to keep shrimp cold, then place bowl in refrigerator. Shrimp are best when eaten freshly poached, but will keep in the refrigerator 2–3 days. Drain and dry before serving.

SHRIMP COCKTAIL

Makes 2 servings*
About 1 cup shredded lettuce
2 tablespoons thinly sliced celery
8–10 cold Poached Shrimp
   (preceding)
Cocktail Sauce (page 41)
2 lemon wedges

Divide lettuce between 2 small bowls or salad plates. Sprinkle celery over lettuce and arrange shrimp on top. Spoon Cocktail Sauce over shrimp and garnish with lemon wedges.

SHRIMP WITH REMOULADE SAUCE

Makes 2 servings*
Lettuce leaves
10 cold Poached Shrimp
   (preceding)
1 tomato, cut in wedges
1 hard-cooked egg, peeled and
   quartered
Remoulade Sauce (following)
2 lemon wedges
2 sprigs parsley (optional)

*This recipe can be easily doubled or tripled.

Line 2 salad plates with lettuce leaves. Arrange shrimp, tomato and egg in pleasing pattern on lettuce. Top with spoonful of Remoulade Sauce and pass remaining sauce at the table. Garnish with lemon wedges and parsley.

REMOULADE SAUCE

Makes 1 cup
1 tablespoon Dijon-style mustard
1/8 teaspoon cayenne pepper
1/2 tablespoon paprika
1/4 teaspoon kosher salt
1 tablespoon distilled white
   vinegar
1–2 green onions, cut in pieces
1 drop Tabasco sauce
2 tablespoons thinly sliced celery
1 large sprig parsley, coarsely
   chopped
2 tablespoons catsup
1 garlic clove, peeled
1 tablespoon fresh lemon juice
1/4 teaspoon prepared
   horseradish
1 cup mayonnaise (preferably
   homemade, page 100)

Place all ingredients except mayonnaise in a blender or a food processor fitted with a steel blade. Process until well blended, scraping down sides of container with rubber scraper as needed. Add mayonnaise and process to blend. Refrigerate overnight to meld flavors. Serve with cold shrimp or crab meat.

SHRIMP AND VEGETABLE TEMPURA

Makes 4 servings
1 medium onion, peeled and
   sliced
1 large sweet potato, peeled and
   thinly sliced
1/4 pound fresh green beans
1 small zucchini (unpeeled), thinly
   sliced
1 pound fresh raw shrimp, peeled,
   deveined and butterflied
4 cups peanut or vegetable oil
Bottled teriyaki sauce

TEMPURA BATTER
2 egg whites or 1 egg
2/3 cup ice water
1/2 cup unbleached flour
1/2 cup cornstarch
1 teaspoon baking soda
Pinch of kosher salt

Prepare vegetables in advance by adding them to a large pot of boiling water and boiling 2–4 minutes. With a slotted spoon, remove vegetables to a bowl of ice water; when cold, drain and keep refrigerated along with the shrimp until ready to fry. Line a jelly-roll pan with paper toweling; preheat oven to 250°F.

To make the batter, beat egg whites in mixing bowl with portable electric mixer until foamy. Add ice water; beat to blend. Sift together flour, cornstarch, baking soda and salt into egg mixture. Beat until blended.

Make sure foods to be fried are cold. Heat oil in wok or deep pan until it registers 360°F on a deep-fat thermometer. Dip foods in batter, let excess batter drip off and add foods to hot oil. Fry until batter turns pale gold, 2–3 minutes. Remove with slotted spoon to lined jelly-roll pan and place in warm oven until all food is fried. Serve with teriyaki sauce for dipping.

LEO WALDMEIER'S WHOLE BOILED LOBSTER

As executive chef of Chicago's incomparable Drake Hotel, Swiss-born Waldmeier supervises food preparation for all the hotel's restaurants, including its award-winning Cape Cod Room where lobsters can be ordered boiled, steamed or broiled. Here's Leo's simple method for at-home preparation.

SELECTING AND STORING LIVE LOBSTER Buying live lobsters can be tricky, as after captivity their meat can shrink within the shell due to lack of feeding. Look for a lively lobster, which signals recent capture and, usually, plump meat. Ask your fishmonger for a female lobster, and the first time around, ask to be shown both a female and male so you can tell them apart in the future. The female is preferable because her roe flavors the cooking liquid and meat. If lobster is packed in seaweed, refrigerate as is. If not, wrap in wet newspapers or a kitchen towel and place in a shallow pan in the refrigerator. In either case, cook as soon as possible.

COOKING THE LOBSTER Use a 12-quart (3-gallon) pot; you can sometimes borrow or rent one from the fish market where you buy the lobsters. Fill pot with 8 quarts water and add 2 cut-up carrots, 1/2 onion, 2 cut-up celery stalks with tops, a few parsley sprigs with stems, one bay leaf, a few very coarsely ground black peppercorns and a handful of rock or kosher salt. Bring to a boil and boil rapidly for 10 minutes.

Holding lobster by the middle, quickly immerse it head first into boiling water. This provides a quick end to the critter. As soon as water returns to a boil, reduce heat so water is gently simmering, cover and cook 12 minutes for a 1–1-1/4-pound lobster; 15 minutes for a 1-1/2–2-pound lobster. With tongs, remove lobster to cutting board. Using a large, sharp chef's knife held almost straight up and down, insert point of knife into middle of head and bring knife blade down in swift, firm motion to split complete length of lobster. Finish splitting head and crack claws by hitting firmly with dull edge of knife blade or with a hammer. Serve with lemon half and melted butter.

TO COOK MORE THAN ONE LOBSTER If pot cannot accommodate more than one completely immersed lobster at a time, remove first lobster after cooking, wrap in a kitchen towel soaked in the cooking liquid and set on a jelly-roll pan in a 200°F oven while second lobster is cooking. Split and serve both lobsters.

MICHAEL CASASANTO'S LOBSTER BAY DELIGHT

This recipe won the 1982 Bays English Muffin Recipe Contest for the very young and creative Michael Casasanto. Serve with fresh fruit for a special brunch.

Makes 2 servings
4 cups water
1/2 teaspoon kosher salt
1/2 carrot, peeled and thinly sliced
1/2 leek, thinly sliced
1/2 celery stalk, thinly sliced
1 tablespoon unsalted butter
1 tablespoon minced onion
1/4 cup dry vermouth or dry white wine
10 ounces (2-1/2 sticks) unsalted butter, cut into 1/2-inch dice
2 teaspoons fresh lemon juice
Kosher salt
Freshly ground white pepper
About 3/4 pound cooked lobster meat, sliced 1/4-inch thick
2 Bays English muffins, split, toasted and buttered
2 teaspoons minced fresh parsley

Bring water to a boil, add 1/2 teaspoon salt, carrot, leek and celery. Boil until vegetables are crisp-tender, about 5 minutes. Remove vegetables with slotted spoon to a bowl; leave water to simmer over low heat.

To make sauce, melt 1 tablespoon butter in a small saucepan over medium heat, add onion and sauté until tender, about 3 minutes. Add vermouth and boil to reduce liquid to 1 tablespoon. Reduce heat to low. With a whisk, whisk in butter 3–4 pieces at a time until all of the butter is incorporated. Add lemon juice and salt and pepper to taste. Keep warm over very low heat.

Drop vegetables and lobster into simmering water for 1–2 minutes. Place split English muffins, buttered sides up, on 2 serving plates. Drain vegetables and lobster well and distribute over muffins evenly. Pour sauce over muffins and sprinkle with parsley.

SCALLOPS IN CREAMY MUSTARD

This piquant treatment for scallops should be prepared at the last minute. Serve over steamed rice or with boiled potatoes.

Makes 2 servings
1/2 cup dry white wine or dry vermouth
1/2 cup bottled clam juice
1 tablespoon Dijon-style mustard
1/4 cup Crème Fraîche (page 74), or whipping cream
3/4 pound fresh sea or bay scallops
1/8 teaspoon Healthful Seasoned Salt (page 99), or purchased seasoned salt
1/2 cup unbleached flour
2 tablespoons unsalted butter
2 tablespoons vegetable or olive oil
1 teaspoon cornstarch
1 tablespoon cold water

In a small saucepan, combine wine and clam juice, bring to a boil over high heat and stir in mustard. Add Crème Fraîche and blend with whisk. Return to a boil, reduce heat and simmer until sauce is reduced by one-fourth, about 15 minutes. Remove sauce from heat and set aside.

Cut each sea scallop in half to form 2 discs; leave bay scallops whole. Cut off tiny tough muscles clinging to scallops. Stir seasoned salt into flour, dust scallops with flour and shake off excess. In a 10-inch frypan, melt butter with oil over medium heat; reduce heat to low and add scallops in single layer. (Cook scallops in 2 batches, if needed.) Cook 1–2 minutes, shaking pan gently. Turn scallops and cook 1 minute more. Remove to a plate. Pour excess butter from pan and stir sauce into pan. Simmer over medium heat about 5 minutes. Combine cornstarch and water, stir into sauce and bring to a boil. Reduce heat to low, add scallops and heat 1 minute. Serve immediately.

STEAMED CLAMS WITH LEMON BUTTER

Ask for steamer clams at your fish market to make this Cape Cod classic. Don't skip the cornmeal step or your clams may be gritty.

Makes 4 servings
3 quarts steamer clams (about 3-1/2 pounds)
Handful of cornmeal
1/4 pound (1 stick) unsalted butter
1 tablespoon fresh lemon juice
3/4 cup beer
1 onion, peeled and chopped
1/2 teaspoon dried thyme, crushed, or 1 sprig thyme
4 black peppercorns

Clean steamers by swishing in large pot of cold water; use stiff brush to remove any foreign materials from shells. Discard any clams that float. Drain off water; cover clams with cold water and stir in handful of cornmeal. Let stand at least 2 hours. Drain again and rinse thoroughly in cold water.

Melt butter in a small saucepan over low heat; add lemon juice and keep warm. Transfer clams to a 5-quart or larger dutch oven or stockpot. Add beer, onion, thyme and peppercorns. Cover and bring to boil over high heat. Cook at a boil, shaking pot until steamers open, 5–10 minutes. With a slotted spoon, remove open clams to serving bowls. Cover and continue cooking until remaining clams open, about 5 minutes. Discard any that do not open. Strain the cooking liquid through 2–3 layers of cheesecloth or a coffee filter into 4 small bowls. Divide lemon butter among 4 other bowls. Serve immediately.

GERRY WALLACE'S CRAB FONDUE

This creamy, rich fondue is a favorite of Gerry, a television talk-show host in Stockton, California.

Makes 2 servings
2 jars (5 ounces *each*) Old English cheddar cheese
1 package (8 ounces) cream cheese, softened
1/4 cup milk
1/2 pound crab meat (fresh or frozen and thawed)
2 dashes Worcestershire sauce
1/8 teaspoon cayenne pepper
1/4 teaspoon garlic powder
Pinch of kosher salt
1 loaf sourdough or french bread

Melt cheeses with milk in an electric fondue pot or a small saucepan set in a frypan filled with hot water. Stir to blend and add more milk if needed to make a smooth mixture. As cheese melts, add Worcestershire sauce, pepper, garlic powder and salt. When mixture is smooth, gently stir in crab meat. If using fondue forks, cut bread into 1-inch cubes; if dipping by hand, cut into larger pieces. Serve immediately.

NOTE This fondue mixture can also be served at room temperature as a chip or vegetable dip.

POULTRY

BUYING AND HANDLING POULTRY

• Patronize a supermarket or meat market with high poultry turnover to get the freshest birds. Or seek out a poultry farm or market in your community where chickens are killed upon order placement.

• Remember that a frozen product is better than an *old* fresh product. If you suspect turnover of a particular item, such as capon or duck, to be slow, by all means buy it frozen. It will have been frozen at the peak of freshness.

• Allow 1/2 to 3/4 pound per serving. This allows for bone and waste.

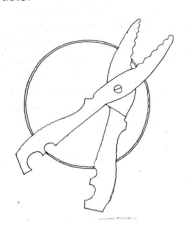

CHICKEN

• Cook fresh poultry as soon as possible after purchase. It can be kept in its packaging one to two days in the refrigerator. For longer storage, remove pieces from store packaging, wrap tightly (to eliminate as much air as possible) in freezer wrap or plastic wrap in desired quantities and freeze up to two months.

• When buying whole or cut-up prepackaged chicken, look for plump broiler-fryers (usually 2-1/2 to 3-1/2 pounds *each*) unless recipe specifies otherwise. The skin should be white-yellow and the meat should be pink. Dark colors and dryness around the edges can mean the chicken was packaged several days earlier. The fat and skin in roasting and stewing chickens (usually 5 to 6-1/2 pounds) will be a deeper yellow than in broiler-fryers.

• An accumulation of juices in the package can mean that poultry has been wrapped several days. Look for packages with as little air space and liquid as possible.

TURKEY

• Fresh turkeys can be ordered from butchers; ask for young hens or toms. Frozen turkeys are also of good quality, readily available year round and less expensive than fresh. Special turkey cuts such as rolled breasts, "baby" sizes and deboned turkey are also available frozen.

• In the fresh prepacked category, fresh turkey parts and even white meat turkey slices are now available. They are great convenience products that allow small families and individuals to enjoy turkey without buying a whole bird. Look for meat that is pink and moist.

DUCK AND CAPON

• If these items do not have a high turnover, in other words, the same item is in the case the last two or three times you visited your supermarket, order the item in advance to be delivered the day you need it, or select a frozen product.

CORNISH GAME HEN

This fowl is almost always available only frozen, usually individually wrapped and priced. Allow one hen per person.

HOW TO TRUSS A CHICKEN

This is a simplified trussing technique. No trussing needle is necessary; instead bamboo picks are used. (Look for these picks at supermarkets, fish markets and gourmet shops.) This method can be used on stuffed or unstuffed chickens, as well as capons, ducks and turkeys.

1. If chicken is wet, pat dry with paper toweling. (Never rinse a fresh chicken or chicken pieces unless you detect an aroma that does not smack of freshness.) Turn chicken breast side down and, if desired, stuff neck cavity loosely. Pull skin flap up and over neck opening and pin in place with bamboo pick. Remove excess pick length by scoring with scissors or knife and breaking it off.

2. Turn chicken breast side up. Tuck wings under chicken, bringing wing tips toward neck end before sliding them under the chicken. Wings will hold in place when this tucking is done properly.

3. Stuff chicken, if desired. Pull flap of skin over opening and pin in place with pick. Break off pick as explained in step 2.

4. With an eighteen-inch length of kitchen string, tie drumsticks together using a figure eight and a knot. Trim off excess string. Chicken is ready to roast.

5. Place chicken on elevated rack in shallow pan to roast.

SAUTE—WHAT'S IN A WORD?

The word sauté came to us from the French, and French cooking remains the greatest influence on American sauté dishes. The term has three commonly applied meanings. First, to sauté is to cook food in a frypan in a small amount of fat or oil over low to medium heat. It is a gentle style of cooking that does not shock delicately textured foods like fish and poultry into a rubbery condition. (Foods cooked in a small amount of oil at high heat are fried.) Often, foods to be sautéed are lightly dusted with flour, a technique the French call meunière (as in sole meunière). This method is sometimes called a simple sauté.

The second meaning of sauté refers to cooking food through the simple sauté stage, then adding liquid and other ingredients, such as vegetables and herbs, covering the pan and allowing the ingredients to cook and the flavors to blend. This is actually a braising step, but it is a component of the general sauté procedure. Finally, sauté can refer to the finished dish, such as What's-On-Hand Chicken Sauté, which follows.

There are many versions of chicken sauté. Talk with ten French-trained chefs and you'll get fifty chicken sauté recipes, each one more interesting than the last. But other foods also take well to sautéing; Brandied Steak for Two, Sherried Liver with Onions and P.Q.'s Simple Steak au Poivre are just a few examples, all found in Chapter 1.

WHAT'S-ON-HAND CHICKEN SAUTE

Chef Yves Schmidt was once challenged to create a French dinner using only those ingredients stocked in a randomly selected homemaker's kitchen. He came up with this marvelous burgundy-flavored sauté as the main course.

Makes 4 servings
1 broiler-fryer chicken (about 3-1/2 pounds), cut into serving pieces
3/4 teaspoon kosher salt
1/4 teaspoon freshly ground black pepper
2 tablespoons unsalted butter
2 tablespoons olive or vegetable oil
4 garlic cloves, unpeeled
2 bay leaves, crumbled
1/2 teaspoon dried thyme
7 green onions, sliced 1/4-inch thick
2-1/2 cups burgundy jug wine
1 tablespoon unbleached flour

Pat chicken dry with paper toweling. Rub salt and pepper over chicken pieces. In a 12-inch frypan, melt 1 tablespoon of the butter with the oil over medium heat. Add chicken pieces skin side down; then add garlic, bay leaves and thyme. Raise heat to medium high and cook chicken until well browned, about 5 minutes per side. Transfer chicken to platter.

Pour out excess oil from pan, add remaining 1 tablespoon butter and melt over medium heat. Add onions and cook, stirring, 1 minute. Add wine, bring to a boil and boil about 5 minutes. Return chicken to pan, sprinkle with flour, turn pieces over, cover pan and cook over low heat until chicken is tender, 15–20 minutes. Remove chicken to platter and keep warm. Boil wine sauce in pan about 5 minutes, scraping up bits from the bottom of pan. Pour sauce over chicken and serve.

HAITIAN CHICKEN

A sauté flavored with the zesty spices of the Caribbean.

Makes 4 servings
1 broiler-fryer chicken (about 3-1/2 pounds), cut into serving pieces
1-1/2 teaspoons kosher salt
Freshly ground black pepper
1 cup unbleached flour
2 tablespoons unsalted butter
2 tablespoons olive oil
4 medium onions, peeled and sliced
3 garlic cloves, peeled and minced
2 teaspoons curry powder
1/8 teaspoon ground turmeric
1–1-1/2 teaspoons red pepper flakes
2 cups chicken stock (canned or made from chicken base)
2 teaspoons cornstarch
2 tablespoons golden rum
1 fresh lime, halved
Lime wedges for garnish

Pat chicken dry with paper toweling. Rub with 1 teaspoon of the salt and the pepper. Put flour in a plastic bag; add chicken pieces, a couple at a time, and shake to coat. In a large frypan, melt butter with oil over medium heat. Add chicken to pan, skin side down, and cook about 20 minutes, turning to brown both sides. Remove chicken to plate.

Add onions and garlic to pan, and cook, stirring, until onions are golden and soft, about 5 minutes. Stir in curry powder, turmeric, red pepper flakes and remaining 1/2 teaspoon salt. Pour 2 tablespoons of the chicken stock into a small bowl and set aside. Add remaining stock to pan, stir and heat to boiling. Add chicken, reduce heat, cover and simmer 10 minutes. Uncover and simmer 5 minutes. Remove chicken to platter or individual serving plates and keep warm. Stir cornstarch into reserved chicken stock and then stir into pan along with rum. Bring sauce to a boil and squeeze in a lime half; squeeze remaining lime half over chicken. Pour sauce over chicken and garnish with lime wedges.

MIKE GORDON'S ROAST CHICKEN WITH NATURAL GRAVY

As an advertising executive with Campbell-Mithum, Chicago, Mike works on food accounts and carries his culinary interest home much to the delight of his son Josh and wife Deborah, owner of her own public relations firm. His "coated" roast chicken is a family favorite.

Makes 4 servings
1 whole broiler-fryer chicken* with giblets (about 3-1/2 pounds)
1 large onion, peeled and minced
2 garlic cloves, peeled and minced
1/2 cup chicken stock (canned or made from chicken base)

POULTRY SEASONING PASTE
5 tablespoons Healthful Seasoned Salt (page 99), or purchased seasoned salt
1 tablespoon paprika
2 teaspoons onion powder
1 teaspoon garlic powder
1/2 teaspoon freshly ground black pepper
Vegetable oil

Preheat standard or convection oven to 350°F. Stir together dry Poultry Seasoning Paste ingredients, then add enough oil to make a thin paste. Remove giblets from chicken and reserve. Pat chicken dry with paper toweling; cut off tail and wing tips (at last joint) and set aside. Rub Poultry Seasoning Paste over chicken to cover entire surface. Put reserved giblets, tail and wing tips, onion, garlic and chicken stock in a shallow roasting pan. Place meat rack in roasting pan, set chicken on rack and roast in the preheated 350°F oven 1-1/4–1-1/2 hours (50–60 minutes in a convection oven) or until instant-read thermometer registers 160°F when inserted in meat between drumstick and breast bone. Remove from oven and let rest in a warm place 10 minutes before serving. Discard giblets (or eat them!), tail and wing tips. Skim excess fat from pan drippings, if necessary, and serve drippings in a gravy boat.

*Substitute a 6-pound roasting chicken or capon, if desired. Increase roasting time by 30–35 minutes, 20–25 minutes in a convection oven.

STUFFED ROAST CHICKEN
Before rubbing seasoning paste on chicken, stuff loosely with Bud Nardecchia's Cornbread Dressing (page 50). Truss chicken and roast as above.

BUD NARDECCHIA'S CORNBREAD DRESSING

Bud, an accountant from Palatine, Illinois, who likes to cook four or more times a week, was a student in the original "Cooking for Men Only" classes in 1977. Here he shares his from-scratch cornbread dressing recipe, which he serves with chicken, turkey and Cornish game hens.

Makes enough stuffing for one 3-1/2 pound chicken or 4 Cornish game hens*
1/2 pound ground pork or bulk pork sausage
1 recipe From-Scratch Cornbread (following), cut into 1/2-inch dice
4–5 celery stalks with tops, thinly sliced
1 large onion, peeled and chopped
2 garlic cloves, peeled and crushed
2–3 sprigs parsley, minced
Kosher salt
Freshly ground black pepper
1/2 cup pitted green olives
Chicken stock (canned or made from chicken base) or water

*Prepare a double recipe and use to stuff a 12-pound turkey.

In a 10-inch frypan, brown sausage over medium heat until crumbly. Add remaining ingredients, moistening with chicken stock until dressing begins to hold its shape. Loose pack into prepared bird(s) and cook according to recipe directions.

NOTE To cook dressing by itself as a side dish, add enough chicken stock to give dressing a mushy consistency. Pack into a greased shallow baking pan and bake in a preheated 325°F oven 25–35 minutes or until crusty on the top but still moist inside.

FROM-SCRATCH CORNBREAD

Can be made a day ahead.

Makes one 8-inch square*
2 cups yellow cornmeal
1 tablespoon sugar
2 teaspoons baking powder
1 teaspoon baking soda
1 teaspoon kosher salt
1 large egg, lightly beaten
2 cups buttermilk
2 tablespoons vegetable oil
Oil for greasing pan
About 1 tablespoon cornmeal for dusting pan

Preheat oven to 425°F. In a mixing bowl, stir together all dry ingredients. Add egg, buttermilk and 2 tablespoons oil; stir just enough to moisten dry ingredients. *Do not overmix.* Brush oil on bottom and sides of an 8-inch square baking pan or other 1-1/2-quart shallow baking pan. Dust pan with cornmeal, shake out excess and pour batter into pan. Bake in preheated oven 30–35 minutes or until wooden pick inserted in center comes out clean.

*This recipe can be easily doubled. Bake in a shallow 3-quart pan.

STUART BROWN'S BLACK TURKEY

No, it's not burned—just an ebony shade from the soy sauce and bourbon marinade. Thanks to Stuart Brown, president of Century Electric of St. Louis, for this delightful recipe. He recommends cooking it on the grill.

Makes 12 servings, with leftovers
One 12–14 pound turkey, fresh or frozen and thawed

1/4 pound (1 stick) unsalted butter, softened
Garlic salt

MARINADE
1 cup soy sauce
1 cup bourbon
1/2–3/4 cup lightly packed brown sugar
1 tablespoon minced fresh ginger root
1 garlic clove, peeled and crushed

Mix together all marinade ingredients. Remove giblets from turkey and pat bird dry inside and out with paper toweling. Place turkey in a large shallow glass or enamel pan, pour marinade over turkey, rub it into the skin and baste turkey 3–4 minutes with a large spoon. Refrigerate turkey 6 hours or overnight, basting and turning occasionally.

Prepare outdoor grill (with cover) and preheat until coals are medium hot. Remove turkey from marinade and rub all over with softened butter and garlic salt. Place on grill, cover and cook 11–13 minutes per pound or until instant-read thermometer registers 170°F when inserted in breast meat between drumstick and breast bone. Remove from grill; let rest 10 minutes before carving.

CHU YEN LUKE'S CHINESE ROAST DUCK

This duck literally hangs around your kitchen before roasting! The air drying adds to the skin's crispness, and the unusual roasting technique devised by Chinese cooking teacher Chu Yen Luke simulates the vertical roasting ovens used in Chinese restaurants.

Makes 4 servings
One 4-1/2–5-pound duck
Plum, sweet and sour, or oyster sauce for dipping

MASSAGING SOLUTION
3 tablespoons honey
3 tablespoons dry Chinese cooking wine or dry sherry
3 tablespoons distilled white vinegar
1/2 teaspoon kosher salt
1 cup water, boiling

Remove giblets from duck cavity. Pat duck dry inside and out with paper toweling. In a large mixing bowl, stir together all Massaging Solution ingredients until honey dissolves. Separate duck skin from meat by inserting your fingers under the skin of the neck cavity and working them as far around the body as possible. Place duck in the bowl of Massaging Solution. Baste the bird for 5–7 minutes by grasping a drumstick and rotating the duck in the solution and by using a large spoon to ladle the solution over it. Cut a 2-foot length of kitchen twine and tie it around the neck skin, loop it around the wings and then tie another knot around the neck. Hang the duck by the string from a pot rack or other spot in the kitchen where air can circulate around the bird for 5–6 hours.

Fill a roasting pan half full of water and place on floor or lowest rack of oven. Position a rack in the middle of the oven and preheat the oven to 350°F. Place the duck, breast side up, directly on the middle rack so it sits above the pan of water. (The water-filled pan provides moisture and collects the duck drippings.) Roast 1-1/2– 1-3/4 hours. Remove from the oven and let cool to room temperature. Cut into small serving pieces through the bone with a heavy cleaver or poultry shears. Serve with one or more of the suggested dipping sauces.

ROASTED CORNISH GAME HENS TARRAGON

Cornish game hens are one of the easiest and quickest-cooking roasts. Each hen is a self-contained portion and looks wonderful on a plate when surrounded with colorful vegetables.

Makes 1 or more servings
1 Cornish game hen per serving
Kosher salt or Healthful Seasoned
Salt (page 99)
Freshly ground black pepper
Tarragon sprigs or dried tarragon
Rosemary sprigs or dried
rosemary
Juniper berries
Softened unsalted butter

Preheat standard oven to 350°F, or convection oven to 325°F. Thaw hen; remove giblets from cavity and reserve for another use. Pat hen dry with paper toweling and rub cavity with salt and pepper. Add a sprig of tarragon (or a generous pinch of dried tarragon), a sprig of rosemary (or a pinch of dried rosemary) and 2 juniper berries to the hen cavity. Truss the hen or simply tuck wings under body.

Rub hen all over with salt, pepper and butter. If roasting 1 hen, place on cooling rack set on a jelly-roll pan; if roasting more than 1 hen, use a meat rack. Pour a thin film of water in pan and roast hen in the preheated oven 1–1-1/4 hours (45–60 minutes in a convection oven). The hen is done when a drumstick can be wiggled easily, or when juices from cavity run clear. Remove from oven and let rest in a warm place 5 minutes. Serve whole or cut in half with kitchen shears and serve cut sides down on individual serving plates.

STUFFED CORNISH HENS Omit tarragon, rosemary and juniper berries. Stuff loosely with Bud Nardecchia's Cornbread Dressing (page 50). Roast as above.

JUANITA'S SOUTHERN FRIED CHICKEN WITH CREAM GRAVY

Kentucky Colonel, eat your heart out! This is fried chicken the old-fashioned way, with cream gravy. Team this with On-the-Square Buttermilk Biscuits (page 72) and you'll make a hit with Southerners and Yankees alike.

Makes 4 servings
1 cup unbleached flour
1/2 teaspoon Healthful Seasoned
Salt (page 99), or purchased
seasoned salt
2 eggs
1/2 cup milk
1 pound lard*
1 broiler-fryer chicken (about 3
pounds), cut into serving pieces
2 teaspoons kosher salt
Freshly ground black pepper

GRAVY
2 tablespoons pan drippings (from
frying chicken)
2 tablespoons unbleached flour
3/4 cup chicken stock (canned or
made from chicken base)
1/2 cup half-and-half
Kosher salt and freshly ground
black pepper to taste

Line a jelly-roll pan with paper toweling; preheat oven to 250°F. In a shallow bowl, stir together flour and seasoned salt. Set aside next to the range. In a separate bowl, beat together eggs and milk. Set aside next to the flour. Cut lard into 4 equal pieces, place in a 12-inch cast-iron frypan and set over low heat to melt. When lard is melted (depth should be 1/2 inch), increase heat to medium and continue to heat until a bit of celery or bread sizzles when added to the lard. Then, working quickly, coat the chicken as follows: Sprinkle with salt and pepper, rubbing seasonings in well. Beginning with dark meat pieces (drumsticks and thighs), dip each piece in the egg mixture, and then in the flour mixture, patting flour onto chicken so it coats well. Shake off excess flour and immediately add to lard, skin side down. Add breasts and wings last, as they take less time to cook. Fry about 10 minutes, turn with tongs and fry another 10–15 minutes. Pieces should be a deep golden brown. Remove chicken to lined jelly-roll pan in a single layer and keep warm in preheated oven while making gravy.

To make gravy, pour all but 2 tablespoons of the drippings from the frypan.* Return pan to medium heat, add flour and stir until smooth. Cook and stir for 2 minutes. Whisk in chicken stock, and then half-and-half. Allow gravy to simmer 3–4 minutes, stirring to prevent sticking. Taste and correct seasonings with salt and pepper. Pour into gravy boat and serve with the chicken. Gravy is also great on biscuits.

*A NOTE ON LARD With America's interest in light dining growing, lard has almost become a dirty word. But if you taste this recipe and others that utilize lard properly, you will realize that that attitude is a "trendy" mistake. Lard has wonderful flavor, browns beautifully and is a relatively inexpensive fat to buy. It should be used in certain dishes, like this one, where it makes a noticeable difference in the end result. It must be noted, however, that lard is high in cholesterol and should not be used frequently by anyone on a reduced-cholesterol diet. Substitute vegetable oil.

Here are a few tips to keep in mind when using lard: Do not cook over heat any higher than medium. When making a gravy with lard, be aware that it tends to get lumpy as it cools; to rectify, bring to a boil and whisk vigorously. To keep a lard-based gravy from forming a crusty film, cover with a lid. Lard from frying can be reused; strain through a coffee filter or paper toweling while still hot and pourable, then store in the refrigerator and use within 4 weeks.

GOBBLER GRAPE SALAD

The perfect recipe for leftover turkey or chicken.

Makes 2–4 servings
2 cups diced cooked turkey or chicken
1/4 cup thinly sliced celery
1/4 cup thinly sliced carrot
2 tablespoons thinly sliced green onion
1/4 cup seedless grapes, cut in half lengthwise
1/4 cup roasted peanuts (page 98 or purchased)

DRESSING
6 tablespoons mayonnaise (homemade, page 100, or purchased)
2 tablespoons fresh lemon juice
Several grindings of black pepper

Toss together turkey, celery, carrot, green onion and grapes. Make Dressing by stirring together mayonnaise, lemon juice and pepper. Toss turkey mixture with Dressing. Stir in peanuts just before serving. Mound salad on a lettuce leaf, or use as a filling for pita bread.

DEVIL'S WINGS

Just like the Devil, these wings are hot stuff.

Makes 4 servings
3 pounds chicken wings

BASTING SAUCE
1/4 cup vegetable oil
1 teaspoon chili powder
1 teaspoon paprika
1 teaspoon kosher salt
1/2 teaspoon dry mustard
1/8–1/4 teaspoon cayenne pepper

Preheat broiler or prepare outdoor grill; set grid 3–4 inches from heat source. In mixing bowl, whisk together Basting Sauce ingredients. Brush sauce over chicken wings as you put them on the grill. Broil about 15 minutes, turning to brown evenly and basting with additional sauce if desired.

BARBECUED CHICKEN WITH DOWN-HOME BARBECUE SAUCE

Makes 4 servings
1 broiler-fryer chicken (about 3-1/2 pounds), cut into serving pieces
Kosher salt or Healthful Seasoned Salt (page 99)
Freshly ground black pepper
Down-Home Barbecue Sauce (following), or bottled barbecue sauce

Prepare broiler or outdoor grill or preheat convection oven on "broil." Pat chicken dry with paper toweling. Remove any chunks of fat that may be loosely attached to pieces. Excess fat can cause flare-ups when broiling or grilling. Sprinkle chicken with salt and pepper and rub seasonings in well. Place skin side down on outdoor grill, or skin side up in kitchen broiler, so chicken is 4–5 inches from heat source. If using convection oven, place in middle of oven, skin side up. Cook 20–25 minutes, turning 2–3 times to brown evenly (the chicken need not be turned in a convection oven). Brush with barbecue sauce during last 5 minutes of cooking.

DOWN-HOME BARBECUE SAUCE

More subtle and flavorful than bottled! Use on chicken, ribs, hamburgers, even steaks.

Makes about 3 cups
1 tablespoon bacon drippings or vegetable oil
1 medium onion, peeled and minced
1/2 cup bottled chili sauce
1-1/4 cups catsup
2/3 cup lager or dark beer (not light beer)
1/4 cup fresh lemon juice (about 1 lemon)
2 tablespoons red wine vinegar
2 tablespoons Worcestershire sauce
2 tablespoons honey
3 tablespoons prepared horseradish
1 tablespoon soy sauce
2 teaspoons chili powder
1/2 teaspoon paprika
1/4–1/2 teaspoon cayenne pepper
1/4 teaspoon dry mustard
1/4 teaspoon ground cumin

In a medium saucepan, heat bacon drippings, add onion and cook, stirring, over medium-high heat until onion is lightly browned, 5–7 minutes. Add all remaining ingredients, stir and simmer uncovered 20–30 minutes. Cool and store in the refrigerator in a screw-top jar or other air-tight container. Best when made a few days in advance. May be stored for up to 6 weeks.

TURKEY PARMIGIANA

Fresh breast of turkey slices, now available in many supermarkets, make this recipe a snap.

Makes 3–4 servings
1 egg
2 tablespoons vegetable oil
1/2 cup seasoned bread crumbs
1 package (about 1 pound) turkey
    breast slices
About 1 cup All-Purpose Tomato
    Sauce (page 82), or bottled
    pizza sauce
4 ounces mozzarella cheese,
    shredded
1–2 tablespoons grated parmesan
    or romano cheese

Preheat oven to 450°F. In a mixing bowl, beat together egg and oil. Pour bread crumbs into a pie plate or shallow dish. Dip turkey slices in egg mixture, then in bread crumbs, patting with fingertips so crumbs stick. Arrange breaded slices in a single layer on a jelly-roll pan. Bake in the preheated oven 8–10 minutes or until golden brown.

While turkey is baking, heat tomato sauce. Transfer turkey to a small shallow casserole, overlapping slices slightly. Top with tomato sauce, then mozzarella and parmesan; return to oven for 3–5 minutes or until cheese melts.

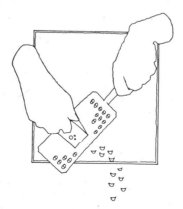

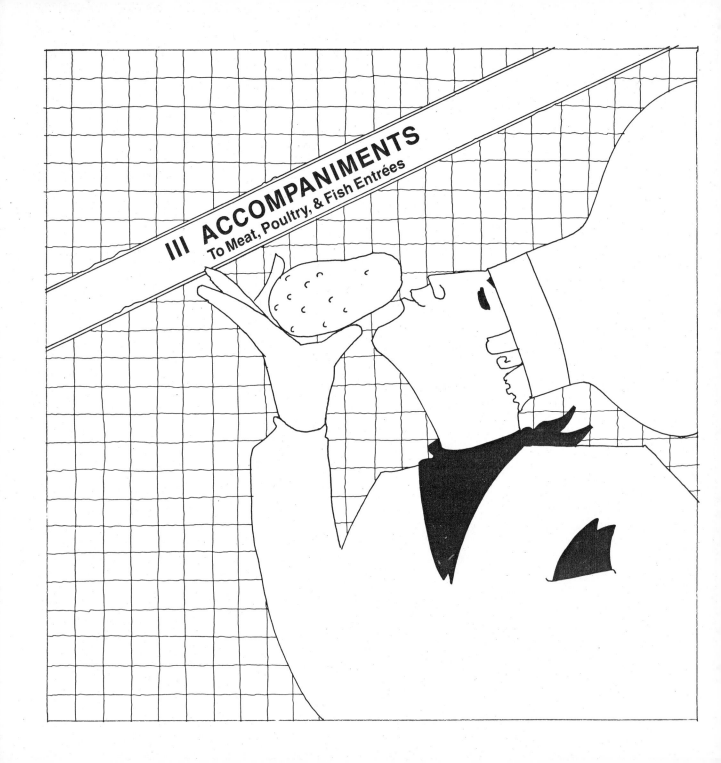

III **ACCOMPANIMENTS**
To Meat, Poultry, & Fish Entrées

A BALANCED MEAL

Though vegetables, rice, pasta, bread and salads are generally known as side dishes, their influence in meals is not incidental. Whether cooking for a houseful of friends or just yourself, you will find that side dishes turn eating into dining.

A memorable, well-balanced meal will be made up of a variety of colors, textures and flavors. If you learn to vary these elements, you will receive rave reviews from diners and will probably do as well nutritionally as someone who plans a meal by spending hours poring over nutrition books.

Varying flavors (sweet, sour, salty, piquant, spicy, bland), colors (green, yellow, red, orange, brown, white) and textures (soft, crisp, firm, mushy, tender, oily, crunchy, creamy, fibrous) will probably lead you almost inadvertently to selecting foods from all Four Basic Food Groups. The groups and examples of what makes them up follow.

THE FOUR BASIC FOOD GROUPS

THE MEAT GROUP: Can be firm, white, red, brown, oily
(2 servings per day)

Red meat	Fish/Seafood
Poultry	Peanuts/peanut
Eggs	butter

THE MILK GROUP: Can be soft, liquid, creamy, firm, white, yellow, orange
(2 servings per day for adults)

| Milk | Ice Cream |
| Cheese | Yogurt |

THE FRUIT/VEGETABLE GROUP: Can be green, yellow, red, white, fibrous, firm, soft, juicy
(4 servings per day)

| Fruits | Vegetables |

THE GRAIN GROUP: Can be white, brown, soft, firm, crunchy, fibrous, chewy
(4 servings per day)

Breads	Pasta
Crackers	Rice
Cereals	

To see how the "balanced meal" works, look at the Casual Dinner menu. You can see that it supplies foods from each of the Four Basic Food Groups and has a variety of flavors, colors and textures.

CASUAL DINNER

Clam Chowder (Meat, Milk, Fruit/ Vegetable)
The Detroit Burger on buns (Meat, Grain, Milk)
Cottage Fries (Fruit/Vegetable)
Lemon Crunch Pie (Grain)

You do not have to labor over nutrition to eat wisely. Let your eyes help by looking for colors, and your tastebuds help by detecting flavors and textures. Remember to vary your selections, both at home and in restaurants, throughout the basic food groups. If you have trouble remembering the groups, create an anagram like Men Go For Meat—MGFM—for Milk, Grain, Fruit/Vegetable and Meat. And for tips on eating for greater fitness in a common-sense way, see Chapter 5.

SUGGESTED MENUS

ELEGANT ITALIAN DINNER

For two
*Italian Salad, 67
Exquisite Fettuccine Alfredo, 74
Garlic Bread, 69
Flaming Drambuie over Fruit, 131

LIGHT LUNCH

For two
Bulgur and Greens Salad, 107
*Quick-Rise Herb Bread, 71

For more menus for two, see
Chapter 7.

CHINESE DINNER

For four
Devil's Wings, 54
Hot and Sour Soup, 84
Steak with Green Pepper, 17
Steamed Rice, 73

SOUTHERN SOJOURN

For four
Snap Bean Fat Salad, 66
Juanita's Southern Fried Chicken
  with Cream Gravy, 52
Mashed Potatoes, 60
On-the-Square Buttermilk Bis-
  cuits, 72

CONTINENTAL MENU

For four
*Cynthia's Veal Chops with Pecan
  Butter, 16
Shoestring Potatoes (see
  French-Fried Potatoes), 60
Zucchini Parmesan, 65
Haagen-Dazs Demitasse, 128

FISH FRY MENU

For four
Tom Slough's Tabasco-Fried Cat-
  fish, 39
*Hush Puppies, 40
*Tartare Sauce, 41
*Creamy Cole Slaw, 69
*Donald McIntyre's Prize-Winning
  Apple Pie, 122

COMPANY DINNER

For four
French Vinaigrette In-the-Bowl
  Salad, 106
Mike Gordon's Roast Chicken with
  Natural Gravy, 49
Boiled Potatoes, 60
Steamed Broccoli, 64
Berries with Crème Chantilly, 131
  (double the recipe)

KIDS COOK DINNER

For four
Green Goodness Salad, 120
Pizza Pockets, 117 (See recipe
  note on dividing recipe in half.)
*Good-as-Gold Nuggets, 124

GREEK SEAFOOD DINNER

For four
Greek Salad, 67
Greek-Style Swordfish Kabobs,
  38
Rice with Tomatoes and Mush-
  rooms, 73
Summer Sweet Corn, 64

CASUAL DINNER

For four
Detroit Burgers, 14
Cottage Fries (see French-Fried
  Potatoes), 60
*Lemon Crunch Pie, 121

TEX-MEX TREAT

For six
Frozen Margaritas (for the adults),
  127
Orange Banana (for the kids), 125
*Cheese Nachos with Guacamole,
  143
*Ronnie Bull's Texas Burritos, 118

CLASSIC AMERICAN DINNER

For four
Steamed Clams with Lemon Butter, 45
Caesar Salad, 66
Broiled Steaks, 11
*Jerry G. Bishop's Showstopper Steak Sauce, 12
*Double-Baked Potatoes, 61
Boiled Asparagus, 64
*Clark Weber's Chocolate Mousse à la Blender, 133

OUTSIDE-INSIDE DINNER

For six
Ken Filewicz's Pot Roast on the Grill, 13
*Mrs. Kriz's Potato Pancakes with Homemade Applesauce, 62
Steamed Carrots, 64
*Strawberry Sorbet, 123

THE BRUNCH BUNCH

For eight
Brian Buda's Strawberry Bolé, 127 (double the recipe)
Sticky Breakfast Bites, 139
*Lindsey Kesman's Fresh Fruit Salad, 107
*Skillet Pancake with Sausage Filling, 140

HOLIDAY DINNER

For six
*Don Roth's Spinning Blackhawk Salad, 68
*Stuart Brown's Black Turkey, 50
*Baked Sweet Potatoes with Yogurt Topping, 63
*Classic Cranberry Relish, 69
*Steve Jenk's From-Scratch White Bread, 70
Whole Cauliflower Boiled in Stock with Carrots, 64
*Choco-Pink Pie, 121

OUTDOOR BARBECUE

*For twelve***
Jim Kriz's Dynamite Finger Food, 146
*Sweet and Sour Cucumbers, 67
*Creamy Cole Slaw, 69
*Brad West's Beer-Braised Barbecued Ribs, 15 (double the recipe)
*Barbecued Chicken with Down-Home Barbecue Sauce, 54 (double the recipe)
*Ronnie Bull's Braised Pinto Beans, 82

*Part or all of this recipe can be prepared in advance of serving time.

**Groups of eight or more are best served buffet style, although an experienced cook won't flinch at serving a sit-down dinner to eight or more. When planning a menu for an outdoor barbecue or any buffet situation, include recipes that can be prepared in advance, like the Dynamite Finger Food, Sweet and Sour Cucumbers, Creamy Cole Slaw, Braised Pinto Beans and Down-Home Barbecue Sauce in the Outdoor Barbecue Menu. When planning amounts to prepare, select a main dish recipe or recipes to generously serve the number of people you expect. For example, in the Outdoor Barbecue Menu, a double recipe of Beer-Braised Ribs, which serves eight, and Barbecued Chicken, which also serves eight, will probably serve twelve rather than sixteen since more food is usually consumed at a buffet than at a sit-down dinner. Fill out the menu by preparing double recipes of one or two side dishes, or single recipes of three or four side dishes. Increasing the number of dishes, rather than doubling recipes, gives variety, allows each guest to sample a variety of dishes, and makes a very attractive buffet table.

THE POTATO PRIMER

If you are going to be a meat-and-potatoes man, or if you just like potatoes, you'll want to vary your style of cooking them. As good as a baked potato is, it is not the only satisfying potato preparation. Try the following methods to increase your potato prowess. Be sure to wash potatoes thoroughly before cooking.

BOILED POTATOES

Place small to medium red potatoes, peeled or unpeeled, in a saucepan. Cover with water by at least 1 inch, add kosher salt (about 1/4 teaspoon for each pint of water) and bring to a boil. Boil about 20 minutes or until tender when tested with a fork. Serve topped with butter and snipped chives or parsley. To reduce calories, boil potatoes in chicken or beef stock and serve without butter.

FRENCH-FRIED POTATOES

Both Idaho and red potatoes can be used for french fries. You will find the waxy red potato makes moist, relatively soft fries, while the mealy Idaho makes crisper, drier fries. Experiment with different potatoes to find your favorite. Use peeled or unpeeled potatoes and cut up into french fry (1/4- by 1/4-inch strips), shoestring (1/8- by 1/8-inch strips) or cottage-fry (1/8-inch-thick slices) shapes just before frying. If you must cut them in advance, put the pieces in a bowl of cold water until ready to fry; then drain and blot thoroughly dry with paper toweling.

Line a jelly-roll pan with paper toweling; preheat oven to 250°F. Pour peanut or vegetable oil into a heavy high-sided saucepan (or use a deep-fat fryer) to a depth of 2-1/2 inches or more. Heat oil until it registers 360°–370°F on a deep-fat thermometer, or until a small piece of potato sizzles and floats as it hits the oil. Fry in batches so as not to crowd, according to the following times: french fries, 4–6 minutes; shoestrings and cottage fries, 3–4 minutes.

With a slotted spoon, transfer potatoes to lined jelly-roll pan; sprinkle with salt, celery salt or Healthful Seasoned Salt (page 99). Keep warm in oven until all fries are cooked, then serve immediately. Store oil for another use as described in Chapter 2.

MASHED POTATOES

Once you taste these classic potatoes, you'll never use the boxed kind again.

Makes 4–6 servings
2 pounds red potatoes (about 6 medium), peeled
1-1/2 teaspoons kosher salt
3 tablespoons unsalted butter, cut into pieces
3 tablespoons milk or whipping cream
Kosher salt to taste
About 1/8 teaspoon freshly ground white pepper

Cut potatoes into 1/2-inch dice. You should have about 6 cups. Place in a 3-quart saucepan, cover with water by 1 inch, add 1-1/2 teaspoons salt and set over medium-high heat. Bring to a boil, reduce heat and simmer 15 minutes or until potatoes are very soft when pierced with a fork. Pour into colander or sieve to drain well.

Immediately return potatoes to saucepan set over very low heat. Mash with a fork or potato masher until smooth. With a portable electric mixer, first beat in butter and then milk. Taste and add salt and pepper. Serve immediately.

NOTE To keep warm or reheat, set saucepan of mashed potatoes in frypan placed over very low heat and pour hot water into frypan. If potatoes dry out a bit, stir in water or milk by spoonfuls to desired consistency.

BAKED POTATOES

While Idaho potatoes are most frequently identified with baking, red potatoes can also be used and will yield moist, waxy potato meat. To bake either kind, preheat oven or convection oven to 375°F. Scrub potatoes with water and a vegetable brush or plastic pad, dry and, with a fork or paring knife, poke 1 or 2 holes in them. If you like soft skins, rub potatoes lightly with vegetable oil. For crispier skin, bake as is. For a slightly moister potato with a soft skin, wrap each spud in aluminum foil. Place potatoes on jelly-roll pan or directly on oven rack. Bake at 375°F about 1-1/4 hours in a standard oven, or 45 minutes–1 hour in a convection oven. Test by inserting tines of fork; when potato is soft to the center, it is done.

DOUBLE-BAKED POTATOES

Makes 4 servings
4 just-baked Idaho potatoes (6–8 ounces *each*)
4–6 tablespoons unsalted butter
4–6 tablespoons sour cream
1/4 cup milk
1–1-1/4 teaspoons Healthful Seasoned Salt (page 99), or purchased seasoned salt
1/8 teaspoon freshly ground white pepper
2 tablespoons dehydrated minced onion

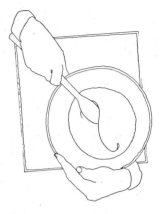

Set oven temperature at 475°F. Cut 1/2-inch-thick slice off the top of each baked potato. With a teaspoon, scoop out potato meat into a mixing bowl, being careful not to break the skin. Set potato shells aside. Mash potato with a fork, add all remaining ingredients and beat until smooth. Mixture should be soft and creamy. Fill potato shells with mixture, mounding and fluffing top with fork. Place potatoes on jelly-roll pan and bake in the preheated 475°F oven about 5 minutes or until tops brown lightly. Serve immediately.

To make ahead, fill and leave at room temperature 1 hour before baking; increase cooking time to 10–15 minutes. Test for internal temperature of 150°F with instant-read thermometer, if desired.

MOM'S BACON-FRIED POTATOES

This old-fashioned recipe is fattening, but it's so delicious it's worth it!

Makes 2–3 servings for normal people, or 1 serving for the ravenous potato lover
4 slices bacon, cut into 1/2-inch pieces*
3 medium red potatoes, peeled and sliced 1/8 inch thick (about 3 cups)
1/8 teaspoon onion powder
Kosher salt to taste
1 medium onion, peeled and chopped

Cook bacon in a 10-inch frypan over medium heat, stirring occasionally until it browns lightly. Remove bacon pieces with a slotted spoon and set aside. Add potato slices to drippings in frypan and cook over medium heat 8–10 minutes, using a pancake turner to stir and turn potatoes so they brown lightly. Add onion powder, cover and cook over low heat 10 minutes, stirring and turning once about midway through cooking period. Sprinkle with salt, chopped onion and reserved bacon pieces; stir, breaking up potato slices into chunks with edge of turner. Cover and cook about 5 minutes. Remove cover and cook another 5–10 minutes until potatoes are browned, stirring occasionally. Serve immediately.

*If you have bacon drippings on hand, omit the bacon and use about 3 tablespoons drippings.

MRS. KRIZ'S POTATO PANCAKES WITH HOMEMADE APPLESAUCE

To duplicate these legendary pancakes, use a wire grater to grate the potatoes, and make your batter just before frying. Double or triple the recipe, if desired.

Makes about 12 medium pancakes
1 pound Idaho or red potatoes (about 3 medium), peeled
1 small onion, peeled
1 egg
1 teaspoon baking powder
1 garlic clove, peeled and crushed
About 1 teaspoon kosher salt
4–5 tablespoons unbleached flour
Bacon drippings or vegetable oil
1 recipe Homemade Applesauce (following)

On a wire grater, grate the potatoes and then the onion into a mixing bowl. Stir in egg, baking powder, garlic and salt. Gradually stir in flour until soupy consistency is achieved. Line a jelly-roll pan with paper toweling.

Melt bacon drippings to a depth of 1/4 inch in a 12-inch frypan placed over medium-high heat. Spoon potato batter into hot fat by heaping tablespoonfuls, then smooth out into flat shapes. Fat should sizzle when batter is added. Do not crowd pancakes in pan. Fry over medium-high heat 3–5 minutes per side or until crispy and golden brown. Drain on lined jelly-roll pan in single layer; keep warm in 250°F oven until all pancakes are fried. Serve immediately with Homemade Applesauce.

HOMEMADE APPLESAUCE

*Makes about 3 cups**
8 medium MacIntosh or Winesap
 apples, peeled, cored and cut in
 1/2-inch dice
Water
1–2 tablespoons sugar

Place apples in medium saucepan
and add water to a depth of 1/2
inch. Cover and cook over medium heat until soft, about 20 minutes, stirring occasionally. Mash
apples with potato masher or fork.
Stir in sugar to taste; amount depends upon sweetness of apples.
Cook uncovered 5–10 minutes
more or until thick and saucy. Remove from heat and let cool
slightly. Serve warm or at room
temperature with Potato Pancakes. Refrigerate any leftover applesauce in screwtop jar. Serve as
condiment with chicken or pork.

*This recipe can be cut in half.

BAKED SWEET POTATOES WITH YOGURT TOPPING

There is no evident similarity between fresh and canned sweet potatoes other than sharing the
same name. Fresh baked sweet
potatoes are wonderful—and
easy!

Scrub potatoes, pat dry and puncture skin with a fork. Bake in a preheated 375°F oven 30–60 minutes, depending on size of potato.
Test by inserting tines of a fork;
potatoes are done when they are
soft to the center. Slit lengthwise
to open, push ends together to
loosen pulp and top with Yogurt
Topping (following).

YOGURT TOPPING

Makes about 1-1/3 cups
1 cup plain yogurt
3 tablespoons lightly packed
 brown sugar
3 tablespoons Canadian whiskey

Stir together all ingredients to
blend well. Serve on Baked Sweet
Potatoes. Store remainder covered in refrigerator.

VEGETABLES

BOILING AND STEAMING VEGETABLES

Boiling and steaming bring out the
fresh flavors and colors of vegetables. It is impossible to give exact
cooking times for these techniques, as they will vary with the
size and natural tenderness of the
vegetable, and the desired degree
of doneness. To test, remove one
piece from pot and pierce with a
paring knife, or cool slightly and
taste. For best results, cook vegetables only until crisp-tender or
slightly beyond. Use the following
techniques and times as guidelines.

BOILING METHOD In a large
stainless-steel, anodized-aluminum or enameled cast iron saucepan, bring to a boil two quarts of
water or stock for each pound of
vegetable. When water reaches a
boil, add a teaspoon of kosher salt
for each quart. Add vegetables
and start timing when water returns to a boil. Cook according to

times listed below or to desired doneness. Pour into colander to drain. Serve immediately, or place in a bowl of ice water if vegetable is to be served cold.

STEAMING METHOD Add water to steamer pot to a level just below height of steaming basket. Place basket in pot and add vegetables to basket. Heat water to a gentle boil or until you can see steam rising from basket. Cover and steam according to times below or to desired doneness. Serve hot, or plunge in bowl of ice water to chill and serve cold.

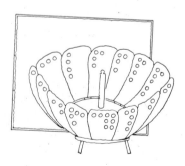

ASPARAGUS Rinse in bowl of cool water to remove grit and cut or snap off tough white ends. Use vegetable peeler to peel tough skin from bottom two-thirds of each stalk, if desired. Stalks can be tied in bundles with kitchen twine and cooked as explained in Boiling Method, or they can be cooked by this easier technique: select a frypan that will accommodate stalks in a single or double layer. Cover stalks with water, add 1/4 teaspoon kosher salt for each cup of water, bring to a boil over high heat and boil 5–10 minutes, depending upon thickness of stalks. To test for doneness, use tongs to lift one stalk from pan; it should be bright green and droop slightly. *Do not overcook*. Drain and serve with butter and lemon wedges. To serve cold, plunge stalks in bowl of ice water; when cold, cover and refrigerate.

BROCCOLI Wash and cut into stalks or florets. If stems are very thick, pierce in several places with knife blade. Boil 5–10 minutes; steam 10–15 minutes.

CARROTS Peel and cut to desired size. Boil slices 5–10 minutes, halves or large pieces 10–15 min-

utes. Steam slices 10–15 minutes, halves or large pieces 15–20 minutes.

CAULIFLOWER Boil whole head 15–25 minutes, cut-up head 5–10 minutes. Steam whole head 25–35 minutes, cut-up head 20–25 minutes. (For an impressive yet simple presentation, boil whole cauliflower and carrot pieces in beef stock, place drained cauliflower on platter, surround with carrots and drizzle with melted unsalted butter and minced fresh parsley.)

GREEN BEANS Trim off ends. Boil whole beans 5–10 minutes, cut-up beans 6–8 minutes. Steam whole beans 10-15 minutes, cut-up beans 7–10 minutes.

SUMMER SWEET CORN

The most crucial aspects of cooking sweet corn are the corn itself and the temperature of the water. Some corn species in markets are labeled as "sweet" when they are not. A true sweet corn will not be tough and gummy if properly cooked by a gentle simmer. Hard boiling only toughens corn and turns it pasty orange. Try this method and look for a corn called Super Sweet. It appears only for two to four weeks near the end of each summer, but is worth the hunt! Always cook corn as soon after picking as possible.

Bring a large pot of water (amount depends on number of ears you are cooking) to a gentle simmer and add 1 teaspoon sugar for each quart of water. With tongs, add ears of corn and cook at a very gentle simmer 3–6 minutes, depending upon natural sweetness of corn. (You can test sweetness by cutting off and tasting one raw kernel.) Remove ears to colander with tongs, let drain 1 minute and serve with unsalted butter.

ZUCCHINI PARMESAN

Makes 2–4 servings*
2 tablespoons unsalted butter
1 tablespoon olive oil
3 small zucchini (peeled or unpeeled), sliced 1/8 inch thick
Few grindings of black pepper
Pinch of kosher salt
1 tablespoon grated parmesan cheese (preferably freshly grated)

In a 10-inch frypan, melt butter with oil over medium heat. Add zucchini and pepper and cook, stirring occasionally, until zucchini softens slightly, 5–7 minutes. Add salt, stir and cook 1 minute. Sprinkle with parmesan, reduce heat to low, cover and cook 2 minutes. Serve immediately.

*This recipe can be easily doubled or halved.

UNADULTERATED ONION RINGS

A true onion lover doesn't need breading or batter on his onion rings. They only mask the delightful flavor of this zesty bulb!

Makes 4 servings*
4 large yellow, Spanish or white onions, peeled
Milk
4 cups peanut or vegetable oil
About 1 cup unbleached flour

Slice onions 1/4 inch thick, place in mixing bowl, cover with milk and let soak 30 minutes to 1 hour. Drain; reserve milk for use in soups, if desired. Line a jelly-roll pan with paper toweling; preheat oven to 250°F.

Heat peanut oil in a heavy, high-sided saucepan to 375°F. Test with a deep-fat thermometer, or by adding a bit of onion; if it sizzles and floats, the oil is ready. Put flour in a paper or plastic bag. In batches, add drained onions to bag. Shake to coat, remove onion slices from bag, shake off excess flour and add slices to hot oil. Fry 3–4 minutes or until golden brown. Remove with slotted spoon to lined jelly-roll pan and spread in a single layer. Keep warm in oven until all rings are fried. (Store oil for other use; see Deep-frying Guidelines in Chapter 2.)

*This recipe can be easily halved or doubled.

NOTE If preparing both french fries (page 60) and onion rings, fry the potatoes first and keep warm in oven.

SAUTE OF CELERY AND CARROTS

This dish was born of necessity. A fastidious hostess found herself with an unexpected dinner guest and carrots and celery the only fresh vegetables in the house. This simple dish is what resulted—with resounding success, I might add.

Makes 2 servings
1 celery stalk
1 large carrot, peeled
2 tablespoons unsalted butter
2 tablespoons water
2 tablespoons minced fresh parsley or mint

Cut celery and carrot into julienne strips (1/8 by 1/8 by 2 inches), or into thin slices on the diagonal. In a 9-inch frypan, melt butter over medium heat; add celery and carrot pieces and cook, stirring, 2–3 minutes. Add water, cover and cook 2–3 minutes. Remove and cook until liquid evaporates, 1–2 minutes. Stir in parsley just before serving.

SALADS AND RELISHES

SNAP BEAN FAT SALAD

The Southern origin of this salad makes it an ideal accompaniment to fried or barbecued chicken or baked ham.

Makes 4 servings
About 1/2 pound green (snap) beans, cut into 1-inch pieces
1 small head romaine, cut into bite-size pieces
2 tablespoons snipped fresh parsley
2 tablespoons snipped fresh chives
1/4 cup thinly sliced mild onion
1/4–1/2 teaspoon salt
Freshly ground black pepper to taste
1/4 pound bacon, chopped
1/2 cup distilled white vinegar

Bring pot of water to a rolling boil, add beans and boil 7–10 minutes or until beans are crisp-tender. Drain, rinse under cold running water and set aside. Place romaine in a large salad bowl. Pat beans dry with paper toweling and sprinkle over romaine. Add parsley, chives, onion and salt and pepper to bowl and toss lightly.

In a 9-inch skillet, cook bacon over medium heat until it has rendered its fat and the bits are crisp. Remove from heat, stir in vinegar and pour over the salad. Toss and serve immediately.

CAESAR SALAD

A special-occasion salad.

Makes 4–6 servings
1 garlic clove, peeled and cut in half
1/2 cup best-quality olive oil
2 small heads romaine, cut or torn into bite-size pieces
Kosher salt
Freshly ground black pepper
1/2 cup grated parmesan cheese (preferably freshly grated)
Juice of 2 lemons
1 egg, coddled*
Worcestershire Sauce
1 cup Caroline's Homemade Croutons (page 101)

Put garlic in olive oil; set aside for several hours or overnight. Place romaine in large salad bowl. Sprinkle with salt and pepper to taste and the parmesan cheese;

toss. Add lemon juice and toss. Remove garlic from oil, pour oil over greens and toss once or twice. Break egg into small bowl, beat with fork to blend, pour over greens and toss well. Add a few dashes Worcestershire sauce, taste and correct seasonings. Top with croutons and serve.

*Coddle egg by placing in a measuring cup, covering with boiling water and letting stand 2 minutes.

ITALIAN AND GREEK SALADS

With a basic dressing and some common elements, you can always be ready to make an Italian or Greek salad by varying some of the salad ingredients.

Each salad makes 4 servings

BASIC DRESSING
1 garlic clove, peeled
1/4 teaspoon kosher salt
2 tablespoons red wine vinegar
1/2 teaspoon dry mustard
1/2 cup best-quality olive oil
1/4 teaspoon dried oregano, crushed
Freshly ground black pepper to taste

ITALIAN SALAD BOWL
1 head romaine, cut into bite-size pieces across the rib
1 small zucchini (unpeeled), sliced
1/4 pound fresh mushrooms, sliced
1 small red onion, peeled and thinly sliced
1/4 cup Italian olives (Crispi Ponentine)
1 tablespoon grated parmesan (preferably freshly grated)

GREEK SALAD BOWL
1 head romaine, cut into bite-size pieces across the rib
4 green onions, thinly sliced
2 tomatoes, diced
1 small cucumber, peeled, seeded and sliced
1/2 pound feta cheese, cut in 1/2-inch dice
1/4 cup Greek olives (Calamata)

BASIC GARNISH
About 1/4 cup mild pepperoncini, drained
4 anchovy fillets

To make Basic Dressing, mash garlic clove and salt in a glass jar with a fork. Add remaining dressing ingredients, top jar with a tight-fitting lid and shake vigorously to blend. In a large salad bowl, toss together either the Italian Salad Bowl ingredients or the Greek Salad Bowl ingredients. Pour on desired amount of dressing, toss and top with Basic Garnish. Store any remaining dressing in the refrigerator.

SWEET AND SOUR CUCUMBERS

Serve in small bowls or as part of a buffet.

Makes 4–6 servings
2 medium cucumbers, peeled and seeded
1/4–1/2 teaspoon kosher salt
2 tablespoons distilled white vinegar
2 teaspoons sugar

Slice cucumbers very thinly and place in mixing bowl; sprinkle with salt and stir. Let stand 15–30 minutes or until moisture is drawn from cucumbers. Mix and break up cucumbers by squeezing with your hand. Do not drain. Stir in vinegar and sugar. Taste and adjust seasonings, if desired.

DON ROTH'S SPINNING BLACKHAWK SALAD

Innovative restaurateur Don Roth is a Chicago institution. For years, his spinning salad was served exclusively at his Blackhawk Restaurant—tossed tableside with a short incantation about the "twenty-one secret ingredients." This salad's exceptional flavor comes from a blending of two homemade dressings, each delicious by itself, fabulous together.

Makes 4–6 servings

BLUE CHEESE DRESSING
1 package (3 ounces) cream cheese, softened
3 ounces blue cheese, crumbled
5–6 tablespoons water

"SECRET" DRESSING
1 egg
1-1/2 tablespoons fresh lemon juice
1 cup vegetable oil
1/4 cup red wine vinegar
1/4 teaspoon Dijon-style or other sharp mustard
3/4 teaspoon paprika
3/4 teaspoon kosher salt
1/4 teaspoon garlic powder
1/4 teaspoon freshly ground white pepper
1 tablespoon sugar
2 tablespoons snipped fresh chives
1-1/2 teaspoons Worcestershire sauce
2 tablespoons Durkee's sandwich and salad sauce

THE SALAD
8 cups mixed salad greens in bite-size pieces (iceberg, romaine, bibb lettuces, endive or any combination)
Healthful Seasoned Salt (page 99), or purchased seasoned salt
Freshly ground black pepper
4–6 anchovy fillets

To make Blue Cheese Dressing, beat together cream cheese and blue cheese; beat in water, a tablespoon at a time, until dressing is of pouring consistency. Or blend in food processor until smooth. Set aside.

To make "Secret" Dressing, process egg, lemon juice and 1/4 cup of the oil in a blender or food processor until well blended. With blender on "high" setting or food processor running, add the rest of the oil in a slow steady stream.

Clean down sides of container with rubber scraper. Add vinegar, mustard, seasonings, sugar, chives, Worcestershire sauce and Durkee's sauce. Blend on "high" until smooth. Place greens in a large salad bowl. Pour "Secret" Dressing over greens in desired amount and sprinkle with seasoned salt and pepper to taste. Toss gently 3–4 times. Add 2–4 tablespoons Blue Cheese Dressing, toss to coat, sprinkle with chopped egg, toss again and garnish with anchovy fillets. Store the unused portion of each dressing in an air-tight container in the refrigerator up to 2 weeks.

NOTE If making dressings ahead, refrigerate until 30 minutes before serving time, then bring to room temperature.

CREAMY COLE SLAW

Since there is no mayo in this cole slaw, it is ideal for picnics and cookouts. Serve with fried or grilled fish or chicken, or with sandwiches.

Makes 4–6 servings*
1/2 head cabbage, shredded
1 carrot, peeled and grated
1 small sweet green pepper, seeded and minced
2 green onions, minced

DRESSING
1/2–3/4 cup creamy salad dressing (Miracle Whip or similar brand)
2–4 teaspoons milk or water
Pinch of kosher salt
Freshly ground black pepper
Paprika

In a large bowl, toss together cabbage, carrot, green pepper and onion. Thin salad dressing with milk and stir in salt and pepper. Pour over cabbage, toss to coat and then sprinkle with paprika.

*This recipe can be easily doubled.

CLASSIC CRANBERRY RELISH

So simple, you'll make it year-round.

Makes about 3 cups
2 packages (12 ounces *each*) fresh or frozen cranberries*
2 cups water
1-1/4–1-3/4 cups sugar
3 tablespoons blackberry-flavored brandy (optional)

Rinse cranberries; place in large saucepan with water and 1-1/4 cups sugar. Bring to a boil, stirring occasionally; adjust heat and boil until all the cranberries "pop" (you'll hear their skins pop open), stirring occasionally, 5–10 minutes. Taste, stir in additional sugar if desired, and boil 2–3 minutes more. Remove from heat, stir in brandy and pour into serving bowl. Let cool, then cover and refrigerate at least 4 hours or up to 1 week. Serve with roasted pork, chicken, turkey or other fowl.

*To freeze fresh cranberries for later use, simply place unopened bag of berries in freezer.

BREADS

GARLIC BREAD

Makes 1 loaf
1/4 pound (1 stick) unsalted butter, softened
2 garlic cloves (or more), peeled and crushed, or 1/4–1/2 teaspoon garlic powder
1 loaf French- or Italian-style bread

Preheat oven to 400°F. In a small mixing bowl, beat butter until light. Beat in garlic. Let stand at least 15 minutes to blend flavors. Slice bread into 1-inch-thick slices, cutting only three-fourths of the way through loaf. Spread slices with garlic butter and spread any remaining butter on top of loaf. Wrap loaf in aluminum foil, leaving 2 inches of crust exposed along the top. Let stand 10 minutes. Bake on oven rack or jelly-roll pan in the preheated oven 10 minutes or until top browns. Serve warm.

STEVE JENKS'S FROM-SCRATCH WHITE BREAD

Steve, who is with the Portsmouth Consulting Group in Durham, New Hampshire, began cooking in 1971 when his wife broke her leg in a skiing mishap. Since then, he has become quite proficient and now cooks for relaxation and a "sense of accomplishment." He shares cooking tasks with his wife and two daughters and prides himself on never using mixes. Here's his favorite bread recipe.

Makes three 9- by 5-inch loaves*
2 cups hot milk
1/4 cup honey
1 tablespoon kosher salt
3 tablespoons Crisco hydrogenated shortening
2 cups warm water (105°–110°F)
2 packages (1 tablespoon *each*) active dry yeast
Pinch of sugar
8 cups unbleached flour
1-1/2 cups whole-wheat flour
1/2 cup wheat germ
Additional Crisco for greasing

In a large mixing bowl, stir together milk, honey, salt and shortening until shortening melts; let cool. In a 2-cup glass measuring cup, stir together 1/2 cup of the warm water, yeast and sugar; let sit 5 minutes or until doubled in bulk. While yeast mixture is doubling, set aside 2 cups of the unbleached flour. Combine remaining 6 cups unbleached flour with whole-wheat flour and wheat germ; set aside.

When yeast mixture is ready, add it to the milk mixture with the

Kneading dough

remaining 1-1/2 cups warm water. Stir in the flour mixture, adding additional unbleached flour from the reserved 2 cups if needed to form a dough ball. Turn dough out onto a lightly floured board and knead until smooth and elastic (10–12 minutes), adding more of the reserved flour as needed to keep the ball from being sticky. Or mix and knead in a heavy-duty electric mixer fitted with a dough hook. Grease a large clean bowl with shortening, place dough in bowl, turn over to coat with grease, cover bowl with linen towel and let dough rise in a warm place** 1-1/2–2 hours, or until doubled in bulk. With a fist, punch down dough and turn out on a floured board; knead a few strokes and then cut into thirds.

Grease three 9- by 5-inch loaf pans with shortening. Preheat standard oven to 325°F, or a convection oven to 300°F. Pat or roll out piece of dough into a 1/2-inch-thick rectangle about 9 inches wide. Starting at one 9-inch edge, roll up into a cylinder and pinch seam and ends closed. Place in greased loaf pan, seam side down, tucking under ends. Repeat with remaining pieces of dough. Let loaves rise in a warm place about 1 hour.

Bake loaves in the preheated standard oven 40 minutes, or the convection oven 30–40 minutes. Loaves are ready when a wooden pick inserted in the center comes out clean. Cool in pan 5 minutes, then remove loaves to cooling rack. Eat 1 loaf and wrap and freeze the others, if desired. Thaw at room temperature and heat briefly in 300°F oven, if desired.

*Halve this recipe and bake two 4- by 7-inch loaves.

**Warm places to set dough for rising include the top of a pilot-light gas range, the inside of a turned-off gas oven with a pilot light, and the center of a turned-off electric oven with a bowl of hot tap water sitting on the bottom shelf.

QUICK-RISE HERB BREAD

This bread toasts beautifully for sandwiches.

Makes one 9- by 5-inch loaf
3-1/4–3-1/2 cups unbleached flour
1-1/2 tablespoons sugar
1/2 teaspoon kosher salt
2 teaspoons dried oregano
2 teaspoons dried basil
1 teaspoon garlic powder
1 package (scant 1 tablespoon) rapid rising yeast
2 tablespoons margarine or butter, softened
1 cup hot water (125°–130°F)

Set aside 1 cup flour. Stir together remaining flour, sugar, salt, herbs, garlic powder and yeast in a large mixing bowl. Test water temperature with instant-read thermometer. If tap water does not reach 125°–130°F, add some boiling water until proper temperature is reached. Stir margarine and hot water into flour mixture. Mix in just enough of the reserved flour to make a dough. Turn dough out onto lightly floured board; knead until smooth and elastic (adding remaining flour as needed to keep dough from sticking), about 5 min-utes. Or mix and knead in a heavy-duty electric mixer with a dough hook. Return dough to bowl, cover with linen towel and let rest 10 minutes.

Grease a 9- by 5-inch loaf pan with margarine. Preheat standard oven to 400°F, or a convection oven to 375°F. With a fist, punch down dough and turn out on a lightly floured board. With a rolling pin, roll dough in a 12- by 8-inch rectangle. Starting at 8-inch edge, roll up into cylinder and pinch seam and ends to seal. Place in greased loaf pan, seam side down. Cover and let rise in a warm place* until doubled in bulk, 30–40 minutes.

Bake loaf in the preheated stan-dard oven 25–30 minutes, or in the convection oven 20–30 min-utes. Loaf is ready when a wooden pick inserted in the center comes out clean. Cool in pan 5 minutes, then remove loaf to cool-ing rack.

*See double-asterisked note on Steve Jenks's From-Scratch White Bread (preceding).

ON-THE-SQUARE BUTTERMILK BISCUITS

Southern cooks have long known that lard brings tenderness and flavor to biscuits. This recipe, which uses a simple cutting-by-knife technique, rises righ and can be eaten slathered with Cream Gravy (page 52).

Makes 12 biscuits
Margarine
1-3/4 cups unbleached flour
1 tablespoon baking powder
1 teaspoon kosher salt
1/3 cup chilled lard
2/3 cup buttermilk
Additional flour

Preheat oven to 450°F and lightly grease a baking sheet (without sides) with margarine. Sift together flour, baking powder and salt into a medium mixing bowl. Cut lard into several pieces, add to flour mixture and use fingers of both hands to pinch lard into flour, breaking it into smaller and smaller pieces as you go. When mixture resembles coarse meal, stir in buttermilk, then gather dough into ball with hands and turn out onto lightly floured board. If dough is sticky, knead in additional flour little by little until dough is no longer sticky and is firm but not hard. Pat dough into 1/2-inch-thick square on a lightly floured board. Cut dough into 2–2-1/2-inch squares with a knife. Place on greased baking sheet with space between biscuits for hard sides, or next to one another for soft sides. Bake in center of the preheated oven 10–12 minutes, or until a light golden brown. Serve with gravy or butter and honey.

PANSY LUKE'S MANDARIN ONION PIES

Pansy is a talented and delightfully humorous cooking teacher who runs a market and catering business in Chicago with her husband Chu Yen. She also escorts groups on culinary tours of China, her homeland. (For information on the tours, write to Oriental Food Market, listed in Mail-Order Sources.) Pansy loves teaching her students how to make these onion pies, which are a good alternative to rice in northern Chinese menus.

Makes 6 pies, 3–6 servings
3 cups unbleached flour
1 cup water, boiling
1/2 cup cold water
2 tablespoons Crisco hydrogenated shortening
1 tablespoon kosher salt
3 green onions, chopped
About 1/2 cup vegetable oil

To make the dough, place flour in a large mixing bowl, stir in boiling water with a fork, add cold water and work dough with your hands until it comes together in a ball. Turn out on a lightly floured board and knead until smooth, about 5 minutes. Place in bowl, cover bowl with a damp towel or paper toweling and let rest 15–30 minutes.

To shape pies, cut dough into 6 equal pieces. Knead each piece lightly on floured board; keep pieces you are not working with covered with damp clean towel. With rolling pin, roll dough into an 8-inch circle, rub 1 teaspoon shortening over the circle, and then sprinkle with 1/2 teaspoon salt and a generous tablespoonful green onion. Roll up into a cylinder and pinch ends closed. Pick up roll and set it on one of its ends; twist from top with one hand, holding onto the bottom with the other hand, to make a tight coil. From the top, press down with palm to flatten coil into a round. With a rolling pin, roll round to a 3/16-inch thickness. Repeat with remaining pieces of dough.

Preheat oven to 250°F. Line a jelly-roll pan with paper toweling. Heat 1-1/2 tablespoons oil in frypan (not wok) over high heat. Add an onion pie and cook uncovered 1 minute. Turn, cover and cook over medium heat 2 minutes. Remove cover, turn pie and fry until golden. Drain on lined jelly-roll pan. Place in warm oven while frying remaining pancakes. Cut into wedges and serve with stir-fry dishes or any meat dish.

RICE, PASTA AND DUMPLINGS

STEAMED RICE

Makes about 3 cups
1 cup long-grain white rice
2 cups water
1/2–1 teaspoon kosher salt

Stir together ingredients in medium saucepan, bring to a boil, cover and reduce heat to low. Cook about 18 minutes without lifting the lid. Fluff with a fork before serving.

RICE WITH TOMATOES AND MUSHROOMS

Makes 4 servings*
5 tablespoons unsalted butter
1/2 pound fresh mushrooms, sliced
1 cup long-grain white rice
1 small onion, peeled and minced
1 can (16 ounces) whole tomatoes, broken up with a spoon, and their juice
1 teaspoon kosher salt
1/4 teaspoon freshly ground black pepper
2 cups chicken stock (canned or made from chicken base)

In a 9-inch frypan, melt 2 tablespoons of the butter, add mushrooms and sauté over medium heat, stirring constantly until tender, about 5 minutes. Set aside. In a 10-inch frypan, melt remaining 3 tablespoons butter over medium heat. Add rice and cook, stirring, until all rice grains turn opaque, about 5 minutes. Add remaining ingredients, including sautéed mushrooms, stir and bring to a boil. Cover and reduce heat to low. Cook 20–25 minutes or until all the liquid is absorbed. If rice is tender but soupy, cook uncovered until liquid is reduced.

*This recipe can be easily halved to serve two.

EXQUISITE FETTUCCINE ALFREDO

Crème fraîche gives this famous dish extra body and a subtle nut-like tartness.

Makes 2 main-course or 4 first-course servings
1 recipe Crème Fraîche (following)
3 quarts water
2 teaspoons kosher salt
1/2 pound dried fettuccine noodles
3 tablespoons unsalted butter
Few grindings of white pepper
Dash of ground nutmeg
1/2–3/4 cup freshly grated parmesan cheese

Make Crème Fraîche a day or more in advance. Bring water to a rapid boil in a 5-quart saucepan and add 1-1/2 teaspoons of the salt. Add noodles and cook until *al dente* (soft but slightly resistant to the bite), 10–15 minutes. Taste a noodle to test for doneness.

While pasta is cooking, stir together Crème Fraîche and butter in a 10-inch frypan over medium heat until butter melts and mixture comes to a boil. Add 1/2 teaspoon salt, pepper and nutmeg and simmer 2–3 minutes. Drain and rinse fettuccine, add to frypan mixture, stir, taste and correct seasonings. Simmer about 2 minutes or until fettuccine is hot throughout. Sprinkle with 1/2 cup of the parmesan, stir and serve immediately. Pass remaining parmesan.

CREME FRAICHE

Makes 1-1/3 cups
1 cup (1 carton) whipping cream
1/3 cup sour cream, or 2 tablespoons buttermilk

Combine ingredients in a tightly covered jar or plastic container and shake to blend well. Loosen lid and allow to rest on jar top. Leave out at room temperature 8 to 24 hours or until cream has thickened. Stir, tighten lid and store in refrigerator until ready to use. Keeps refrigerated for up to 1 week.

NOTE Crème Fraîche makes a rich topping for berries and ice cream sundaes.

FRANKIE D'S PASTA PROSCIUTTO CARBONARA

This recipe is a specialty at Frankie D'Agostino's marvelously Italian Caffé Columbus in Springfield, Massachusetts. He gladly shared it with me over an after-dinner liqueur, cautioning me to use a top-quality prosciutto like the one he gets from Peter Carando's plant just across town.

Makes 2 main-course or 4 first-course servings
3 quarts water
1-1/2 teaspoons kosher salt
1/2 pound dried linguine noodles
1/4 pound prosciutto, thinly sliced and cut into 1/4-inch pieces
1–2 garlic cloves, peeled and crushed
2 eggs
1/4 cup freshly grated parmesan cheese
Additional grated parmesan cheese

Bring water to a rapid boil in 5-quart saucepan, add salt and then noodles. Cook until *al dente* (soft but slightly resistant to the bite), 10–15 minutes. Taste one noodle to test.

While pasta is cooking, heat prosciutto and garlic in a dry frypan over medium-high heat, stirring frequently, until fat is rendered. Keep warm. In a mixing bowl, beat eggs with whisk to blend well; stir in 1/4 cup parmesan. Drain cooked noodles, add hot noodles to egg and cheese in bowl and toss to coat pasta. Reheat prosciutto to sizzling, pour over noodles and toss. Add more parmesan if desired. Serve on warm plates and pass additional cheese.

SAUCY PASTA TWISTS WITH ZUCCHINI

An Italian stir fry, this dish can be made with freshly cooked or leftover pasta, freshly cooked or leftover sauce. It is a quick and easy entrée that can be teamed with Garlic Bread and Italian Salad for last-minute dinner guests.

*Makes 1 main-course serving**
1-1/2 tablespoons unsalted butter
1-1/2 tablespoons olive oil
1 shallot or garlic clove, peeled and minced
1 small zucchini (unpeeled), thinly sliced (about 1 cup)
Pinch of dried oregano
2–2-1/2 cups cooked pasta twists or shells
1/2 cup All-Purpose Tomato Sauce (page 82), Simple Savory Pasta Sauce (page 83) or purchased spaghetti sauce of choice
2 tablespoons grated parmesan cheese (preferably freshly grated)

In a 10-inch frypan, melt butter with oil over medium heat. Add shallot and cook, stirring, until tender, about 3 minutes. Add zucchini and oregano and sauté until zucchini is crisp-tender, about 5 minutes. Stir in cooked pasta until it is hot throughout, add sauce and stir to coat. Stir in half of the parmesan. Serve on a warm plate, sprinkled with remaining cheese.

*This recipe can be easily doubled or tripled.

HALUSKY (BOHEMIAN BATTER DUMPLINGS)

Great with braised meats or anything served with gravy.

Makes 4 servings
3/4 cup milk
1 egg
2 cups unbleached flour
1 teaspoon kosher salt
3–4 quarts water

Pour milk into a measuring cup and stir in egg. Put flour in a mixing bowl and stir in salt. Gradually add milk mixture to flour, stirring constantly to make a thick batter. Beat by hand until smooth, about 30 seconds. Let batter rest 10–15 minutes.

Bring water to a medium boil in a 5-quart pot. Tip bowl so batter flows to the edge as if you are going to pour it out of the bowl. Hold bowl over boiling water, dip a knife into the boiling water and cut off a 1/2-inch-wide sliver of batter against the edge of the bowl; allow sliver to fall into boiling water. Continue to cut dumplings in this manner until all the batter is used, dipping knife in water after each cut. Boil dumplings 12–15 minutes until they rise to the top and are no longer doughy in the center; drain. Serve hot with gravy.

IV MAKE-AHEAD COOKERY

Braised Dishes, Soups, & Casseroles

BRAISED MEATS, STEWS AND SAUCES

Braising is cooking with moist heat. That's the definition one might hear in a high-school home economics class, but it doesn't do justice to the wonderful dishes prepared using this technique! I prefer to think of braising as a platter of corned beef and cabbage, a bowl of spicy red chili or a plate brimming with shrimp-studded jambalaya. To me, a braised dish is one in which solid foods are simmered in liquid for an exchange of flavors. That takes in chunky sauces, soups, and browned and nonbrowned meat and vegetable dishes.

Braising is usually done in a covered dutch oven or other pot, but the pot can be uncovered if the recipe so specifies. A braised dish can be prepared on the range top or in the oven. But best of all, these dishes can be made one day and served another, and they actually improve upon reheating. Make a pot of Potage Parmentier today and it's delicious. Serve the remainder of it tomorrow and it tastes even better. Dishes like chili, spaghetti sauce and soups can be made in big batches, refrigerated or frozen in smaller amounts and used as needed. While braised dishes may take a long time to cook, they are great time-savers in the long run.

THE ROLE OF WATER IN COOKING

Since braising utilizes water and other liquids that are mostly water, this is a good place to explain the role of water in cooking. It was that extraordinary chef and teacher Jacques Pépin who first made me aware of the importance of understanding what happens to water during cooking. He said, "If you understand this, cooking will become easy."

Water in cooking has two roles: it is both a carrier of flavors and a cooking agent, but not always at the same time. In braising, water (liquid) is both a carrier and the cooking agent; in roasting, the small amount of water in the bottom of the pan becomes a carrier as juices drip into it; in boiling or steaming, it is mainly a cooking agent, but there is some transfer of flavors; in sauce making, it is a carrier.

As water boils or simmers, it reduces; the steam that rises off a simmering liquid is water lost to the air. But, back in the pot, there are still the same foodstuffs, spices and flavoring agents that were there before the water cooked away. This means the flavors in the pot have become more concentrated. This simple process of boiling away liquid is called "reduction" and is utilized in braising, the making of sauces and gravies and in any dish where you end up with less liquid than that with which you started. What makes any of these dishes taste good is the concentration of flavors in the liquid, which brings up the practical application of this theory: if a braised dish, gravy or sauce *tastes weak* and diluted, reduce it to concentrate flavors. If the dish tastes too strong, add water to lighten the flavors.

Why does a braised dish taste better the second (or third) time around? It is due to the prolonged blending of flavors and to the evaporation of liquid that occurs in refrigeration or freezing, both forms of "natural reduction."

MRS. KRIZ'S BRAISED SMOKED BUTT AND PEA SOUP

In a Bohemian kitchen, everything is utilized to the utmost. This recipe from my mother's repertoire shows how one small cut of meat and some vegetables make both the soup and the main course of a hearty cold-weather meal. Smoked butt, a slightly obscure cut which is actually smoked pork shoulder, also makes great sandwiches with tomatoes and rye bread the next day.

Makes 4 servings, with leftovers
1 smoked pork butt, about 2 pounds (blade butt is leaner; boneless butt slices easier)
2 large carrots, peeled and sliced
1 celery stalk, sliced
1 medium onion, peeled and coarsely chopped
2–3 sprigs parsley, chopped
1/2 small cabbage, chopped (optional)
1 medium potato, peeled and diced
8 ounces (1 cup) dry split peas
3 tablespoons bacon drippings
6 tablespoons unbleached flour

ONION GRAVY
1 slice bacon, cut into 1/4-inch-wide strips
1 large onion, peeled and chopped
1 cup cooled reserved cooking liquid
1 tablespoon unbleached flour

Cover the smoked butt with water in a 5-quart dutch oven, bring to a boil and remove the smoked butt. Reserve 1 cup of the cooking liquid for making the gravy; discard the remainder. Rinse the dutch oven, return meat to pot, add vegetables, split peas and water to cover. Bring to a boil, reduce heat, cover and simmer about 2 hours or until meat is fork tender. Remove meat to a platter, cover with aluminum foil and keep warm.

In a small pan, melt bacon drippings over medium heat, stir in flour and cook and stir 2–3 minutes. Whisk flour mixture into boiling soup to thicken. To finish soup, put liquid and vegetables through a food mill, process in a food processor fitted with a steel blade, or push through a sieve with a large spoon. Return soup to heat and keep warm while making gravy.

To make gravy, place bacon in a 9-inch frypan over medium heat and cook until fat is rendered and bacon begins to brown. Add onion and cook until transparent, about 5 minutes. Add 3/4 cup of the reserved cooking liquid and bring to a boil. Stir flour into remaining 1/4 cup cooking liquid, whisk mixture into boiling gravy and let boil 2 minutes. Serve soup as first course or reserve for another day. Slice smoked butt 1/4 inch thick and serve with gravy. Boiled potatoes make a good accompaniment.

CORNED BEEF BOILED DINNER

Don't wait for St. Patrick's Day to try this.

Makes 4–6 servings
One 3–5 pound corned beef brisket
1 onion, peeled and sliced
4 whole cloves
6 black peppercorns
2 bay leaves
6 small potatoes, peeled
3 medium carrots, peeled and cut in half
1 small head cabbage, cut into wedges

Rinse corned beef under cold running water, place in a 5-quart dutch oven and cover with water by 2 inches. Add onion and spices. Bring to a boil, reduce heat, cover and simmer about 40 minutes per pound or until corned beef is fork tender, adding water as needed to keep corned beef immersed. Add potatoes and carrots during the last 30 minutes of cooking; add cabbage during the last 15 minutes.

To serve, slice corned beef thinly across the grain. Spoon cooking liquid over meat and vegetables, if desired.

ALVIN RAY'S BRAISED LAMB WITH RED CABBAGE

Cooking enthusiast Alvin Ray likes to serve this hearty oven-braised dish with green salad, steamed rice and lots of dark beer.

Makes 6–8 servings
One 5–6 pound boned rolled leg of lamb
Olive oil for rubbing on lamb
3 garlic cloves, peeled and cut into slivers
3 cups (two 12-ounce bottles) dark beer
3 onions, peeled and thinly sliced
3 sprigs parsley, with stems
1 bay leaf
1/2 teaspoon dried rosemary, crushed
1/4 teaspoon dried thyme, crushed
6 tablespoons olive oil
1-1/2 cups beef stock (canned or made from beef base)
4 tablespoons (1/2 stick) unsalted butter
1/4 cup unbleached flour
Kosher salt
Freshly ground black pepper
Double recipe Steamed Rice (page 73), hot
Braised Red Cabbage (following)

Rub lamb with olive oil, slit in several places with paring-knife tip and insert garlic slivers. Place lamb in a large glass or stainless-steel bowl or a baking dish and add beer, onion slices, parsley, bay leaf, rosemary and thyme. Cover with plastic wrap and refrigerate at least 12 hours, turning occasionally. Remove lamb from marinade, reserving marinade. Preheat oven to 300°F.

In a large ovenproof dutch oven, heat 6 tablespoons olive oil, add lamb and brown over medium-high heat on all sides. Add marinade and beef stock. Cover with a large piece of aluminum foil gently pressed against meat and liquid, then up the insides of the pan and over the edges. Cover pot with a lid and bake in the preheated oven 2-1/2–2-3/4 hours or until fork tender. (Lamb can be cooked over low heat on the range top, if desired.) Remove lamb to platter, cover with foil and keep warm.

Strain cooking liquid and return 4 cups to dutch oven. Melt butter in a 9-inch frypan, add flour and cook, stirring, until flour just *begins* to brown. Whisk flour mixture into liquid in dutch oven and heat to boiling; simmer 2 minutes. Add salt and pepper to taste. Arrange rice around lamb on platter. Serve Braised Red Cabbage and gravy separately.

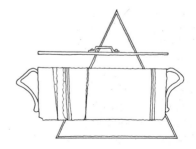

BRAISED RED CABBAGE

Makes 6–8 servings
2 heads red cabbage (about 2
    pounds *each*)
1-1/2 teaspoons salt
1/4 pound (1 stick) unsalted butter
1/2 teaspoon freshly ground black
    pepper
1 cup dry red wine
2 tablespoons caraway seeds
2 tablespoons firmly packed
    brown sugar
1 tablespoon red wine vinegar

Shred cabbage coarsely by slicing
1/4 inch thick. Place cabbage in 1
or 2 large bowls, cover with cold
water and stir in 1 teaspoon of the
salt. Soak 30 minutes, then drain
well. Melt butter in a large saucepan, add cabbage and cook and
stir 5 minutes. Stir in the remaining 1/2 teaspoon salt, pepper,
wine and caraway seeds. Heat to
boiling, reduce heat and simmer 5
minutes. Stir in brown sugar and
vinegar, cover and simmer until
tender, about 30 minutes.

JAMBALAYA

Braised rice studded with shrimp,
ham and bacon from the heart of
the Deep South.

Makes 4–6 servings
1/4 pound sliced bacon, cut into
    1-inch pieces
1 small onion, peeled and
    chopped
1–2 garlic cloves, peeled and
    crushed
1 large sweet green pepper,
    seeded and cut into 1/2-inch-
    wide strips
2 tablespoons minced fresh
    parsley
1/2 pound smoked ham, cut into
    1/4-inch-wide strips
1 cup long-grain rice
1 can (20 ounces) whole toma-
    toes, coarsely chopped and
    liquid reserved
1/2 teaspoon dried thyme,
    crushed
Pinch of red pepper flakes
1 teaspoon kosher salt
Freshly ground black pepper
1-1/2–2 cups chicken stock
    (canned or made from chicken
    base)
1 pound raw medium shrimp,
    shelled and deveined

In a deep frypan or Dutch oven,
cook bacon over medium heat until fat is rendered and bacon is
brown but not crisp. Remove with
a slotted spoon and reserve. Add
the onion to the pan with the drippings and cook, stirring, until
transparent, about 5 minutes. Stir
in the garlic, green pepper, half
the parsley and the ham. Cook,
stirring, until peppers soften,
about 3 minutes. Add rice and stir
to coat with fat; cook, stirring, until
rice turns milky white, 2–3 minutes. Add the reserved bacon, tomatoes and their liquid, thyme,
pepper flakes, salt, black pepper
and 1-1/2 cups chicken stock.
Bring to a boil, cover and cook
over low heat 15–20 minutes, or
until rice has absorbed the
chicken stock. Add additional 1/2
cup stock if all liquid is absorbed
but rice is not yet tender. Add
shrimp to pan, pushing them down
into the rice; cover and continue to
cook for about 5 minutes. Sprinkle
with remaining parsley and serve
piping hot.

BACK-FOR-MORE CHILI

Use fresh or canned hot peppers to spice this chunky-style chili flavored with Canadian whiskey. The spiciness will mellow after a few days in the refrigerator. Serve with Ronnie Bull's Flour Tortillas (page 119).

Makes 8 servings
2 tablespoons vegetable oil
3 pounds beef chuck, cut into
   1/2-inch cubes
2 medium onions, peeled and
   coarsely chopped
1 cup Canadian blended whiskey
3-1/2 cups beef stock (canned or
   made from beef base)
2 cans (28 ounces *each*) whole tomatoes, chopped, with their
   liquid
1 can (6 ounces) tomato paste
1 or more fresh chili peppers,
   seeded and chopped,* or
   chopped canned chili peppers
1 teaspoon salt
2 tablespoons ground cumin
2 tablespoons dried oregano
   (preferably Mexican)

2 teaspoons sugar
5–7 garlic cloves, peeled and
   minced
1 can (15-1/4 ounces) chili beans,
   or about 2 cups Ronnie Bull's
   Braised Pinto Beans (page 82,
   optional)
Condiments: shredded cheddar
   cheese, chopped onions and
   sour cream

In a 5-quart dutch oven, heat oil over medium heat, add beef and onion and cook, stirring constantly, until meat browns lightly. Brown in 2 batches, if necessary. Return all meat to pot, add whiskey and beef stock and simmer over medium heat uncovered for 30 minutes. Add all remaining ingredients except beans and condi-

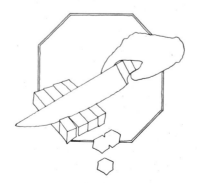

ments. Simmer uncovered over low heat 2 hours, stirring occasionally.

Taste and correct seasonings. Stir in beans and simmer another 15 minutes. If chili appears too thick, add water. If chili is too thin, continue to simmer. Top with cheddar cheese, onions and/or sour cream.

*When handling fresh chili peppers, do not touch your fingers to your lips or eyes before thoroughly washing your hands. To diminish some of the chili pepper's spiciness, remove the seeds, as they are the hottest part. To seed, cut pepper in half lengthwise and scrape out seeds with knife tip. Cut off stem and chop pepper as directed. When selecting fresh chili peppers, remember that jalapeño peppers are the hottest, finger peppers generate a lesser degree of heat and banana peppers are mildly spicy.

RONNIE BULL'S BRAISED PINTO BEANS

Mash some of the beans for Ronnie Bull's Texas Burritos (page 118), and use the remainder as a soup.

Makes about 6 cups
1 pound (2 cups) pinto beans
6 cups water
3 medium onions, peeled and coarsely chopped
3 garlic cloves, peeled and minced
1 teaspoon kosher salt
1 tablespoon chili powder
1 teaspoon paprika
1/2 teaspoon freshly ground black pepper
1 tablespoon lemon pepper

Rinse beans and pick over to remove any stones. Soak beans in 6 cups water overnight. (For quick-soak method, add beans to 6 cups rapidly boiling water, boil 2 minutes, remove from heat, cover and let stand 1 hour.) Add all remaining ingredients to water and beans, bring to a boil, reduce heat, cover and boil gently for 2 hours or until beans are tender. With a slotted spoon, remove 2–3 cups of beans to a frypan. Add 1/4–1/2 cup bean liquid and mash beans with a fork or potato masher to a paste. Keep warm over low heat until ready to fill burritos.

ALL-PURPOSE TOMATO SAUCE

A thick and zesty sauce for pasta, pizza and sandwiches.

Makes about 7 cups
1/4 cup olive oil
1-1/2 cups finely chopped onion (about 2 medium)
4–6 garlic cloves, peeled and minced
2 cans (28 ounces *each*) crushed Italian tomatoes with added purée*
1 can (6 ounces) tomato paste
1 cup beef stock (canned or made with beef base)
2–3 bay leaves
3 tablespoons minced fresh oregano, or 1-1/2 tablespoons dried oregano, crushed
2 tablespoons minced fresh basil, or 1 tablespoon dried basil, crushed
2 teaspoons sugar
2 teaspoons kosher salt
1/2 teaspoon freshly ground black pepper

In a 3-quart saucepan, heat olive oil over medium heat, add onions and cook, stirring, about 5 minutes or until transparent and slightly soft. Add garlic and cook 2 minutes. Add all remaining ingredients, bring to a boil, reduce heat and simmer uncovered about 1 hour. Use as is, or freeze in 1-cup portions as described in plastic bags entry in Cleanup and Storage section of Equipping the Kitchen.

*Two cans (28 ounces *each*) Italian plum tomatoes can be used. Chop tomatoes coarsely and add them to pan with their liquid.

SIMPLE SAVORY PASTA SAUCE

Use convenient store-bought ingredients or your own homemade ones in this simple recipe. Freeze leftover sauce for another meal.

Makes about 5 cups
1/2 pound Savory or Hot Italian Sausage (page 103), or purchased Italian sausage
4 cups All-Purpose Tomato Sauce (preceding), or bottled meatless spaghetti sauce of choice

In a 10-inch frypan, brown sausage over medium heat until crumbly and all pink color is gone, about 10 minutes. Add tomato sauce, stir and bring to a simmer. Serve over cooked pasta.

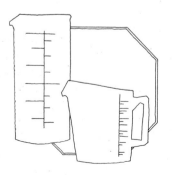

SOUPS

JOHN CONNERS'S DAY-AFTER TURKEY SOUP

As vice-chairman of Beatrice Foods, John deals with food on the corporate level during the day, then cooks at home in the evenings for relaxation. Here he shares a delightful soup that puts the turkey carcass to good use.

Makes about 4–5 quarts
1/2 pound (2 sticks) unsalted butter
1 cup unbleached flour
Yellow food coloring (optional)
1/2 cup chopped sweet green pepper
1/2 cup chopped carrot
1/2 cup chopped onion
1/2 cup sliced celery
1 small jar or can (2 ounces) chopped pimiento
1–2 cups chopped leftover turkey meat

SOUP STOCK
One leftover turkey carcass (from a 15-pound roasted bird), with all the bones
4 carrots, peeled and cut in half
4 celery stalks with tops, cut in half
2 onions, peeled and cut in half
1 tablespoon kosher salt

To make stock, place turkey carcass in a 7-quart dutch oven or stockpot, chopping carcass up to make it fit. Add remaining stock ingredients and enough water to cover completely, about 5 quarts. Bring to a boil, reduce heat, cover with a tight-fitting lid and simmer 8 hours. Replenish water as it evaporates. Strain stock by pouring into a colander set over a large saucepan.

In a frypan, melt butter over medium heat, stir in flour, bring to a boil and cook, stirring, 2–3 minutes to make a roux. Bring strained stock to a boil and whisk in roux a little at a time until stock reaches desired consistency. (Refrigerate remaining roux and use to thicken soups and sauces.) Add a few drops food coloring if desired. Stir in vegetables and turkey and simmer until vegetables are just tender, about 15 minutes.

ARTHUR GLADSTONE'S NOBLE MEAT SOUP

Arthur is one of America's most prolific novelists, but don't look for his name on the bookshelf. He writes under no fewer than four pen names!

*Makes 4–6 servings**
1 beef brisket (about 3 pounds)
2 teaspoons kosher salt
3 carrots, peeled and cut into 1-inch pieces
3 celery stalks, cut into 1-inch pieces
3–4 sprigs parsley
1 large onion, peeled and quartered
1 small bay leaf
2–3 black peppercorns
3 large potatoes, peeled and quartered

Trim fat from beef; cut meat into serving-size pieces. Fill a 3-quart saucepan two-thirds full of water and bring to a boil. Add beef and all remaining ingredients except potatoes. Cover, bring to a boil, reduce heat and simmer until meat is tender, about 5 hours. Add potatoes during last hour of cooking.

Serve meat and vegetables in soup plates with some of the stock. Refrigerate remaining stock; lift off congealed fat before using in recipes calling for beef stock.

*" . . . depending upon the magnitude of the sundry assembled appetites," according to Arthur.

HOT AND SOUR SOUP

Like most Chinese dishes, this Mandarin-style soup takes some preparation time, then cooks in just minutes. Experiment with the white pepper and vinegar to find the desired balance between hot and sour.

Makes 4–6 servings
1/4 cup distilled white vinegar
1/2 teaspoon white pepper powder
1-1/2 teaspoons Oriental sesame oil
1/2 ounce dried Chinese black mushrooms (about 1/3 cup)*
1/2 ounce lily flowers (about 1/3 cup)
1/4 ounce cloud ears (about 1/4 cup)
1/2 pound fresh bean curd cakes (tofu)
1/4 pound boneless pork shoulder, partially frozen
About 2 ounces whole bamboo shoots
1 tablespoon light soy sauce
1 teaspoon sugar
1 teaspoon kosher salt
2 tablespoons cornstarch
6 tablespoons cold water
1 egg
3 green onions
6–8 cups chicken stock (canned or made from chicken base)

Preparation: Stir together vinegar, white pepper and sesame oil in a large serving bowl; set aside. Soak black mushrooms, lily flowers and cloud ears in separate bowls of water until soft, 30–40 minutes; drain, pressing out excess moisture. Cut hard stems from mushrooms and shred caps; shred cloud ears. Cut bean curd into 3/8-inch dice. Shred pork and bamboo shoots by slicing 1/8-inch thick, stacking slices and cutting into 1/8-inch-wide matchstick pieces. In a small bowl, stir together soy sauce, sugar and salt; in a separate bowl, stir together cornstarch and cold water. Beat egg with a fork in another small bowl. Slice green onions thinly. Assemble all ingredients near range.

To cook: In a large saucepan, bring chicken stock to a boil. Add the pork, bean curd, bamboo shoots, mushrooms, lily flowers and cloud ears. Simmer 5 minutes, add soy sauce mixture, return to a boil and add the cornstarch mixture while stirring constantly. Add the egg and green onions, remove from the heat and let stand 30 seconds; do not stir. Ladle soup into serving bowl containing vinegar mixture. Stir and serve immediately.

*Dried Chinese black mushrooms can be purchased whole or shredded. If you have purchased shredded ones, they can be soaked in the same manner as described for the whole ones.

SOPI DI YUWANA (IGUANA SOUP)

The natives of Aruba in the Netherland Antilles claim that iguana promotes man's virility. I must agree. Any cook who captures an iguana for his dinner is man enough for me!

Makes 4–6 servings
6 cups chicken stock (canned or made from chicken base)
1 garlic clove, unpeeled
1 leek, very thinly sliced
1 onion, peeled and studded with 3 whole cloves
1 tomato, seeded and chopped
1 sweet green pepper, seeded and chopped
1/4 head cabbage
1 plump iguana,* skinned and cut into serving-size pieces
1 teaspoon ground cumin
Kosher salt
Freshly ground black pepper
Pinch of ground nutmeg
2–3 ounces vermicelli

In a large saucepan, combine chicken stock, garlic and vegetables and simmer uncovered about 30 minutes. Add the iguana and simmer another 30 minutes. Strain the stock, discard vegetables and remove the iguana meat from the bones. Return stock to the heat and add the spices and vermicelli. Simmer 5–10 minutes or until vermicelli is tender. Add iguana meat, heat through and serve.

*Substitute 1 broiler-fryer chicken (about 3 pounds) for the iguana, if desired.

QUICK CLAM CHOWDER

*Makes 2 servings**
2 tablespoons unsalted butter
1 small onion, peeled and chopped
1/4 cup minced celery
1/4 cup minced carrot
1 can (6-1/2 ounces) minced clams
1 medium potato, peeled and diced
1/4 teaspoon kosher salt
Freshly ground white pepper
1 cup half-and-half cream
1/2 cup milk, chicken stock or bottled clam juice
1 teaspoon cornstarch

In a medium saucepan, melt butter over medium heat. Add onion, celery and carrot and cook, stirring, until tender, about 5 minutes. Drain clam liquid from can into the pan and add potato, salt and pepper. Cover and simmer 12 minutes. Stir in half-and-half and 1/4 cup of the milk and the minced clams. Simmer 5 minutes. Taste and correct seasonings. Stir cornstarch into remaining 1/4 cup milk, stir into simmering soup, bring to a boil and serve.

*This dish can be easily doubled.

POTAGE PARMENTIER

Potage Parmentier, potato and leek soup, is the hot cousin to the famous cold vichyssoise. While not as well known as the chilled delicacy, it is an absolutely delicious soup that is so simple to make, you'll do it often. Prepare with leeks whenever possible for truest flavor.

Makes about 2 quarts
4 cups diced peeled potatoes
   (about 4 large)
3 cups thinly sliced leeks* (use white part plus 2 inches of green), or 2 cups thinly sliced onions
2 quarts chicken stock (canned or made from chicken base)
Salt and freshly ground black pepper to taste
1/2 cup whipping cream
Caroline's Homemade Croutons
   (page 101)

In a 5-quart saucepan, stir together potatoes, leeks and chicken stock. Bring to a boil, reduce heat and simmer uncovered for about 50 minutes or until potatoes and leeks are tender.

With a slotted spoon, remove potatoes and leeks to food processor, blender or food mill and process with just enough of the liquid in the pan to form a purée. Return purée to liquid in saucepan, taste and season with salt and pepper. Stir in whipping cream and bring to serving temperature over low heat. Serve with croutons.

VICHYSSOISE Make Potage Parmentier, but increase whipping cream to 1-1/2 cups. Season highly with salt and pepper since chilling will diminish seasoning flavors. Refrigerate until very cold. Serve in chilled small bowls sprinkled with freshly snipped chives. Omit croutons.

*To clean leeks of their hidden dirt, slit down into white and rinse under cold running water.

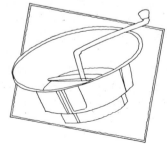

CASSEROLES

STUART SILVERMAN'S VEAL AND GRAPEFRUIT CURRY

Stuart is an English teacher and free-lance writer who loves to experiment in the kitchen. He created this unusual flavor combination and received compliments for his effort.

*Makes 2–3 servings**
2 tablespoons unsalted butter
2 tablespoons olive oil
3/4 pound boneless veal, cut in 1-inch cubes
5–6 shallots, peeled and sliced
Pinch of kosher salt
1 grapefruit, peeled, sectioned and drained
3 tablespoons lemon or lime honey
4–6 fresh mint leaves (optional)
1 small tomato, seeded and chopped
Pinch of chili powder
Pinch of curry powder
Pinch of ground nutmeg
1/2 teaspoon freshly grated lemon rind
2–3 teaspoons brandy
2–3 ounces pastina (barley-size pasta)

In a 10-inch frypan, melt 1 tablespoon of the butter and the oil over medium heat. Add veal and shallots; cook, stirring, until veal is browned, 3–5 minutes. Sprinkle with salt, stir and set aside.

In a 9-inch frypan, melt remaining 1 tablespoon butter, add grapefruit sections and sauté about 1 minute. Add honey, mint, tomato, spices, lemon rind and brandy. Simmer over medium-low heat until mixture is reduced to a light syrup, 5–7 minutes. Set aside.

Preheat the oven to 400°F. Cook pastina in boiling salted water until *al dente* (tender but slightly resistant to the bite). Drain in colander and rinse with water. To assemble casserole, stir together veal, grapefruit and pasta. Spoon into a 6-cup casserole, place in the preheated oven and reduce the heat to 325°F. Bake about 45 minutes or until veal is tender.

*This recipe can be easily doubled.

TED MAIER'S
LAMB SHANKS DELUXE

Ted, recently retired from the men's clothing business, now spends his time living on Chicago's glamorous Gold Coast and traveling with his wife Phyllis. So far they have eaten their way through fifty-three countries, but must return home to have this favorite. Mashed Potatoes (page 60) are an excellent accompaniment.

Makes 4 servings
4 meaty lamb shanks
1/2 lemon
1/4 teaspoon garlic powder
1 cup unbleached flour
2 teaspoons kosher salt
1/2 teaspoon freshly ground black pepper
1/2 cup vegetable oil
1 can (10-1/2 ounces) condensed beef broth
1 cup water
1/2 cup dry vermouth
1 medium onion, peeled and chopped
4 carrots, peeled and sliced into 1-inch chunks
4 celery stalks, sliced into 1-inch chunks

Rub lamb shanks with cut side of lemon and sprinkle with garlic powder; let stand 10 minutes. Combine flour, salt and pepper in a paper or plastic bag. Add shanks, one at a time, and shake to coat with flour. Reserve flour.

Preheat the oven to 350°F. In a heavy 10-inch frypan, heat oil and brown shanks. Remove shanks to a shallow casserole, arranging in a single layer. Add 1/4 cup of the reserved flour to the pan drippings and whisk over heat until well blended and mixture begins to brown slightly. Add condensed broth, water and vermouth; cook, stirring, until slightly thickened. Stir in onion and pour over shanks in casserole dish. (Dish can be covered and refrigerated at this point and cooked later.) Bake shanks in the preheated oven for about 1 hour. Turn shanks, stir in carrots and celery and bake another hour or until meat is fork tender.

EASY CURRIED TURKEY

When time is short, turn convenient frozen turkey slices into this exotic dish with little effort. Serve with steamed rice.

Makes 4 servings
1 package (2 pounds) frozen
  sliced turkey and gravy
2 tablespoons unsalted butter
1 medium onion, peeled and
  chopped
2 garlic cloves, peeled and
  crushed
1 teaspoon curry powder
Plain yogurt
Sweet chutney of choice
2 green onions, thinly sliced

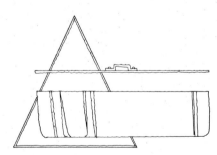

Heat frozen turkey and gravy in container on a jelly-roll pan in oven according to package directions, reducing time to 40 minutes. While turkey is heating, melt butter in a 9-inch frypan, add onion and garlic and cook, stirring, until onions are transparent and slightly tender, about 5 minutes. Add curry powder and cook, stirring, 1 minute; set aside.

Remove turkey from oven and stir curry mixture into gravy in pan. Return turkey to oven and heat an additional 10–15 minutes. Top each serving with a dollop of yogurt, a spoonful of chutney and a sprinkle of green onion, or pass them separately.

NORMAN MARK'S SPINACH-RICOTTA CASSEROLE

Norman is a busy Los Angeles-based television personality who currently co-hosts the nationally syndicated "Breakaway" show. A self-proclaimed Italian food freak, Norman likes this lasagna-like dish because he can cook the noodles in the morning and keep them refrigerated in water until it's time to assemble the casserole.

Makes 8 servings
1 package (16 ounces) lasagna
  noodles
1 package (10 ounces) frozen
  chopped spinach, thawed
1 large egg, beaten
1 pound mozzarella cheese,
  shredded
1 pound ricotta cheese
1 tablespoon unsalted butter
1 cup bottled pizza sauce, or All-
  Purpose Tomato Sauce
  (page 82)
2 cups grated parmesan cheese
  (preferably freshly grated)

Cook noodles according to package directions, drain and rinse under cold water. (If cooking ahead, place in a shallow casserole dish, cover with cold water and refrigerate.) Preheat oven to 350°F.

Squeeze excess water from spinach by pressing with a spoon in a sieve. In a mixing bowl, beat egg and stir in spinach, mozzarella and ricotta until well mixed. Butter a 13- by 9- by 2-inch baking pan. Arrange one-third of the drained noodles over bottom of pan and spoon half of the spinach mixture over the noodles. Top with half of the remaining noodles, spoon on the rest of the spinach mixture and then top with the remaining noodles. Pour sauce over the top, sprinkle with parmesan cheese and bake in the preheated oven about 20 minutes or until top is bubbly and lightly browned. Let stand 5 minutes, then cut into squares to serve.

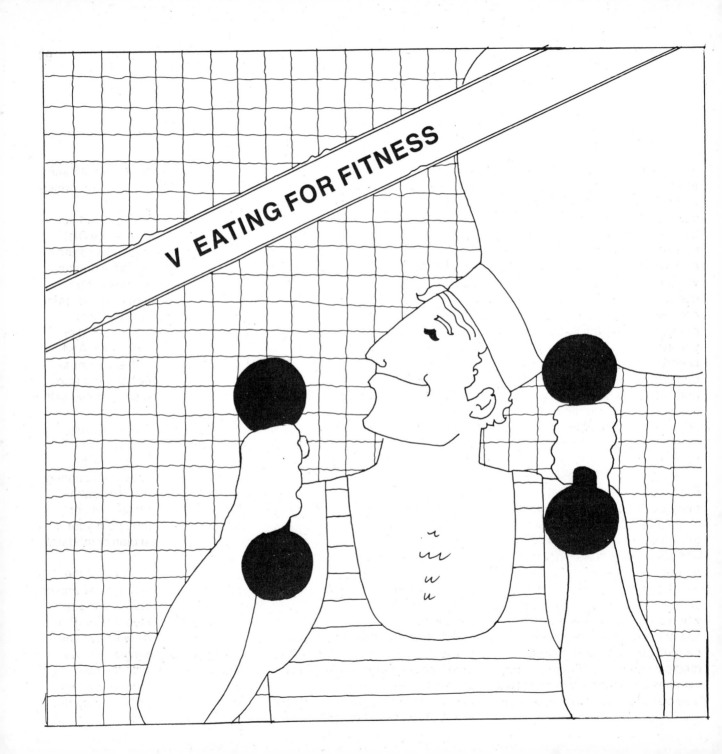

This is a chapter for people who are concerned about their health and their weight, for those who want to look trim and feel good. Many of the principles contained here are reflected in the recipes throughout the book. If you have a weight problem that is due to or complicated by a health problem, consult a physician for a proper dietary plan. If, on the other hand, you are anywhere from five to twenty-five pounds overweight and the problem is due to what and how much you eat, you can change your eating habits and bring your weight down to stay—and the process is almost painless!

The Common Sense Fitness Eating Plan (CSFEP), with its emphasis on controlling fat and salt in the diet, can be beneficial to a fitness-conscious person of any age. Older people may need to alter decades-old eating habits, but the changes suggested in this chapter are easy to implement when compared to the drastic no-salt and low-cholesterol diets handed out by doctors to treat medical conditions. People in their twenties and thirties, whose tastes may be more open to change, can

benefit the most. Following the CSFEP today may mean they won't have to go on drastic diets in their later years.

THE COMMON SENSE FITNESS EATING PLAN

Eating for fitness is part of the life style of the 1980s. Never before have so many products been labeled "low salt," "low fat," "low sugar," "natural" and "real." And never before have so many people been so hell-bent on looking better. At the same time, never have so many consumers been so confused and misled.

The sad fact is that the food industry today, including diet-book publishing, is often characterized by extremes and extremists who would have people eating ridiculous, even hazardous combinations of foods with the promise of weight loss and glamor gain.

With all the diet-book and diet-product hype going on, it is crucial to remember that the healthful approach to diet is the one that is based on common sense, and that is exactly what this chapter has to

offer: a plan to reduce weight and feel better through common-sense eating.

Forget what can be called, for lack of a better term, "The Diet Syndrome." Everyone has seen—or done—it! You go on a drastic diet for four to six weeks, then lapse into bad habits, only to gain back the weight that was lost. Then you go on the drastic diet again, only to lapse again. And again, and again. It is a vicious cycle that not only hampers true weight loss, but also destroys self-confidence.

The Common Sense Fitness Eating Plan outlined here and illustrated by the recipes in this chapter will not have you counting calories, eating bizarre health foods like kelp and tempeh, or eliminating anything from your current diet. It is a plan of moderation, not abstinence.

The comforting aspect of the CSFEP is that following any one of its points will probably help you look trimmer and feel better. Practicing all the points will have you looking and feeling great for as long as you stay with the plan, which, because there is nothing drastic about it, can be a lifetime.

Your commitment to CSFEP boils down (excuse the culinary pun) to behavior modification in the most positive sense. You will see results that will cause you to follow the plan more steadfastly, thereby modifying your eating behavior a bit more, which will in turn produce more positive results, and so on. This is a rewarding cycle.

THE PLAN'S FOCUS

The Common Sense Fitness Eating Plan helps reduce the two food substances that cause men the most health problems: salt (more specifically the sodium in salt) and fat. No one need recount to today's aware male how salt and fat contribute to heart disease and stroke. The facts and accompanying case histories receive generous coverage in newspapers, magazines and health publications. Refined sugar, while by no means a lesser evil, is of less importance here. This is because the CSFEP is geared to men, who as a group are generally not sweets eaters and on the average consume only low to moderate amounts of sugar.

No matter what your current style of cooking and eating is, the Common Sense Fitness Eating Plan can be implemented in full or in part. Try to follow these guidelines when dining out as well as at home.

REDUCE YOUR INTAKE OF SALT
The Five-Point Plan

This simple five-step plan will gradually fine tune your palate to be happy with less salt than it now finds satisfying. The taste for salt is an acquired one, and it can be reduced slowly and easily. Don't try to go off salt "cold turkey." The drastic flavor change will be so unpleasant that it will only dissuade you from ever seriously trying to lower your salt intake. (This plan does not apply to individuals who have been put on a no-sodium or low-sodium diet by their doctors.)

1. *Use only unsalted butter and/or unsalted margarine in cooking and at table.* You might want to ease into this by first using unsalted butter for cooking, then extending that use to the table. Because your tastebuds are accustomed to the salted variety, you may at first not like the flavor of the unsalted. But stay with it, and you will soon recognize butter's smooth, creamy flavor in a way you have never known it. In addition to reducing your salt intake, unsalted butter imparts a particularly good flavor to baked goods and sautéed foods.

Using unsalted butter may seem like a small step in the overall scheme to reduce salt intake, but it is a critical one that begins the palate adjustment that must be made if you are to eat less salt and prefer it. And its use does make a greater difference than one might suspect: one tablespoon of what is euphemistically termed "lightly salted" butter contains 102 calories and 116 milligrams sodium, while one tablespoon of unsalted butter contains 102 calories and 2 milligrams sodium.

Unsalted butter is more readily available than unsalted margarine. If you are stocking up on butter, or use it very slowly, store the excess in the freezer. It should also be noted that all the recipes in this book were developed with unsalted butter.

2. *Reduce the salt you use in recipes.* This step, done gradually, will help your palate come alive to the true flavors of foods. If you now

add 1 teaspoon of salt to a particular recipe, reduce it to 3/4 teaspoon for one to two months, then to 1/2 teaspoon, and so on, until you reach a level that satisfies both your palate and fitness consciousness. If you are able to eliminate salt from the recipe completely, bravo! If you can only cut it in half, it's still bravo! You've reduced salt intake from cooking by a very significant 50 percent.

3. *Reduce consumption of commercial condiments and convenience foods.* Commercially made condiments like catsup, mustard, pickles, barbecue sauce, salsa, soy sauce, steak sauce, mayonnaise, peanut butter, salad dressing, croutons and all their relatives on the supermarket shelf rely heavily on salt and other sodium additives for their flavor, processing and shelf life. So do convenience foods like dry soup mixes; condensed soups; bouillon cubes; biscuit mixes; some cereals; vegetable and tomato juices; canned fish and seafood like anchovies, crab meat, sardines and tuna; canned vegetables like sauerkraut, green beans, kernel and creamed corn; canned baked beans; and pasta in tomato sauce.

The list could go on, but it is easier to learn how to spot salt through labeling than it is to memorize dozens of foods. If you have a question about the amount of salt in a given product, look at the ingredient list on the label. Ingredients are listed in the order of the amount of their presence. For example, if a jar of chicken bouillon cubes lists salt first, it means there is more salt in that product than any other ingredient, including chicken. If salt is listed second, it has the second highest presence, and so on. Try to avoid those products that list salt among the first three or four ingredients, and those that list one or more other sodium additives: sodium nitrite (impedes dangerous microbial growth and improves colors in cured meats), monosodium glutamate (a flavor enhancer; also causes an allergic reaction in some people that is known as the "Chinese restaurant syndrome"), sodium saccharin (a sweetener), and sodium benzoate (a preservative in relishes, sauces and salad dressings).

Cut back on the consumption of these condiments and convenience foods by using less, by buying low-salt varieties or by making your own. There are several recipes in this chapter to get you off to a good healthy start. And because many condiments are also high in sugar, you will cut sugar intake at the same time.

4. *Reduce consumption of salty snack foods.* Run down a list of America's favorite snack foods and it reads like a salt freak's *Who's Who.* Peanuts, popcorn, pretzels, potato chips, crackers, tortilla chips are all usually both coated with salt and made with salt. Some food-processing companies are cooperating by offering certain products in "salt free" or "unsalted" forms. Such products readily available today include saltine crackers with unsalted tops and unsalted roasted peanuts, potato chips and pretzels.

The majority of popularly priced snack foods, however, are still heavy with salt. But that doesn't mean you must give up all those goodies. Learn to make your own. It's simple and you will soon come to realize how much delicious natural flavor is masked by salt. And believe it or not, you'll save money when you make your own.

5. *Reduce consumption of processed meats.* Cut back on ham, corned beef, pastrami, bacon, all sausages, hot dogs and cold cuts. This phase of the five-point plan is probably the toughest to uphold because these products are so thoroughly woven into our food culture. But the fact remains that smoked, cured and pickled meats are high in salt compared to fresh products. They also contain nitrate and nitrite additives that are considered harmful by many in the medical community.

If your standard lunch is a ham sandwich, try one of turkey white meat twice a week. If you can't live without breakfast sausage, make your own (see the recipe in this chapter), or find a butcher who will make it for you with low salt and no nitrates. (Remember, these reduced-additive products do not have the shelf life of regular commercial products and spoil more quickly.) If sandwiches are a big part of your diet, it will be difficult to reduce consumption of processed meats at first and, possibly, for several months. But once your palate is tuned, you may find many of these products too salty to your "new" taste.

SODIUM CONTENT OF FOODS*

FOODSTUFF	AMOUNT	SODIUM IN MILLIGRAMS	CALORIES
Cottage cheese	1/2 cup	457	117
Buttermilk	1 cup	257	99
American cheese	1 ounce (1 slice)	406	116
**Yogurt, plain, low fat	1 cup	125	123
Whole milk	1 cup	120	150
Vegetable-juice cocktail	6 fluid ounces	665	30
Tomato juice	6 fluid ounces	659	36
Orange juice, frozen	6 fluid ounces	4	92
Pineapple juice	6 fluid ounces	3	69
Apple juice	6 fluid ounces	4	87
Fresh grapefruit	1/2 grapefruit	1	26
French salad dressing (commercial)	1 tablespoon	214	66
Blue cheese or Roquefort salad dressing (commercial)	1 tablespoon	153	76
Thousand Island salad dressing (commercial)	1 tablespoon	109	80
Oil and vinegar (home blend)	1 tablespoon	Trace	62

*From "Straight Talk About Salt," The Salt Institute, 206 North Washington, Alexandria, VA 22314.

**From "Morton Salt Helps You Measure," Morton Salt, 110 North Wacker Drive, Chicago IL 60606.

GUIDE TO SODIUM IN FOODSTUFFS

To check the amount of sodium in your diet, or to identify those foods that have the highest sodium content, send for "Straight Talk About Salt/What You Should Know About Salt and Sodium In Your Diet," a booklet published as a service to consumers by The Salt Institute in cooperation with The Food and Drug Administration. To receive a free copy, send a stamped self-addressed envelope to The Salt Institute, 206 North Washington Street, Alexandria, Virginia 22314.

When you consult "Straight Talk About Salt," it may surprise you to find that many of the foods long touted as "diet foods" have high sodium levels. How many times have you seen dieters eating cottage cheese, drinking vegetable-juice cocktail and munching on salads with commercially prepared salad dressings? While they may be cutting calories, they are not eating healthfully. On the preceding page are some examples of high-sodium foods frequently used by dieters, as compared to those with moderate to light sodium levels.

CONTROL YOUR INTAKE OF FATTY FOODS

Foods high in fat include bacon, butter, margarine, well-marbled red meats, sour cream, mayonnaise, whipping cream (often called heavy cream in recipes), oil (e.g., vegetable and olive) and foods fried in oil, and cheese (especially soft cheeses, which tend to have a higher fat content). Most rich-tasting foods and dishes are high in fat or have sufficient fat content to advise a judicious approach.

Substitute fresh lemon juice for oil in salads and other preparations. Use plain low-fat yogurt instead of sour cream whenever possible, including on baked potatoes; if tasting tart yogurt instead of rich sour cream on your potato is too drastic a change, combine sour cream and yogurt and gradually increase the proportion of yogurt as your palate adjusts to the flavor. Cut back on the use of butter; there is no satisfying substitute for the delicious flavor of unsalted butter.

Reduce the number of times per week you eat red meat, bacon and sausage. Certain foods high in fat, like bacon, sausage, cheese and mayonnaise, are also high in salt and should be consumed in limited and constantly decreasing amounts if good health and fitness are your goals.

STRIVE TO EAT ONLY FRESH PRODUCE Canned and frozen vegetables and fruits often contain salt and/or sugar, so use fresh produce whenever possible. If you must use frozen vegetables, avoid those prepared in sauces. Select canned fruits packed in their own juices rather than in heavy or light syrup. (See Handling Fresh Fruits and Vegetables.)

INCREASE CONSUMPTION OF SALADS, POULTRY, SEAFOOD, PASTA, FRUITS AND VEGETABLES Use these items as substitutes for red meat as you decrease your consumption of it. If salad doesn't appeal to you as an entrée, add a can of water-packed tuna or strips of lean roast beef, turkey or chicken to the greens. Salads need not be made of lettuce: create your own versions using your favorite vegetables (raw or steamed). Learn to properly prepare seafood, fish and poultry. The most common problem with these foods is overcooking, which dries them out and makes them unpalatable (see Chapter 2).

MAKE YOUR OWN SALAD DRESS-INGS Look at the label on a commercially made salad dressing and you will see "salt" high on the ingredient list, not to mention the food additives used as stabilizers and emulsifiers. When you make your own dressings, you control the salt and fat contents and can continue to reduce them as your palate adjusts to less.

USE LOW-FAT COOKING TECH-NIQUES Steaming, boiling, poaching and stir frying are all low-fat cooking techniques. Steaming, used primarily for vegetables and reheating foods, cooks with moist heat that does not dry food out. Boiling is also good for vegetables. Poultry, fish and seafood are good candidates for poaching (see Cooking Terms and Techniques), and stir frying is suited to meat, vegetables, shellfish and chicken (see Chapter 1).

TO STEAM Place the proper amount of water in the pot. If using a saucepan and footed steam basket, the water level should not touch the bottom of the basket and will consequently be about 3/4 inch deep. If using a large steamer pot with basket insert, several inches of water can be used. The simmering water must not touch the bottom of the basket, however, or the bottom of the cooking food will become soggy.

Bring water to a boil, then lower heat so it boils gently (not rolling). Put the basket in the pot and place the food to be steamed in it, making sure it will not touch the pot lid; cover the pot. Reheating cooked foods will take from two to five minutes, depending on the size of the pieces. Cooking raw vegetables will take from five to fifteen minutes, according to their size and texture.

When opening a steamer, lift the lid so that the steam is directed away from you. Test foods for doneness by allowing the steam to clear momentarily, then inserting the point of a paring knife into the food.

USE A FRYPAN WITH NONSTICK SURFACE Silverstone, Teflon and T-Fal pans allow you to fry foods successfully with a minimum of oil.

DRINK WATER OR FRUIT JUICE AT MEALS Whether you opt for the tap, carbonated or pure bottled variety, water is a wise substitution for more caloric beverages at meals or snack time. For if we are what we eat, we are also what we drink. Fruit juices are healthful but not necessarily low in calories. If you now consume soft drinks regularly, you will want to come down from that sugar high gradually. Try switching to tonic, then regular club soda (which contains salt), and finally to unsalted carbonated water, tap water or pure bottled water. A well-squeezed wedge of lemon or lime will do wonders for a glass of ice water, a drink that complements anything you eat. Forget about "fruit drinks." They are made of low percentages of fruit juice, water and added sugar and are often as expensive as pure fruit juice.

REDUCE YOUR INTAKE OF LI-QUOR AND BEER If you drink hard liquor and/or beer regularly, occasionally substitute wine, then gradually increase the number of times you choose wine over the others. Wine is lower in calories and aids digestion. If you find most table wines too namby-pamby, try the gutsier-flavored sherries, from *fino* (very dry) to *oloroso* (full and robust).

REDUCE YOUR INTAKE OF SWEETS Reduce the amount of jam, candy, cookies, pastries and desserts you eat. Substitute a freshly sectioned grapefruit or other fresh fruit for dessert.

WATCH YOUR INTAKE OF DAIRY PRODUCTS Some dairy products are high in fat; others are high in sodium. It seems to be a trade-off. Those low in calories (fat) and often touted as diet foods, like cottage cheese and buttermilk, are high in sodium. Those high-fat products like whipping cream and sour cream are, by comparison, high in calories and low in sodium. Cheeses of all types tend to have substantial sodium content, especially the aged hard varieties like parmesan and the veined varieties like blue.

USE KITCHEN EQUIPMENT THAT HELPS YOU EAT FIT

There are certain pieces of kitchen equipment that can help you stay on this or any eating-for-fitness plan. Refer to the section on Equipping the Kitchen for additional information on the following items.

CONVECTION OVENS help by roasting and broiling meats and poultry with no added fat. The surging air sears foods and seals in natural juices so gravies and sauces are unnecessary.

MECHANICAL MEAT TENDERIZERS allow you to eat leaner cuts of meat cooked in low-fat fashion. You can take a lean, unmarbled cut like a round steak, treat it with a mechanical meat tenderizer and then broil or pan sear it to a juicy, tender finish. Some of the most flavorful cuts are the less tender, lean ones that usually have to be cooked by more caloric methods like braising. In addition, the tenderizer saves 30 to 40 percent cooking time.

FOOD PROCESSORS help save time in preparing fresh fruits and vegetables, but more significantly can chop fresh meats for sausage making and can aid in salad-dressing preparation by emulsifying ingredients so they do not readily separate.

STEAMERS come in many configurations, from a simple steaming basket to multitiered pots. They can be used for cooking vegetables, meats, fish and poultry quickly and without fat or oil, and produce a moist product every time. Steamers are also great for reheating rolls, meat, pasta or anything that should have a moist, soft surface.

DIET AND CANCER

There has been much discussion in the media of diet's relationship to cancer. At this time there is no such thing as a diet that will prevent cancer, but the Common Sense Fitness Plan is similar to the National Research Council's guidelines on a prudent diet to "reduce anxiety" about cancer. The council's recommendations include reducing fat intake to not more than 30 to 40 percent of total caloric consumption; eating whole grains; eating raw vegetables and fruits; drinking alcohol in moderation; and avoiding pickled, smoked and salt-cured foods such as sausage, smoked fish, ham and bacon.

BASIC INGREDIENTS AND SNACKS

ROASTED NUTS

Freshly roasted nuts of all kinds make nutritious and delicious snacks and additions to salads, stir fries and desserts. To buy the freshest, best-quality nuts, look for a wholesale nut firm or grain company in your community. Often they will have retail outlets where you can purchase raw (unroasted) nuts for more reasonable prices than you will find in supermarkets for the salted, roasted product.

Using raw nuts allows you to roast only as many as needed for snacking or cooking at the moment, and to salt them lightly or not at all. At first, unsalted nuts may seem bland to you. But after a while, you will come to love the true nut flavors that are discernable only when you roast at home without oil and salt.

Arrange raw nuts in a single layer on a jelly-roll pan. Place the pan in a preheated 325°F oven and roast according to the following timetable. Remember, nuts scorch easily, so watch carefully and note any timing differences peculiar to your oven. Cool before using.

TYPE OF NUT	ROASTING TIME
Almonds, slivered blanched	12–16 minutes
Almonds, whole blanched	16–20 minutes
Cashews, whole	12–16 minutes
Filberts, whole blanched	16–20 minutes
Peanuts, Spanish, with or without skins	20–25 minutes
Peanuts, Virginia blanched	16–20 minutes
Sunflower seeds, raw	10–15 minutes

NOTE If using a convection oven, roast at 325°F and reduce times by 5 minutes.

SALT STAND-INS

Salting foods is not an easy habit to give up, or even reduce. Some food scientists claim salt dependency is acquired during one's childhood; others say the link goes back to preprimate times when man evolved from ocean-habitat creatures. While academicians may argue over this, those of us trying to stay in shape need only worry about one thing: reducing salt in our diets without sacrificing flavor.

Chemical salt substitutes, which can be found in supermarkets, are made principally of potassium chloride, with the substance constituting as much as 97 percent in some brands. Young people without health problems could probably use these potassium chloride products in place of the salt in their diets without any ill effects. However, their use is not advised for whole families or older individuals, especially those with heart or kidney disease, or anyone watching his or her blood-pressure level. This is because potassium levels affect the body's regulation of heartbeat, and changes in heart rhythm can be very hazardous to the more mature body. Undiagnosed kidney disease could result in the diminished ability of the kidneys to rid themselves of a potassium overload.

It is much safer to simply reduce salt intake than to worry about a new chemical imbalance in your body. The following are spices and food substances that can be used as salt stand-ins.

AROMATIC BITTERS You may have been stocking your bar with bitters for years, but have you thought of keeping a bottle in the kitchen? That is the perfect home for this product, which is a nonalcoholic blend of herbs and spices.

Use it to replace part or all of the salt in recipes; add three or four dashes for each cup of gravy, or about 1/4 teaspoon per cup of salad dressing. Mix a few dashes with melted unsalted butter and drizzle on cooked vegetables. Adjust these amounts to suit your taste, and give free rein to your imagination to come up with more ways to use bitters.

DRY VERMOUTH Another product from the bar cache. This one is frequently used in place of dry white wine in cooking, but it can take on a new role when used as a flavoring agent in salad dressings and marinades in which salt has been reduced. A tablespoon or so will also give new character to seafood and poultry dishes.

HOME BLEND SEASONING MIXTURES Mixing salt with other spices and herbs, as in Healthful Seasoned Salt (following), maximizes a small amount of salt by combining it with other flavors. The use of these mixtures enhances the herbal flavors while cutting back salt consumption. Make up your own blends using your favorite flavors; gradually

lessen the amount of salt you add to reduce its intake further.

HEALTHFUL SEASONED SALT

This mixture, which can be used in place of plain salt, is similar in taste to the most popular commercial seasoned salt. Unlike supermarket varieties, however, it contains no MSG (monosodium glutamate), a substance that causes an allergic reaction in some people.

Kosher salt is pure salt and contains as much sodium as other (table) salts. What makes this recipe healthful is that less than 27 percent of the mixture is salt. When used in the same quantity as salt in recipes, Healthful Seasoned Salt will help you reduce salt intake dramatically.

Healthful Seasoned Salt imparts more flavor than plain salt to food because of its blend of spices. Those who like pepper will want to add freshly ground black or white pepper to dishes in addition to this mixture.

Makes about 1-1/4 cups
1/4 cup kosher salt
1/4 cup onion powder

2 tablespoons paprika
2 tablespoons garlic powder or granulated garlic
1 tablespoon white pepper powder
2 teaspoons sugar
1 tablespoon ground thyme

In a small mixing bowl, stir together all ingredients. (For a finer blend, crush ingredients in mortar with pestle in small batches until all are blended.) Store in screwtop jar or other air-tight container.

QUICK BEEF STOCK

Makes about 1 cup
1 cup beef stock (canned or made from beef base)
About 1/4 teaspoon *each* dried basil, marjoram, oregano, thyme and rosemary

Combine all ingredients in a small saucepan. Boil until reduced to 2/3 cup, then strain. Double or triple this recipe, if desired, but always reduce by one-third of original volume.

NOTE Do not use beef stock made from bouillon cubes, which contain far too much salt. Reducing stocks made with bouillon cubes concentrates the salt as well as the beef flavor, and may make your dish too salty.

CHICKEN STOCK

Chicken stock can be made in any quantity, and with bones or whole pieces. The secret to good chicken stock is the same as for any homemade stock: cook it down to concentrate the flavor. Never salt the stock until it is completely cooked, as it will become saltier as the liquid reduces.

Makes about 1 quart
About 2 pounds chicken necks, bones and wings (in any combination)
1 carrot, cut into 1-inch pieces
1 leafy celery top
About 6 black peppercorns
1–2 shallots, peeled and halved
Kosher salt to taste

Place chicken pieces in a 3-quart saucepan, add cold water to just cover and bring to a simmer over medium heat. With a large spoon, skim off the scum that will rise to the top for about the first 5 minutes. Add remaining ingredients, except salt, cover with a slightly tilted lid and simmer for about 1 hour. Taste; if flavor is satisfying, add salt to taste and simmer another 2 minutes. If flavor seems weak, continue to simmer another 15 minutes before adding salt. Remember, the salt will help bring out the chicken flavor, so taste carefully. You cannot reduce a stock too much; if the flavor seems too concentrated, simply add water.

Remove the chicken; the meaty parts may, of course, be eaten. Pour the liquid through a sieve, then cool and refrigerate up to 1 week, or freeze in 1-cup portions up to 2 months. (See plastic bags entry in Storage and Cleanup section of Equipping the Kitchen for handy freezing directions.)

HOMEMADE MAYONNAISE

Once you start making your own mayonnaise, you will never want to go back to the ''plastic'' variety found on supermarket shelves. A word of caution: this mayonnaise will not keep more than four or five days in the refrigerator, so make it in quantities you can use up quickly.

Makes 3/4 to 1 cup
1 egg
1/2 tablespoon sherry or red wine vinegar
1/2 tablespoon Dijon-style mustard
Scant 1/2 teaspoon salt, or less
1/4 teaspoon freshly ground white pepper
About 1 cup vegetable or olive oil, or a combination

In a blender or a food processor fitted with a steel blade, place all ingredients except oil. Process briefly to blend. With machine running, pour in oil in a slow, steady stream until mixture thickens and is of mayonnaise consistency. If using a blender, stop machine once or twice to scrape down sides of container. Store in a scrupulously clean air-tight container in the refrigerator.

ZESTY GREEN MAYONNAISE Add 2 tablespoons sliced green onions (green portion only) and 4 sprigs parsley, coarsely cut, to completed mayonnaise and continue to process until the mayonnaise turns a uniform green.

DO-IT-YOURSELF CATSUP

Basically, catsup is a reduction of tomatoes with spices added, but don't expect this version to taste like the supermarket variety. It will be slightly thinner than commercial catsup, and not as bland because the spices will come through more clearly.

This is a recipe for those who are serious about reducing salt in their diets, as no salt measure is included. Salt is present, however, in some of the ingredients.

Makes about 3-3/4 cups
2 cans (28 ounces *each*) Italian plum tomatoes, with their liquid
2 cans (6 ounces *each*) tomato paste
1/2 cup chopped onion
4–5 garlic cloves, peeled and minced
1/2 cup firmly packed brown sugar
1/2 cup malt vinegar
2 bay leaves
1/4 teaspoon ground cloves
1/4 teaspoon ground allspice
1/4 teaspoon ground mace
1/4 teaspoon freshly ground black pepper
1 teaspoon dry mustard
1 teaspoon Worcestershire sauce

Put tomatoes and their liquid in a stainless-steel or anodized-aluminum 5-quart dutch oven; break tomatoes up with a wooden spoon. Stir in tomato paste, onion and garlic. Heat to boiling, reduce heat and simmer uncovered 45 minutes. In batches, purée in blender or food processor fitted with a steel blade; or put through the fine blade of a food mill. Return to dutch oven, add all remaining ingredients and simmer uncovered about 1-1/2 hours or until thickened. Cool and store in refrigerator in a screw-top jar. Use as you would store-bought catsup.

CAROLINE'S HOMEMADE CROUTONS

These crisp, flavorful croutons are simple to make. Prepare them in big batches and keep in a twist-tie plastic bag in the cupboard. With these delicious croutons on hand, you will eat salads more often. For an herb-flavored version, use Quick-Rise Herb Bread (page 71).

Makes about 4 cups
About 4 cups day-old bread cubes (1/2-inch squares), made from french bread, sourdough bread or Quick-Rise Herb Bread
6 tablespoons unsalted butter
1/4 cup olive oil
4–6 garlic cloves, peeled and bruised

Arrange bread cubes in a single layer on a large jelly-roll pan. Toast cubes in a 250°F oven 15–20 minutes, or until they are completely dry but not brown.* Pour cubes into large bowl. Raise oven heat to 325°F.

In a small pan, melt butter with the olive oil. Add garlic and cook over low heat 3–4 minutes. Pour over bread cubes and toss to coat. Return cubes to jelly-roll pan and toast in the 325°F oven 5–7 minutes, or until brown. Cool before using, then add to salads and soups. You will never go back to the boxed kind!

*For a crouton that is both low salt and low fat, stop here and use the toasted bread cubes. These croutons are especially good when made with herb bread or any flavored bread.

HOMEMADE TORTILLA CHIPS

Shop for tortillas in Hispanic groceries where they are available fresh every day. Avoid those found in the refrigerator section of the supermarket; they are frequently thick and tasteless. Day-old tortillas are the best to use for this munchy snack food.

To stock up on tortillas, buy several packages, wrap them well in plastic and freeze; thaw at room temperature before cutting and frying.

Makes about 72 chips
1 package (10 ounces) corn
   tortillas
About 3/4 cup vegetable or peanut
   oil
Salt (optional)

Cut tortillas in half, then cut each half into thirds to form triangles. Line a jelly-roll pan with paper toweling. Pour oil into a 10-inch (preferably nonstick) frypan and heat until a scrap of tortilla added to the oil sizzles. Add tortilla triangles to hot oil in a single layer, and fry about 2 minutes per side or until golden brown and crisp. Remove to a lined jelly-roll pan to drain. If desired, sprinkle with salt. Serve with salsa, or use to make Cheese Nachos with Guacamole (page 143). Store any leftover chips at room temperature in a container with a tight-fitting lid.

LOW-FAT DIP

While this dip is low in fat, it is not low in salt. Serve with crackers or raw vegetable "dippers."

Makes about 1 cup
1 cup low-fat small-curd cottage
   cheese
2 teaspoons freeze-dried chives
1 tablespoon canned vegetable-
   juice cocktail or tomato juice
1 tablespoon Dijon-style mustard
1 teaspoon grated onion

Stir together all ingredients. Cover and refrigerate at least 1 hour before serving to allow flavors to blend.

ON MAKING SAUSAGE

If you love sausage but need or wish to watch your consumption of salt, fat and/or chemical additives, you have two alternatives: (1) stop eating sausage, or (2) begin making it yourself.

Making sausage is not difficult and the results are rewarding. Best of all, you know exactly what is in the homemade product.

The recipes that follow are for bulk sausage and sausage patties, so the need for casings is eliminated. If you wish to make sausages with casings, there are cookbooks that specifically deal with that topic.

A particularly important aspect of sausage making is cleanliness. Because the meat is ground and has so many exposed surfaces, it is very susceptible to potential bacteria, making clean work surfaces and equipment mandatory.

For the recipes included here you will need meat, spices, a grinder, ice cubes (to chill the meat and clear the grinder blades), plastic wrap, mixing bowls and a large metal spoon or electric mixer.

The grinder merits some discussion. There are hand-operated

ones, electric ones, and grinder attachments for heavy-duty electric mixers. When selecting a grinder, make sure it has both coarse and fine grind plates. A food processor can be used to chop the meat, but it is likely to yield a texture that is different—probably finer—than that to which you are accustomed. The uniformity of only very fine textures can be controlled when using a processor.

These sausage recipes were inspired by Bertie Selinger, who teaches sausage making in the Chicago area. She is a no-nonsense, back-to-basics cook who also uses her grinder to transform beef chuck into hamburger meat.

SAVORY ITALIAN SAUSAGE

Makes 2 pounds bulk sausage
2 pounds pork shoulder, including
   about 25 percent fat
2 ice cubes
1–1-1/2 teaspoons fennel seeds
2 teaspoons kosher salt
1/2 teaspoon paprika
1/2 teaspoon freshly ground
   coarse black pepper
1/4 teaspoon cayenne pepper
1/2 teaspoon sugar

Cut pork shoulder into strips, 1/2 by 1/2 by 3 inches each. Put ice cubes in a plastic bag and hit firmly with a hammer or the dull edge of a heavy knife to break them into pieces. (Never do this with the sharp edge as you will nick and bend it.) Feed pork strips through grinder fitted with coarse grind (large hole) plate, feeding half of the ice pieces through the grinder in the middle of grinding and the remainder after the last pork strips have been fed. (The moisture will be beneficial to the sausage.) Crush fennel seeds lightly in mortar with pestle, or against the side of a small bowl with a spoon. Stir salt, paprika, peppers and sugar into fennel seeds, add to ground pork and mix thoroughly with a clean spoon or an electric mixer. Cover mixture with plastic wrap pressed close to meat and up along inside of bowl and refrigerate 2 hours.

To test seasoning, sauté a spoonful of the sausage mixture in a dry frypan until thoroughly cooked, i.e., until the pink color has disappeared and sausage just begins to brown. Taste and adjust seasoning by adding more of the

spices, if desired. Store sausage in the refrigerator no longer than 3 days.

To store longer, divide into 4 equal (1/2-pound) portions, wrap well in freezer paper or plastic wrap and freeze up to 1 month. Use in any recipe that calls for bulk sausage.

HOT ITALIAN SAUSAGE

This highly flavored sausage is not recommended for those with delicate palates.

Makes 2 pounds bulk sausage
2 pounds pork shoulder, including
   about 25 percent fat
3 ice cubes
2 teaspoons kosher salt
1-1/2 teaspoons fennel seeds
1 teaspoon sugar
1/2 teaspoon paprika
1/2 teaspoon freshly ground
   coarse black pepper
1/2 teaspoon cayenne pepper
1/2–1 tablespoon red pepper
   flakes

Prepare as for Savory Italian Sausage (preceding recipe), using 2 ice cubes during the grinding and one after. Add pepper flakes with other seasonings.

BERTIE SELINGER'S BREAKFAST SAUSAGE

A recipe Bertie has been serving her healthy, happy family for years. Now she teaches it to her cooking students.

Makes 2 pounds sausage patties
2 pounds pork shoulder, including about 25 percent fat
2 ice cubes
2 teaspoons kosher salt
1/2–1 teaspoon sage
1/2 teaspoon freshly ground coarse black pepper
1/4 teaspoon sugar
1/8 teaspoon paprika
1/8 teaspoon cayenne pepper
1/8 teaspoon celery seeds
Pinch of ground ginger
Pinch of ground nutmeg

Following instructions for Savory Italian Sausage, grind pork, but use small hole plate for fine grind; add spices, mix and test as directed. After adjusting seasonings and when mixture is very cold, encase in plastic wrap as follows: Place two 12-inch pieces of plastic wrap on a clean, flat work surface. Place half of the sausage mixture in a log shape on each piece of plastic wrap. Wrap sausage, roll back and forth to compact meat, and twist ends tightly. Refrigerate at least overnight, or freeze if sausage will not be eaten in 2–3 days.

To serve, slice refrigerated or frozen sausage roll into 1/2-inch-thick slices, pat to reshape if needed, and sauté in a dry frypan until brown on both sides and thoroughly cooked, about 15 minutes. (Cook frozen sausage a few minutes longer.) To test for doneness, insert a wooden pick into sausage and look for clear juices to run.

BURRITO SAUSAGE FILLING

A spicy bulk beef sausage to use as a filling for Ronnie Bull's Texas Burritos (page 118), or purchased taco shells. You can also form this mixture into patties, sauté them and serve on hamburger buns.

Makes 2 pounds bulk sausage
1 tablespoon dehydrated onion
1/4 cup water
2 pounds beef chuck, including 25 percent fat, or a mixture of beef and pork
2 ice cubes
2 teaspoons kosher salt
2–4 teaspoons chili powder (preferably unadulterated)
1/2 teaspoon sugar
1/2–1 teaspoon ground cumin
1/2 teaspoon red pepper flakes

Stir onion into water; set aside a few minutes until onion is soft. Following instructions for Savory Italian Sausage (page 103), grind beef; add salt, spices and onion with water, mix and test as directed.

To prepare for serving, sauté sausage in dry frypan until crumbly and brown, then use as a filling for burritos or purchased taco shells. To store uncooked sausage, cover with plastic wrap pressed close to sausage and up inside of bowl, and refrigerate no longer than 3 days before using.

To store longer, divide into 4 equal (1/2-pound) portions, wrap well in freezer paper or plastic wrap and freeze up to 1 month. To cook, thaw first, then sauté in a dry frypan until sausage is crumbly and brown.

SALADS AND SALAD DRESSINGS

COLD SALMON PLATE

Canned salmon is an attractive ingredient that can be served in cold and hot dishes. It is an excellent source of protein and vitamins and contains little fat. Remember that the liquid, skin and *tiny* bones that canned salmon contains are edible and contribute to the goodness of the fish.

Here chilled salmon is used to make a beautiful "arranged" salad plate with great variety of taste, color and texture.

Makes 2 entrée-salad or 4 salad-course servings
1 pound fresh broccoli
2 tablespoons vegetable oil
1-1/2 tablespoons fresh lemon or lime juice
1/4 teaspoon Healthful Seasoned Salt (page 99)
Few grindings of black pepper
1/4 teaspoon dried tarragon, crushed, or 1 teaspoon snipped fresh tarragon
1 cup plain low-fat yogurt, or 1/2 cup *each* sour cream and plain low-fat yogurt

1 can (15-1/2 ounces) king, pink or red salmon, chilled
Lettuce leaves
2 medium tomatoes, cored and cut into wedges
2 hard-cooked eggs, quartered
1 small cucumber, peeled, seeded and sliced
2 or 4 sprigs parsley

Cut broccoli into spears or, if you prefer smaller pieces, into florets. Steam 4–5 minutes or until bright green and crisp-tender. Rinse with cold water and drain well; arrange in a shallow dish.

In a screw-top jar, shake together oil, lemon juice, seasoned salt and pepper. Pour over broccoli, cover dish and refrigerate at least 1 hour.

Drain the marinade from the broccoli; set the broccoli aside and stir the marinade and tarragon into the yogurt. Drain the chilled salmon and break meat into chunks, discarding the skin if desired. Line salad plates with lettuce leaves. Arrange broccoli, salmon, tomato wedges, egg quarters and cucumber slices on leaves in a pleasing manner. Garnish with parsley sprigs. Serve yogurt dressing on the side.

NO MAYO TUNA SALAD

A low-fat tuna mixture perfect for luncheon salads, sandwiches or snacking.

Makes 2 entrée-salad servings
1 can (6-1/2 ounces) water-packed tuna
1–2 teaspoons pickle relish
1/4 teaspoon onion powder or freshly grated onion
Juice of 1 hefty lemon wedge
Freshly ground black pepper to taste
3 tablespoons chopped celery
3 tablespoons unsalted roasted peanuts or almonds (page 98)
Shredded lettuce
Saltine crackers with unsalted tops

Drain tuna gently, allowing some moisture to remain. Stir together tuna and relish, onion powder, lemon juice, pepper, celery and nuts. Spoon over shredded lettuce and serve with crackers.

NOTE If making tuna mixture ahead, do not add roasted nuts until serving time. If you are eating alone, save half of the salad mixture for a sandwich the next day.

FRENCH VINAIGRETTE IN-THE-BOWL SALAD

Ever since I saw professional chef Yves Schmidt make this salad, it has been a personal favorite. The dressing is made in a large bowl, greens and other vegetables are placed on top and the salad is tossed at the table. To the astonishment of guests, a naked salad suddenly becomes dressed.

Makes 2 entrée-salad or 4 salad-course servings
1 large carrot, peeled
1 large celery stalk (peeled if stringy)
1 cucumber, peeled and seeded
1/2 head iceberg lettuce
3 garlic cloves, peeled
1 tablespoon Dijon-style mustard
1 teaspoon red wine vinegar
1/8 teaspoon ground thyme
Several grindings of black pepper
3 tablespoons olive oil

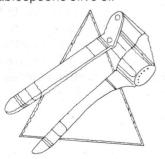

Slice carrot, celery and cucumber thinly on the diagonal. Tear or cut lettuce into bite-size pieces. Set vegetables aside. With garlic press, press garlic into a large salad bowl; add mustard, vinegar, thyme and pepper. Use a small whisk to blend, then add olive oil, a few drops at a time, whisking constantly. Dressing should have a creamy consistency.

Arrange lettuce on top of dressing, then place carrot, celery and cucumber slices in concentric circles over lettuce. To serve, toss, bringing up dressing from the bottom of the bowl.

NOTE Caroline's Homemade Croutons (page 101) are a wonderful addition to this salad.

BRANDY AND SPINACH SALAD

A spinach salad enhanced with a brandy-laced dressing. Lovely for company.

Makes 4 salad-course servings
1 garlic clove, peeled and cut in half lengthwise
3/4 cup olive oil
6 tablespoons cherry-flavored brandy
1/4 cup red wine vinegar
1/4 teaspoon kosher salt (optional)
1/8 teaspoon freshly ground black pepper
1/4 teaspoon dry mustard
About 6 cups spinach leaves, washed and stems removed
2 medium oranges, peeled and sectioned, or 1 can (10 ounces) Mandarin orange sections, drained
4 green onions, thinly sliced
1/2 cup roasted slivered almonds (page 98)

Place halved garlic clove in olive oil and let stand at least 2 hours. Remove and discard garlic; place oil, brandy, vinegar and seasonings in a 16-ounce screw-top jar, cover and shake to blend. Place spinach leaves, orange sections and onions in a large salad bowl. Pour desired amount of dressing over and toss to coat. Sprinkle with almonds. The dressing that remains can be stored in the refrigerator for future use.

BULGUR AND GREENS SALAD

The dressing that accompanies this hearty bulgur-wheat creation is tasty, low in fat and easy to make. It will bring out the true vegetable flavors of any salad.

Makes 2 entrée-salad or 4 salad-course servings
1/2 cup fine bulgur (cracked wheat)
2 cups chopped iceberg lettuce
1 cup chopped tomato
1/2 cup chopped seeded cucumber
1/4 cup chopped onion
1 cup (about 4 ounces) shredded natural swiss cheese

LEMON DRESSING
1/2 cup fresh lemon juice
1/4 cup vegetable oil
Salt to taste
1/4 teaspoon freshly ground black pepper
1/2 cup minced fresh parsley

In a bowl, rinse bulgur in cool water to remove any grittiness. Add enough cold water to bulgur to cover by 1–2 inches, and refrigerate 45 minutes or until wheat is tender. Drain bulgur in a sieve, pressing to remove excess moisture. In a large salad bowl, toss bulgur with lettuce, tomato, cucumber, onion and cheese.

To make dressing, combine lemon juice, oil, salt and pepper in a screw-top jar. Secure top well and shake to blend. Pour over salad, sprinkle with parsley and toss. Serve in salad bowls or use as a filling for pita-bread pockets.

LINDSEY KESMAN'S FRESH FRUIT SALAD

Lindsey is a bright and energetic six-year-old from Oakbrook, Illinois, who loves sledding, skating, biking, tennis, running and climbing anything taller than she is. This fruit salad is her favorite dessert, breakfast fruit, and luncheon salad. She likes it better than ice cream, cookies or pie, and she has a svelte figure to prove it.

Always begin this salad with grapefruit or orange sections, which form a citrus base and keep items like banana and apple from darkening. This recipe makes a generous amount, but because it is made up of your choice of fruits, you can decrease the size easily.

Makes 4–6 servings
1 large white, pink or red grapefruit
2 oranges
1 banana, peeled and sliced

Two or more of the following:
1/2 cantaloupe, peeled and cut into pieces
1 apple, cut into pieces
1 cup strawberries, hulled and cut in half
1/2 pineapple, cut into chunks
1 or 2 kiwi fruits, peeled and sliced
1 cup seedless grapes

Peel and section the grapefruit and oranges into a large bowl, making sure no juices are lost. Add the banana and stir gently. Add two or more of the suggested fruits and stir gently. If fruits were chilled when cut, serve salad immediately by spooning into small bowls, giving each portion some of the juice; if they were not chilled, refrigerate from 30 minutes to 1 hour before serving.

To keep leftover fruit salad in the refrigerator overnight, remove any banana and strawberry pieces, as they will become too soft.

AROMATIC FRENCH DRESSING

A low-salt dressing that gets its flavor impact from aromatic bitters, an ingredient found in every well-stocked bar or kitchen. Use on your favorite combination of greens.

Makes about 3/4 cup
1 garlic clove, peeled and crushed
1/2 cup olive oil
3 tablespoons fresh lemon juice
1 teaspoon aromatic bitters
Few grindings of black pepper
1/4 teaspoon dry mustard
1/4 teaspoon paprika

Place all ingredients in a screw-top jar with a tight-fitting lid. Shake until well blended. Store in a jar on the cupboard shelf if used often, or in the refrigerator if used infrequently. Allow to come to room temperature before pouring over greens.

CELERY SEED DRESSING FOR FRUIT

This dressing is a marvelous blend of sweet and savory. It is best when made several hours ahead so the flavors meld. Serve it over orange or grapefruit sections, sliced avocados or apples, berries or any fruit you choose.

Makes about 3/4 cup
3 tablespoons sugar
1 tablespoon honey
1/2 teaspoon dry mustard
1/4–1/2 teaspoon salt
1/2 teaspoon celery seeds
1/2 tablespoon grated onion
2–3 tablespoons sherry vinegar
1/2 cup vegetable oil

In a blender or food processor fitted with a steel blade, place all ingredients except oil. Process briefly to blend. With machine running, pour in oil in a slow, steady stream. Transfer dressing to screw-top jar or other air-tight container and refrigerate overnight. Bring to room temperature before serving.

FAST SPICY DRESSING

Using yogurt as a substitute for part or all of more fattening ingredients is a simple, effective path to healthier eating. This dressing will put "zip" in green and citrus salads.

Makes about 3/4 cup
1/2 cup mayonnaise (preferably homemade, page 100)
1/4 cup plain low-fat yogurt
1 teaspoon dried tarragon, crushed, or 2–3 teaspoons snipped fresh tarragon
About 1/2 teaspoon dry mustard
Pinch of cayenne pepper

Stir together all ingredients, taste and correct seasonings. Store in an air-tight container in the refrigerator for up to 4 days.

SOUPS

BLENDER GAZPACHO

A combination of fresh vegetables and seasonings that will awaken the palate to the delight of low-salt eating. A perfect summertime lunch when friends drop in.

Makes 8 servings
8 large ripe tomatoes, peeled, seeded and coarsely chopped
2 garlic cloves, peeled
2 small onions, peeled and coarsely chopped
1 sweet green pepper, seeded and coarsely chopped
2 large cucumbers, peeled, seeded and coarsely chopped
1/3 cup best-quality olive oil
1/4 cup cider or white wine vinegar
Juice of 1/2 lemon
1 tablespoon aromatic bitters
Freshly ground black or white pepper to taste
About 1/4 cup thinly sliced green onions, for garnish

In a blender or food processor fitted with a steel blade, purée the tomato chunks in batches, and pour the purée into a large bowl (preferably stainless steel). Place half of the remaining ingredients, except the green onions, in the blender and purée until smooth. Add to the puréed tomatoes. Purée the remaining half of the ingredients and add them to the bowl. Stir well, cover and refrigerate at least 4 hours. Taste and adjust seasoning. Serve in chilled small bowls, garnished with green onions.

BOB DJAHANGUIRI'S COLD YOGURT SOUP

Low-fat yogurt is the flavor base of this cool and refreshing soup adapted from the recipe collection of Chicago restaurateur Bob Djahanguiri.

Makes 4–6 servings
1/2 cup raisins
2 cups warm water
1-1/2 cups fresh asparagus pieces (about 1-1/2-inch lengths)
2 cups plain low-fat yogurt
1 cup half-and-half cream
1 cup chopped walnuts
1 hard-cooked egg, peeled and chopped
1/2 cup thinly sliced green onion
Kosher salt and freshly ground white pepper to taste
Chopped fresh parsley or dill, for garnish

In a large bowl, soak raisins in warm water about 10 minutes. Steam asparagus pieces about 5 minutes, or until bright green and crisp-tender. Stir yogurt and half-and-half into raisins and water, add all remaining ingredients except parsley and stir again gently. Cover and refrigerate 4 hours or until very cold. Taste and adjust seasonings. Serve in chilled small bowls, garnished with parsley or dill.

SUPERB HALIBUT BAKE

Fish is a fast-cooking, satisfying alternative to red meat. See Chapter 2 for more fish and seafood recipes.

*Makes 2 generous servings**
1/4 teaspoon ground mace or
   nutmeg
1/2 teaspoon aromatic bitters
1/2 cup nonfat milk
2 halibut steaks (10 ounces each)

Preheat oven to 400°F. Stir together mace, bitters and milk. Place halibut steaks in a shallow glass baking dish and pour milk mixture over them. Bake in the preheated oven 15 minutes, or until fish flakes but is still moist.

*Halve this recipe for a simple meal for one.

EASY HERB-WRAPPED CHICKEN

This dish is best when made with fresh herbs, but you can substitute dry ones. Use those recommended here, or make up your own combinations.

*Makes 2 generous servings**
4 chicken breast halves, skinned**
4 tablespoons fresh lemon juice
4 tablespoons snipped fresh tarragon, or 2 teaspoons dried tarragon, crushed
2 tablespoons snipped fresh chives, or 1 teaspoon freeze-dried chives
2 teaspoons onion powder
4 tablespoons unsalted butter
4 tablespoons snipped fresh parsley (optional)

Preheat oven to 375°F. Place each chicken breast in the center of a 10-inch square of heavy-duty aluminum foil. Top each chicken piece with 1 tablespoon lemon juice, 1 tablespoon snipped tarragon (or 1/2 teaspoon dried tarragon), 1/2 tablespoon snipped chives (or 1/4 teaspoon dried chives), 1/2 teaspoon onion powder, 1 tablespoon butter and 1 tablespoon parsley. Wrap foil around chicken pieces snugly, making double folds on all edges. Place packets on a jelly-roll pan and bake in the preheated oven 20 minutes. To serve, unwrap each chicken piece, place on plate and pour herb-laced juices from packet over chicken.

*Halve this recipe for a simple meal for one.

**To skin a chicken breast, grasp skin with one hand and pull it gently but firmly away from the flesh. Skinned boned chicken breasts can also be used, if desired. Check for doneness by making a small slash in edge of a breast after 15 minutes in the oven. It should no longer be pink.

BULGUR PATTIES

Bulgur, or cracked wheat, has become very popular of late and can now be found in most supermarkets and in health-food stores. A staple of Middle Eastern cooking, bulgur is actually wheat grains that have been boiled and dried to bring out their cereal flavor. It is available in several grinds, from fine to coarse. Try these patties as a flavorful alternative to red meat.

Makes 8 patties (4 servings)

PATTIES
1/2 cup fine bulgur (cracked wheat)
1/2 cup vegetable oil
1/3 cup minced onion
2–3 glarlic cloves, peeled and minced
1/2 cup currants or chopped golden raisins
1/2 cup finely chopped walnuts
1/3 cup minced fresh parsley or coriander
1 large egg, lightly beaten
2 tablespoons unbleached flour
1/2 teaspoon kosher salt or to taste
Pinch or more of ground cumin

SAUCE
1 cup plain low-fat yogurt, slightly cooler than room temperature
1/8 teaspoon white pepper powder

To make the patties, rinse bulgur in cool water in a bowl to remove any grittiness. Add enough cold water to wheat to cover by 1–2 inches and refrigerate about 45 minutes, or until bulgur is tender. Drain in a sieve, pressing bulgur to remove all excess moisture.

Heat 1 tablespoon of the oil in a small frypan, add onion and garlic and cook and stir over low heat about 3 minutes, or until onion is soft. In medium bowl, stir together onion, garlic and bulgur. Add currants, walnuts, parsley, egg, flour, salt and cumin and mix well with a wooden spoon or your hands. Form slightly heaping 1/4 cupfuls into round patties about 1/2 inch thick.

Heat the remaining oil in a 10-inch frypan until very hot. Test by adding a bit of parsley; if it sizzles, the oil is hot enough. Add patties and fry over medium heat about 3 minutes per side, or until brown. Lift out with slotted utensil and drain on paper toweling.

To make sauce, stir together yogurt and white pepper. Serve patties hot with sauce on the side.

NOTE To reduce the fat, steam the patties for 5 minutes instead of frying them.

BROWN RICE AND ONION RISOTTO

Brown rice is recommended by many nutritionists for its whole-grain goodness. It has a firm texture and nutlike flavor that goes especially well with poultry, lamb and game. You will find brown rice in the rice section of your supermarket, and though it does take longer to cook than most other rices, it is just as easy to prepare.

Makes 4 cups
1/4 cup unsalted butter or olive oil, or a combination
1 cup chopped onion
1 cup brown rice
2 cups Chicken Stock (page 100), or stock made from chicken base
1/4 teaspoon salt
Freshly ground black pepper to taste
1 bay leaf
1/4 cup minced fresh parsley

Heat butter in a 3-quart saucepan, add onion and cook and stir 2 minutes. Add brown rice, stir and add stock, salt, pepper, and bay leaf. Over medium heat, bring to a simmer. Cover saucepan, reduce heat to low and simmer 45 minutes, or until rice absorbs all the liquid. Gently stir parsley into rice just before serving.

BEVERAGES

BANANA BUTTERMILK COOLER

When you get a craving for a thick, fattening shake, try this buttermilk concoction instead. It is low in fat, but does have its share of salt. If you are very concerned about sodium intake, try the Nutritious Cooler, which follows.

*Makes 1 serving**
3/4 cup buttermilk
1 medium banana, peeled and cut into chunks
1 teaspoon sugar (optional)
1 sprig mint, for garnish (optional)

In a blender or food processor fitted with a steel blade, blend together buttermilk, banana chunks and sugar until smooth. Pour into a chilled stemmed glass and garnish with mint, if desired.

*This recipe can be easily doubled.

NOTE For a fancier version (that also contains more sugar), top the glass with a scoop of pineapple sherbet.

NUTRITIOUS COOLER

Fresh natural fruits make this a real treat.

Makes 1 serving
About 1/2 cup chilled fresh orange juice
1/2 tablespoon fresh lemon juice
About 1/2 cup chilled watermelon pulp, in chunks
Thin lemon slice, halved, for garnish

In a blender or a food processor fitted with a steel blade, combine orange and lemon juices and watermelon chunks and blend until smooth. Serve in a chilled glass, garnished with a lemon slice half.

*This recipe can be easily doubled.

NOTE If you prefer your drink well chilled, refrigerate 30 minutes, then just before serving, reblend quickly if it has begun to separate.

VI RECIPES FOR DAD & THE KIDS

Cooking is camaraderie—and not just for adults! There is a togetherness found in the kitchen that is unique to the situation.

Children from age two on up love to help in the kitchen. Sure, it is a time when they can munch on ingredients and lick their fingers. But more importantly, it is an opportunity for them to get to know you better *and* for you to get to know them better. A careful selection of the dishes you prepare with children can help shape wise eating habits and teach basic cooking skills that will stay with them all their lives. Plus, there is the positive feeling of accomplishment a child experiences when those gathered at the dinner table rave about a particular dish and he or she can say, "I helped make it."

Not all recipes are conducive to child-adult cooperation, of course. Complicated recipes, those with liquor as an ingredient, and those too sophisticated to whet a juvenile appetite should be avoided. The recipes in this chapter have been specially developed and written to appeal to children. The method for each is broken down into "kids" and "dad" steps as guidelines to preparation. For ad-ditional help in selecting recipes, see the age categories that follow.

This chapter will be of particular help to separated and divorced fathers who often rack their brains for "fun" things to do with the kids when they have them for the day, weekend or longer. Instead of taking children to the same old fast-food establishments, plan a simple meal at home that you can prepare together. It will be a much more personal experience for everyone.

But remember, children need to be *supervised* in the kitchen. It can be a dangerous place if they are not taught how to use its equipment properly.

TEACHING CHILDREN KITCHEN TASKS

CHILDREN AGES 2–6 Allow children to stir ingredients, toss salads, add ingredients to recipes and begin to measure dry ingredients. At the upper end of the age range, they may be able to use a vegetable peeler, but should not be allowed to use sharp kitchen knives. Place-setting knives and butter spreaders can be safely handled. Children this age also like to play in soapy water, so let them help clean up the dishes. (Once past this age, they may never again volunteer to wash dishes.)

CHILDREN AGES 7–11 Teach children the basics of proper knife use, depending upon their coordination and desire to learn. During this age period, children can begin to work with the range: stirring ingredients on the stove top, preheating the oven, placing foods in the oven, etc. They can also be taught how to operate certain small appliances like toasters, electric mixers and blenders with adult supervision. Proper measuring of dry and liquid ingredients should be mastered.

CHILDREN AGES 12–16 During these years, the proper use of knives and small appliances can be mastered. More sophisticated techniques, like roasting and poaching, can be learned. If children have been involved in cooking tasks for some years, they will need less supervision now and can often be expected to fend for themselves in the kitchen. They may wish to create their own recipes or move on to complicated dishes with several preparation steps. Even at this age, supervision is important.

MUFFIN-TIN MEATLOAVES

Meatloaf is always best when literally mixed by hand. This recipe uses as many hands as are available. Baking time for these individually portioned loaves is short compared to a standard-size meatloaf, so dinner isn't long off.

Makes about 10 muffin-size meatloaves
2–3 slices day-old bread
2 pounds ground beef
1/2 pound bulk pork sausage (plain or sage flavored)
1 egg
3/4 cup milk
1 cup chopped onion, or 1/3 cup dehydrated onion
1-1/2 teaspoons salt
1/4 teaspoon freshly ground black pepper

Dad: Make bread crumbs by tearing day-old bread into small bits to make 1-1/4 cups. Preheat oven to 350°F.

Kids: Put all of the ingredients in a large mixing bowl and use hands (2, 4 or 6) to mix them together

well. Shape mixture into 10 equal balls. Place each ball in an ungreased muffin-tin well.

Dad: Place muffin tins in the preheated oven and bake 20–25 minutes, or until instant-read thermometer inserted in center of a loaf reads 150°–155°F. Remove from oven, let cool slightly, then turn out of tins.

NOTE For a more adult flavor, substitute 2 tablespoons bottled steak sauce for 2 tablespoons of the milk.

JUDITH HINES'S HAM AND CHEESE STACKS

Cooking instructor Judith Dunbar Hines, of the Cooking & Hospitality Institute of Chicago, loves to teach cooking to children. She offers this easy prepare-ahead casserole for breakfast, brunch or lunch. Once it's assembled, it can be refrigerated as long as overnight before baking.

Makes 6–8 servings*
1 tablespoon melted or very soft unsalted butter
8 slices white, wheat or rye bread
8 ounces american, swiss or cheddar cheese

8 teaspoons mustard
8 slices american, swiss or cheddar cheese
8 slices Canadian bacon or ham
8 slices canned pineapple
8 eggs
Paprika (optional)

Kids: Preheat oven to 325°F if casserole is to be baked when assembly is completed. With a pastry brush, lightly grease the sides of a 9- by 13-inch shallow glass baking dish with butter.

Dad: Trim crusts off bread to make neat squares. Shred the 8 ounces of cheese.

Kids: Spread each bread slice with a teaspoon of mustard and place bread in a single layer in the buttered dish. Put a slice of cheese, then a slice of ham on each piece of bread. (You may have to trim ham to fit.)

Dad: Drain pineapple slices well (reserve liquid for drinking later). Place 1 pineapple slice on each "stack" in the pan.

Dad & the kids: Break the eggs into a large mixing bowl. Beat with a whisk or electric mixer until foamy. Pour eggs into baking pan, taking care to keep "stacks" in place. Sprinkle shredded cheese on top, then add a sprinkle of paprika, if desired.** Bake in the pre-heated oven 40 minutes. Remove from oven and let sit 10 minutes before serving. Cut into 8 squares to serve.

*To serve 4, cut all ingredients in half and use an 8-inch square baking pan.

**At this point, casserole can be covered with plastic wrap (pressed against contents) and refrigerated for a few hours or overnight before baking.

PIZZA POCKETS

This is a great dish for Dad to try with older children, as the technique and flavoring may not appeal to younger ones. A tasty and quick alternative to making pizza from scratch, these pockets pack all of the goodies pizza fiends love into a simple format that can be served for lunch or dinner with a green salad.

Makes 8 servings
1/4 cup olive or vegetable oil
2 large onions
2 large sweet green peppers
1/2 pound fresh mushrooms

Several grindings of black pepper
1/4 cup water
1 pound pepperoni
1 teaspoon dried oregano
1 teaspoon dried basil
1 jar (15-1/2 ounces) Prince brand all-natural pizza sauce, or 2 cups All-Purpose Tomato Sauce (page 82)
8 pita bread rounds
6–8 ounces mozzarella cheese

Kids: Measure olive oil into 12-inch frypan. Preheat oven to 400°F.

Dad: Peel and chop the onions, seed and cut the green peppers into 1/4-inch strips, and slice the mushrooms. (Do all of this ahead if you like, and bag and refrigerate.)

Dad & the kids: Heat oil in frypan, add onions and cook and stir over medium heat until softened, 3–4 minutes. Push onions to one side of pan, add green peppers and cook and stir 2–3 minutes. Push peppers aside and add mushrooms and black pepper; cook and stir about 2 minutes. Stir in water, cover and cook 2 minutes, or until peppers are bright green and crisp-tender.

Dad: Cut pepperoni into 1/8-inch-thick slices.

Kids: Crush oregano and basil with thumb in palm of hand and stir into vegetables along with pizza sauce and pepperoni slices. Stir, cover and simmer over low heat 3–4 minutes.

Kids: Cut pita rounds in half. Place 8 halves in a single layer in the center of a large sheet of aluminum foil. Bring the edges of the foil up and fold over to completely wrap breads. Place foil packet on baking sheet or jelly-roll pan and heat in the preheated oven about 4 minutes. Using a grater, shred the mozzarella.

Dad & the kids: To serve, remove pita bread from oven, unwrap and fill each pocket with pepperoni mixture; top with a generous pinch of mozzarella. For second helpings, wrap remaining pita bread in foil and heat as before.

NOTE: The filling can be made up to 2 days in advance, refrigerated and reheated gently before serving. You can plan leftovers by cooking the filling as described and reserving half of it for another meal. Reheat gently in the same manner, adding a few tablespoons of water if mixture is too thick.

RONNIE BULL'S TEXAS BURRITOS

When the name Ronnie Bull is mentioned in and around the Windy City, sports fans of all ages ask "You mean *the* Ronnie Bull?" As NFL Rookie of the Year in 1962 and a star running back for the World Champion Chicago Bears in 1963, Bull became a Chicago favorite early in his career and decided to settle in his adopted city when his playing days ended in 1970. He is now vice-president of marketing for *Pro Football Weekly,* but his culinary heart is back in Bishop, Texas, his hometown and the home of good-eatin' treats like these burritos Bull cooks for himself and his children Randy, Melissa and Melanie.

Makes 4–6 servings
2 tomatoes
1/2 head iceberg lettuce
4–6 ounces cheddar cheese
2 avocados
1/2 lemon
1 recipe Ronnie Bull's Braised Pinto Beans (page 82), or 1 can (16 ounces) refried beans

1 recipe Ronnie Bull's Flour tortillas (page 119)
Bottled salsa of choice

FILLING
1 pound ground beef
1 envelope McCormick taco seasoning mix, or brand of choice
Pinch of ground cumin

Dad: To prepare filling, cook ground beef and taco seasoning mix according to package directions, adding the cumin with the water. Cook until almost all of the liquid has evaporated and the mixture is crumbly.

Kids: Core and chop the tomatoes, slice the lettuce thinly to shred, and shred the cheese. Put each of these ingredients in a separate bowl and set aside.

Dad & the kids: Pit, peel and mash the avocados. Squeeze in the juice of 1/2 lemon, stir gently and set aside.

Dad: With a slotted spoon, transfer pinto beans and a small amount of their liquid to a frypan. Heat to serving temperature, mashing the beans with the back of a wooden spoon to make a somewhat smooth consistency.

(See directions in Braised Pinto Beans recipe.) Heat tortillas according to directions in recipe.

Kids: Line up the bowls of tomato, lettuce, avocado and cheese on counter top or table. Place salsa with condiments.

Dad & the kids: Assemble burritos as follows: Each person puts together his or her own. Begin with a warm tortilla, spread mashed beans over half of it, top with a spoonful of meat mixture, and then cheese, tomato, lettuce and avocado. If desired, spoon on salsa. Fold in half and eat. Yum!

NOTE: Do not discard any leftover ingredients. Use to make Second Day Bean-Burrito Soup, following.

SECOND DAY BEAN-BURRITO SOUP

Leftovers from Ronnie Bull's Texas Burritos, preceding

Dad & the kids: Stir beef filling, mashed beans, tomatoes, lettuce and cheese into unmashed Braised Pinto Beans. Cover and refrigerate. The next day, heat and serve with warmed tortillas as a first-course or main-course soup.

RONNIE BULL'S FLOUR TORTILLAS

Makes 12 tortillas
2 cups unbleached flour
4 teaspoons baking powder
1 teaspoon salt
1/4 cup soft lard
3/4 cup milk

Kids: In a large mixing bowl, measure out and stir together flour, baking powder and salt.

Dad: Cut lard into pieces and add with milk to dry ingredients. Stir with a fork until mixture begins to form a ball. With hands, bring ball together and place on a lightly floured board.

Kids: Knead dough with lightly floured hands, adding small amounts of flour as needed, until dough is no longer sticky to the touch. Divide dough into 12 equal balls and loosely cover balls with a piece of plastic wrap or a damp clean towel.

Dad & the kids: With a rolling pin, roll out each dough ball on a lightly floured board into a thin round (about 1/16 inch thick).

Dad: While last tortillas are being rolled out, heat a dry frypan (preferably nonstick) over medium heat. Line a bread basket or mixing bowl with a linen napkin.

Dad & the kids: Cook tortillas one at a time in dry frypan about 1 minute per side, turning with pancake turner. Tortillas should take on a golden-brown pebbled appearance and puff up slightly. As each tortilla comes off the pan, place it in the linen-lined basket and fold napkin over it to keep the stack warm. Serve immediately or reheat as follows: Place tortillas in single layer on a baking sheet or jelly-roll pan in 300°F oven for 3−4 minutes to soften. Do not heat too long or tortillas will stiffen.

TO FREEZE TORTILLAS: Let cool completely, stack and wrap tightly in plastic wrap, plastic bag or freezer wrap, eliminating as much air as possible. To heat, thaw by removing from wrapping, separating and placing on cooling rack; then follow reheat instructions above.

OINK-OINK PEANUT BUTTER SANDWICHES

A different twist on the peanut butter sandwich.

Makes 4 servings
5−6 slices bacon
8 slices whole-wheat bread
Softened unsalted butter
1/2 cup smooth or chunky peanut butter
4 teaspoons pickle relish

Dad: Fry bacon until crisp; remove to paper toweling to drain.

Kids: Spread 1 side of each bread slice with butter.

Dad & the kids: Crumble cooled bacon. Stir together peanut butter, bacon and pickle relish.

Kids: Spread peanut butter mixture on the buttered sides of 4 of the bread slices and top with remaining bread slices, buttered sides in. With serrated knife, cut sandwiches in half and serve.

GREEN GOODNESS SALAD

All children need to learn how to work with a variety of fresh fruits and vegetables. This salad is a good and colorful beginning for youngsters. See Handling Fresh Fruits and Vegetables for directions on preparing the lettuce and avocado.

Makes 3–4 servings
About 1/2 head iceberg lettuce
2 medium carrots
1 small avocado
The children's favorite store-
    bought or homemade salad
    dressing
About 1 cup Caroline's Home-
    made Croutons (page 101)
Pepper mill

Kids: Pull the large leaves off the lettuce, tear them into bite-size pieces and place in a large salad bowl. With a vegetable peeler, peel the carrots; cut off the ends. Still using the vegetable peeler, shave each carrot into long lengths into the salad bowl, rotating the carrot so it is evenly shaved on all sides. Be careful not to get too close to fingers.

Dad: Cut avocado in half, remove pit, cut pulp into chunks and scoop out into salad bowl.

Dad & the kids: Shake dressing well, then carefully pour over salad in a thin stream. Toss well to coat all ingredients with dressing. Taste a bit of the lettuce and add more dressing if needed. Sprinkle with croutons and serve.

Kids: Place pepper mill on table for those who want to add pepper.

ONE-BOWL BANANA BREAD

An electric mixer makes this moist quick bread a snap to prepare, but the batter can also be mixed by hand. Eat one loaf fresh from the oven; wrap and freeze the second for another day. Serve this scrumptious bread with whipped cream cheese or butter, or all by itself.

Makes 2 loaves
Softened unsalted butter
1-3/4 cups plus 2 tablespoons un-
    bleached flour
1 cup sugar

1 teaspoon baking soda
Pinch of salt (optional)
1/4 teaspoon ground nutmeg
Pinch of ground cloves
2 medium bananas
1 cup chopped walnuts
2 eggs
1/2 cup vegetable oil
1/3 cup buttermilk or orange juice
1 teaspoon vanilla extract

Dad: Preheat oven to 325°F.

Kids: With a pastry brush, coat bottoms and sides of two 7- by 3-1/2-inch loaf pans with soft butter. Add 1 tablespoon flour to each pan and shake about until inner surfaces of pans are completely coated with flour. Tap out excess flour. Set pans aside.

Dad & the kids: In a large mixing bowl, stir together 1-3/4 cups flour, sugar, baking soda, salt, nutmeg and cloves with a wooden spoon.

Dad: Peel bananas. In a food processor or with a bowl and a fork, mash bananas until smooth. If nuts have not been purchased chopped, chop them now.

Kids: Add mashed bananas, eggs, oil, buttermilk and vanilla to the dry ingredients and stir to combine.

Dad: With an electric mixer or a wooden spoon, beat until well blended. Stir in nuts. Pour batter into prepared loaf pans, dividing equally. Bake in the preheated oven about 50 minutes, or until wooden pick inserted in center of loaf comes out clean. Cool in pans about 10 minutes, then invert pans to remove loaves. Set loaves on wire cooling racks to cool completely.

OATS 'N NUTS PIE CRUST

A simple crunchy crust that can be filled with the pudding and pie filling or the ice cream flavor of your choice. Try the Lemon Crunch or Choco-Pink versions here as starters, then create your own fillings and toppings.

Makes one 9-inch crust
1/3 cup finely chopped walnuts, pecans or peanuts
4 tablespoons (1/2 stick) unsalted butter
1 cup quick-cooking oats (uncooked)
1/3 cup firmly packed brown sugar
1/2 teaspoon ground cinnamon
Pinch of ground nutmeg (optional)

Dad: Preheat oven to 375°F. Finely chop whole or broken nutmeats to measure 1/3 cup. Melt butter over low heat.
Kids: Measure the oats and pour into a large mixing bowl. With fingertips, pack brown sugar into a 1/3 cup dry measuring cup. (No fair licking fingers until you've finished packing down sugar!) Add brown sugar, nuts, cinnamon and nutmeg to the oats. Stir to blend well.
Dad: With pastry brush, lightly coat bottom and sides of a 9-inch pie plate with melted butter. Add remaining butter to oat mixture.
Kids: Stir oat mixture until well blended.
Dad & the kids: Turn oat mixture into prepared pie plate. With fingertips, press mixture onto bottom and up sides of plate. Bake in the preheated oven 8–10 minutes, or until golden brown. Remove from oven and place on wire cooling rack. Cool completely before filling.

CHOCO-PINK PIE

Fill cooled Oats 'n Nuts Pie Crust with 2 pints softened peppermint or strawberry ice cream. Freeze 30 minutes. Drizzle chocolate syrup or topping over pie and return to freezer for at least 4 hours before serving. Makes one 9-inch pie.

LEMON CRUNCH PIE

Prepare 3-ounce package of lemon pudding and pie filling according to package directions. Pour into cooled Oats 'n Nuts Pie Crust and refrigerate at least 4 hours. To serve, use aerosol can of whipped cream to make stars around edge of pie filling and one big star in the center. To make stars, hold can vertical to pie (straight up and down) with nozzle about 1/4 inch from surface. Press aerosol nozzle gently and briefly, raising can very slightly at the same time. Each star takes only about 1 second to make. Makes one 9-inch pie.

NOTE: These two pies are best served 4–6 hours after making. Otherwise the crust will not be crisp.

DONALD McINTYRE'S PRIZE-WINNING APPLE PIE

In 1980, I was privileged to be a judge in Carson Pirie Scott's apple pie baking contest in Chicago. No fewer than fifty pies were tasted that day and, when the smoke cleared and the frenzied sampling quieted down, this recipe was the unanimous winner. Everyone was pleasantly surprised to learn the cook who devised and baked this pie was a man—the only male to enter the contest! Donald's award had all his fellow contestants "apple green" with envy. Congratulations, Donald!

Makes one 9-inch pie
1 cup sugar
1/4 teaspoon ground nutmeg
1/2 teaspoon ground cinnamon
2 cups plus 3 tablespoons un-
    bleached flour
7 medium apples (4 Greening, 3
    Paula Reds)
1/2 teaspoon salt
1/2 cup vegetable oil
1/4 cup low-fat milk
2–3 tablespoons unsalted butter
    or margarine
Milk and sugar, for top crust

Kids: In a large bowl, measure out sugar, nutmeg, cinnamon and 3 tablespoons of the flour.

Dad: Preheat oven to 425°F. Peel and core apples, cut into thick slices, then cut slices in half. Add apples to sugar mixture and stir well; set aside.

Kids: Sift remaining 2 cups flour and the salt into another large mixing bowl. Add oil and milk all at once and mix together with a fork until dough forms a ball. Pat dough ball gently with hands, then place ball on board and cut in half. Flatten each half with palm.

Dad & the kids: With a rolling pin, roll out a dough ball between 2 sheets of waxed paper to a diameter of 1 inch larger than pie plate. Peel away top sheet of waxed paper, place bottom sheet dough side down in pie plate, and gently press dough to bottom and sides of plate; peel away second sheet. Roll out remaining dough in same manner; do not remove waxed paper.

Kids: Add apple mixture to lined pie plate, distributing apples evenly. Cut butter in 1/4-inch pieces and dot apples with butter. Remove top sheet of waxed paper from dough circle and place bottom sheet dough side down over apple-filled pie plate. Peel away second sheet.

Dad & the kids: Trim dough all around so that it is 1/2 inch larger than pie plate. Turn dough edge under, and with a fork, press dough edge against pie plate to seal. With a paring knife, slit top crust in several places to make vents. Be decorative if you like. Brush top with milk; sprinkle lightly with sugar, if desired. With 2-inch strips of aluminum foil, cover edge of pie to prevent overbrowning. Bake in the preheated oven 30 minutes.

Dad: Remove foil collar and bake another 15 minutes. Crust should be medium brown and apples should hold their shape and be tender. Cool before cutting.

STRAWBERRY SORBET

"Sorbet" is a fancy French word that children will better understand as sherbet. It is generally the purest essence of a fruit, in this case fresh strawberries, puréed and mixed with liquid, then frozen. Use any type of ice cream machine to make this delightful and cooling dessert. Only be forewarned: once you've made it, you'll be asked to make it again and again!

Makes 6–8 servings
2 pints fresh, best-quality
  strawberries*
1–1-1/3 cups sugar, depending
  upon sweetness of berries
1-1/4 cups orange juice
1/2 cup fresh lemon juice

Kids: Wash strawberries by swishing in a large bowl of cool water set in the sink. Lift berries out with hands and place in a clean bowl.

Dad: Hull berries by cutting around the stem with the point of a paring knife. Cut each berry in half.
Kids: Measure sugar, orange juice and lemon juice and add to berries; stir well. Let stand 2–3 hours so flavors can blend. This is a good time to run errands, go shopping or work on other recipes.
Dad & the kids: In 2 or more batches, purée strawberry mixture in a blender or food processor. Freeze in any type of ice cream maker according to manufacturer's instructions.

*Two packages frozen strawberries in syrup (10 ounces *each*) can be substituted for the fresh berries. Reduce sugar to 1/2 cup.

RASPBERRY ICE CREAM

Grow your own raspberries, buy them at the supermarket or go to one of those berry-picking farms. No matter how you get them, don't let berry season go by without trying this ice cream.

Makes about 1-1/2 quarts
2-1/2–3 cups raspberries
3/4 cup sugar
1-1/2 cups whipping cream
3/4 cup milk
1-1/2 teaspoons vanilla extract

Dad: Rinse raspberries only if they appear to need it. Otherwise, use berries as they are.
Dad & the kids: Stir together berries and sugar, mashing berries gently. Let stand 4–6 hours. This is a good time to play tennis, go to a ballgame or visit the zoo. Put the mixture through the fine blade of a food mill, or press through a sieve until nothing but the raspberry seeds remains in the sieve. Be sure to get as much berry pulp and juice from the seeds as possible; discard seeds. Measure remaining ingredients and stir into raspberry pulp. Freeze in any type of ice cream maker according to manufacturer's instructions.

GOOD-AS-GOLD NUGGETS

Whether you call it a cookie or a candy, this no-bake sweet will be a favorite of dad and kids alike. Sinfully good chocolate is combined with the nutritional goodness of oat flakes and raisins.

Makes about 30 nuggets
1/2 cup extra-chunky peanut butter
3 tablespoons unsalted butter or margarine
2 tablespoons honey
1 package (6 ounces) real semisweet chocolate morsels
1-1/4 cups quick-cooking or old-fashioned rolled oats (uncooked)
1-1/4 cups golden or dark raisins

Dad: Line 1 or more baking sheets with waxed paper. Set a frypan containing about 1 inch of water over low heat.

Kids: Measure out peanut butter, butter and honey and put into a 2-quart saucepan. Add package of chocolate morsels. Cover saucepan and set in water in frypan. Set timer for 15 minutes.

Dad: Measure out rolled oats and raisins.

Dad & the kids: When timer goes off, uncover chocolate pot and stir with a whisk or spoon until well blended. Add oats and raisins; stir with a spoon carefully until everything is chocolate coated. With a teaspoon, scoop out rounded spoonfuls and drop on wax-paper-lined baking sheets. Refrigerate at least 1 hour before sampling. Place nuggets in an airtight container and store in the refrigerator. For best flavor, remove from refrigerator 15 minutes before serving.

TWICE-AS-YUMMY CHOCOLATE SHAKE

A double-rich shake that can be used as a dessert.

Makes 3 servings
3 cups cold milk
1/4 cup chocolate syrup
3 scoops chocolate ice cream

Kids: Measure milk, chocolate syrup and half of the ice cream into a blender container.

Dad & the kids: With pulsing action, whip ingredients in blender until smooth. Add remaining ice cream and whip briefly until thick. Serve with straws, if desired.

THE ORANGE BANANA

So simple and so good that children will start making this for themselves. Serve for breakfast, mid-afternoon snack or bedtime treat.

Makes 2–3 servings
2 cups chilled orange juice
1 banana

Dad: Measure orange juice into blender container, using the calibrations on the side of the container.
   Kids: Peel banana and cut into 1/2-inch chunks. Add to blender.
   Dad & the kids: Purée juice and banana until smooth and frothy. Pour into glasses to serve.

NOTE: When serving to guests, garnish each serving by slitting a strawberry halfway through and placing it on the edge of the glass.

VII **SEXY FOODS**
Drinks, Menus, & Desserts for Romantic Times

DRINKS TO WARM THE HEART

When you have a special guest for dinner, nothing sets the mood like a cocktail. Wine is fine but a mixed-drink concoction is more adventuresome.

BRIAN BUDA'S STRAWBERRY BOLE

As vice-president of Grant/Jacoby Advertising, Brian uses this punch when entertaining large groups, then pares down the recipe for more intimate hosting.

Serves 2
1 cup strawberries, hulled and cut in half
1/2 cup superfine sugar
1/2 cup brandy
1 bottle Rhine or chablis wine
2 whole strawberries

Place halved strawberries in a 32-ounce clear glass pitcher, cover with sugar and stir in brandy. Let sit at room temperature or in the refrigerator for 8–24 hours. Add wine, stir and serve in wineglasses with a whole berry in each glass.

FROZEN MARGARITA

With Mexican food so popular, it would be a sin not to know how to make a good margarita.

Makes 2 servings
1 lime
2 tablespoons kosher salt
1/3 cup tequila
2 tablespoons Triple Sec
1-1/2–1-3/4 cups crushed ice

Squeeze the juice from the lime into a shallow dish. Spread salt in another small shallow dish. Dip the rims of two stemmed glasses first in the lime juice, then in the salt. Refrigerate glasses at least 15 minutes. Put tequila, Triple Sec, 1 tablespoon of the lime juice and the ice in a blender. Starting on low speed and gradually increasing to high, blend for 1 minute. Spoon into prepared glasses.

APRICOT APERITIF

Fruity without being sweet.

Pour equal parts of apricot-flavored brandy and dry vermouth into 2 glasses. Serve straight up or add some rocks. Makes 2 servings.

PINA COLADA

A sweet and mellow favorite.

Makes 2 servings
1/2 cup pineapple juice
1/4 cup cream of coconut*
6 tablespoons white or golden rum
2 cups crushed ice
2 fresh pineapple spears (optional)

Put all ingredients, except pineapple spears, into a blender. Starting at low speed and gradually increasing to high, blend 1 minute. Pour into 2 chilled stemmed glasses and add a pineapple spear to each glass.

*Cream of coconut is a canned purée of coconut and sugar available in supermarkets, liquor stores and frequently in Hispanic markets.

COFFEE COLADA For a change of pace (and a more potent drink!), substitute Tia Maria for the rum, then drizzle about 2 teaspoons Tia Maria on top of each drink.

HAAGEN-DAZS DEMITASSE

Whether you host dinner at home or in a restaurant, the offer of an after-dinner drink is a gracious one. Try this demitasse in either situation. It's so good, even non-coffee drinkers will love it!

Pour equal parts Häagen-Dazs Cream Liqueur and hot coffee into 2 demitasse cups. For a standard-size cup, pour in 1/4 cup of the liqueur, then add hot coffee to fill the cup. Makes 2 servings.

BOURBON MILK PUNCH

Great for breakfast—the adult way to drink your milk!

Makes 2 servings
1-1/2 cups cold milk
1–2 tablespoons powdered sugar
1/4 cup bourbon

Combine all ingredients in a blender container and blend at high speed about 10 seconds. Pour into two 6-ounce glasses and serve immediately. Serve over crushed ice, if desired.

COCKTAILS PLUS

When a meal is too much and a cocktail is too little, try either of these plans.

TAPAS WITH SHERRY

Sherry, the noble wine of Spain, is gaining in popularity in America as a sophisticated drink to serve in the afternoon or evening. Here are the four basic types:
Fino: Very dry to dry, pale and light. Always serve chilled.
Amontillado: Medium dry, nutty, amber, full flavored. Serve chilled or on the rocks.
Oloroso: Deeply golden, gently sweet, fragrant and full bodied; great for cooking and sipping. Serve chilled, on the rocks or at room temperature.
Cream: Velvety brown, sweet, smooth and heavy; good after dinner or with dessert. Serve over ice or at room temperature.
The drier sherries, *fino* and *amontillado*, are excellent aperitifs to be served with the snacks the Spanish call *tapas*, which include anything that's munchable and handy: cubes of cheese, nuts, olives, bits of sausage, or meatballs. For a simple tapas platter, cut cheddar or swiss cheese into cubes and thread on bamboo picks with pimiento-stuffed olives, pepperoni slices and grapes. Arrange on a platter or wooden board with cooled (or leftover) Devil's Wings (page 54), which have been cut apart at the joints for easy handling.

BRIE AND FRUIT WITH CHAMPAGNE

Nothing quite sets off champagne's sparkle and flavor like fruit and cheese. This is a simple, effective way to celebrate those small special occasions for two.

Set a wedge of room-temperature brie (preferably French) on a platter (preferably silver). Surround with strawberries, apple wedges, seedless grapes, sliced peeled kiwis, pineapple spears, or any fruit easily handled with fingers. Add some crackers (preferably water table wafers) and a cheese knife. Serve with chilled champagne (preferably in tulip-shaped glasses).

HOW TO OPEN A BOTTLE OF CHAMPAGNE The proper technique for opening champagne, taught so skillfully by champagne expert Smitty Kogen, is not as glamorous as the explosive, cork-popping renditions seen in the movies. Thank goodness! It does not waste all that lovely bubbly, nor does it dissipate the bubbles. Here is Smitty's drill: Never aggravate or agitate a bottle of champagne, especially just prior to opening. It should always be stored in a reclining position of calm and should be well chilled at time of opening. With your thumb on the cork, remove wire cage. Hold the bottle at a forty-five-degree angle with the cork in one hand and the bottom of the bottle in the other. Firmly grasp the cork and hold it still while turning the bottle slowly. You are not taking the cork from the bottle; you are easing the bottle off the cork. As the bottle turns, you will feel the cork start coming out, sometimes with great pressure. This is where the strength comes in. Do not allow the cork to fly out at will. Keep it under control while turning the bottle until the cork eases all the way out. There should be no loud "pop," just a whisper.

MENUS FOR TWO

My research into romantic-dinner preferences showed great diversity in what people perceive to be sensual dining. Some like light eating so they won't feel filled up, while others prefer heavier creamy dishes for the texture sensations they impart. Some think an elegant dress-up dinner is sexy, while others opt for undershirt-casual. For most, however, their favorite foods in any situation are the same foods they consider to be sexy. Take Gerry Wallace's Crab Fondue (page 45). He used so many "oo's" and "ah's" in the writing of the recipe, one just knows that he'll be in a good mood when he eats it. And there's Jane Hotchkiss's Seafood Serenade. Her smile went from ear to ear when she started describing it.

Planning a menu for a sexy meal boils down to a simple rule of thumb: To assure a relaxed mood, serve light meals to light eaters and hearty meals to lusty eaters. And one more consideration. Food shouldn't get in the way of romance, so remember KISS— Keep It Simple, Sexy! Here are some menus to get you started.

JANE HOTCHKISS'S SEAFOOD SERENADE

Hearty eaters are lovers of life. Enough said.

Quick Clam Chowder, 85
Whole Boiled Lobster (with lots of butter), 43
Zucchini Parmesan, 65
Garlic Bread, 69
Ice cold beer

When your guest arrives, have the chowder cooked, the lobster bouillon made, the zucchini sliced, and the garlic bread ready to pop into the oven.

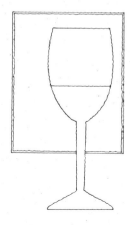

A PICNIC WITH THE BIRDS

There's nothing more romantic than a picnic, as long as you don't set your blanket on an anthill. Pick a secluded spot, preferably at the beach away from grassy fields if either of you has hay fever. There's nothing romantic about a sneezing fit.

Roasted almonds, 98
Carrot sticks with Fast Spicy Dressing, 108
Roasted Cornish Game Hens Tarragon, 52
French bread with unsalted butter
Bunch of green seedless grapes
Dry white wine

Cook the Cornish hens in advance; let cool but do not refrigerate. Pack the butter and the dip in small closed containers. Pack the food in a picnic hamper or basket covered with a check tablecloth. Let the wine bottle and bread peek out of the top for effect. Bring ice for the wine in a cooler. Pack a butter knife but no other eating implements; tear the hens and bread apart and eat Tom Jones style. Pack lots of napkins and don't forget the corkscrew!

GERRY WALLACE'S FONDUE MENU

For gazing into each other's eyes.

Gerry Wallace's Crab Fondue, 45
Sauté of Celery and Carrots, 66
California white wine
Ginny Weissman's Mutually Dipped Strawberries, 130

When your guest arrives, have the fondue mixture heating, the bread cubed, the celery and carrots julienned, the wine chilled, and the strawberries washed.

FITNESS FIEND'S DINNER

If you met on the jogging path and bicycle together twenty miles each weekend.

Bob Djahanguiri's Cold Yogurt Soup
Brown Rice and Onion Risotto
Superb Halibut Bake

When your guest arrives, have the soup made, the rice cooked and the halibut ready to go into the oven.

IF YOUR LOVER HAS A SWEET TOOTH

For dessert lovers, "sweet" and "sexy" are synonymous.

GINNY WEISSMAN'S MUTUALLY DIPPED STRAWBERRIES

Ginny, a Los Angeles-based writer and co-author of *The Dick Van Dyke Show Book*, says her men must satisfy The Three *S*'s—single, solvent and sexy.

Makes 2 servings
A plate of fresh strawberries, with stems intact
A small bowl of Grand Marnier, Valenciana or other orange-flavored liqueur
A small bowl of powdered sugar
A small bowl of brown sugar

Holding a berry by the stem, dip in liqueur, then powdered sugar or brown sugar and feed to your date. Keep feeding until all the berries are gone.

BERRIES WITH CREME CHANTILLY

Simple and elegant. A favorite dessert of those who are watching their weight but who are too weak to say "no" to everything.

Makes 2 servings
1 pint fresh raspberries, blueberries, blackberries or strawberries
1/2 cup whipping cream
1–2 teaspoons powdered sugar
1/4 teaspoon vanilla extract, or
   1 teaspoon coffee- or orange-flavored liqueur

Put stainless-steel mixing bowl and electric-mixer beaters in freezer or refrigerator to chill. Pick over berries and rinse in cool water, if needed. If using strawberries, hull with a paring knife. Dry berries on paper toweling or in a salad spinner. Divide evenly between 2 dessert bowls. In a circular motion, beat together cream, sugar and vanilla in chilled bowl with chilled beaters. When cream just begins to hold its shape, it is ready. It should be thickly saucy, not stiff. Spoon over berries.

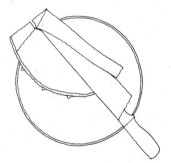

FLAMING DRAMBUIE OVER FRUIT

Dramatic, delicious and simple.

Makes 2 servings
About 2 cups fresh pineapple chunks, orange slices, grapefruit sections or melon chunks, or any combination
1/2 cup Drambuie liqueur

Divide fruit between 2 dessert bowls. Heat Drambuie in a small shallow enameled or stainless-steel frypan until hot but not boiling. Remove from heat and carefully ignite with a lighted match. While flaming, tip pan, scoop up the flaming liqueur with a long-handled spoon and ladle over the fruit. If you wish to extinguish the flames before adding liqueur to fruit, cover pan briefly. The longer the flames burn, the sweeter the resulting sauce will be.

FOR CHOCOHOLICS

Never has chocolate enjoyed such popularity in this country. Strange it should coincide with the most vigorous fitness trend ever witnessed. If there's a chocoholic in your life (and there likely is), you'll want to master some easy chocolate recipes with which to lure and entice. After all, according to food lore, chocolate is an aphrodisiac.

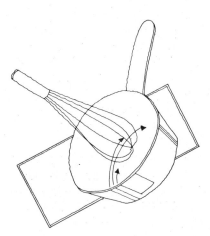

CHOCOLATE SAUCE TO POUR ON EVERYTHING

This sauce can be served warm or at room temperature over cake, ice cream, fruit—anything that you want to taste with chocolate on it. Use your imagination.

Makes about 1/2 cup

1/2 cup (3 ounces) real semisweet chocolate morsels* (or other semisweet cooking chocolate, chopped)
3 tablespoons whipping cream
1 tablespoon Kahlúa coffee liqueur
1 tablespoon unsalted butter

Place chocolate, whipping cream and Kahlúa in a small saucepan and cover with lid. In a 10-inch frypan, heat water to a depth of 1 inch until hot but not simmering. Set saucepan in frypan and keep over low heat 10–15 minutes. Do not let water boil. Uncover and use a small whisk to stir until mixture is smooth and glossy. Remove saucepan from water bath and stir in butter until it melts. Serve sauce warm or at room temperature. Store in an air-tight container in the refrigerator; reheat in a water bath.

*When you start cooking with chocolate, you will find *real* chocolate morsels an excellent ingredient. They have a rich flavor, are convenient to measure and melt evenly. In time, you might want to try some more exotic chocolates with different flavor nuances. Check gourmet food shops, or write to the Madame Chocolate listing in Mail-Order Sources for a free catalog.

CLARK WEBER'S MOUSSE A LA BLENDER

A phenomenon in the radio broadcast business, Clark has been on the air in Chicago continuously for twenty-three years, and currently hosts his own morning show. He likes to make this mousse for his wife, and for a real treat, he even washes the dishes he dirties. This recipe makes two servings for today and two for tomorrow.

Makes 4 servings

1 package (6 ounces) real semi-sweet chocolate morsels
3/4 cup hot milk
2-1/2 tablespoons very hot coffee
2 tablespoons Grand Marnier, Valenciana or other orange-flavored liqueur
2 eggs
Crème Chantilly (page 131)

Place all ingredients except eggs and Crème Chantilly in blender. Begin to blend at high speed, then add eggs through top while blender is running; continue to blend for 2 minutes. Pour into 4 dessert dishes and refrigerate until firm, about 4 hours. Garnish with Crème Chantilly just before serving.

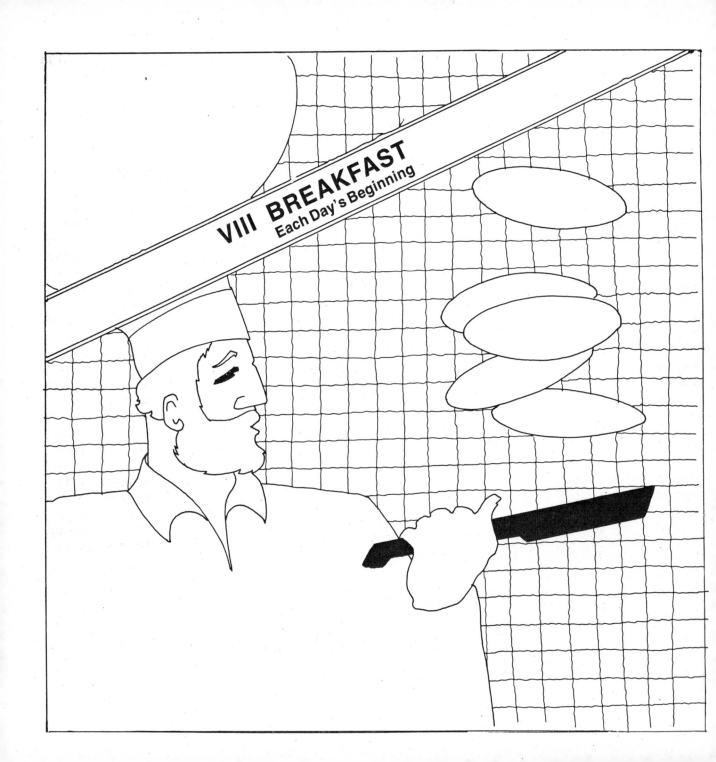

Breakfast can be put together without cooking a thing. Pour the juice, cereal and milk, and spoon on the sugar, and the meal is made in no time at all. While this approach is okay now and then, it isn't the hot breakfast that so many of us need to get through a long, hectic day. Once you learn the basics of cooking eggs and breakfast meats, you can embellish them with fresh fruit and freshly baked breakfast rolls (from the refrigerator section of your supermarket) to dazzle yourself and your guests.

ON COOKING EGGS

Temperature is crucial to cooking eggs successfully. They are very sensitive to heat, and if subjected to sudden or high heat, they will toughen just like meat, poultry and other protein foods. To graphically observe the difference between a harshly cooked and a properly cooked egg, run this little experiment: Prepare two hard-cooked eggs, one according to the method given on page 137, and the other in a pan of boiling water. Peel and cut open the two eggs and compare their texture, color and flavor. You will immediately recognize that it doesn't take much heat to cook an egg. The egg cooked by the latter method will be tougher, discolored and stronger flavored. And that's no egg-xaggeration!

FRIED EGGS

Fry 1 or more eggs at a time, using a pan just big enough to accommodate the desired number. For each egg, melt 1 tablespoon or less bacon drippings, unsalted butter or margarine in frypan over medium-low heat. Break egg into pan and sprinkle with salt and freshly ground black or white pepper. Cook until white is set, 1–2 minutes. Spoon hot fat over yolk until a film forms, or use a pancake turner to flip egg over and cook another 1–2 minutes. Remove from pan to warm plate. Serve immediately.

SCRAMBLED EGGS

Beat 1 or more eggs in mixing bowl with whisk or fork, adding 1 tablespoon water or milk for each egg. Season with salt and freshly ground black or white pepper to taste. Using 1/2 tablespoon for each egg, melt unsalted butter, margarine or bacon drippings over medium-low heat in frypan just large enough to accommodate eggs (8-inch pan for 1 or 2 eggs, 9-inch pan for 3 or 4 eggs, 10-inch pan for 4 or more). Pour in eggs and use a wooden paddle or spoon in a nonstick frypan or the back of a fork in all other frypans to stir eggs while shaking the pan back and forth. (If desired, add shredded cheese, chopped ham or chopped hot peppers to eggs as they begin to cook.) When eggs are desired consistency, remove to warm plate.

TWO-EGG OMELET

With a fork or whisk, beat together 2 large eggs, 2 tablespoons water or milk, salt and freshly ground white or black pepper to taste until well blended. In a 9-inch omelet pan* set over medium-low heat, melt 1/2 tablespoon unsalted butter. Add eggs. As they begin to set around the edge, use a corner of your pancake turner to push them toward the center of the pan and let the still-liquid portion run to fill in the space. Do this, shaking and tipping the pan occasionally, until all the eggs are set and the top is still moist. Let cook about 30 seconds to firm the bottom, then slip pancake turner under one-half of omelet and flip it to fold omelet in half. To firm up runny interior, cover pan and cook 30 seconds to 1 minute, turning omelet at half-way point, if desired. Slide omelet onto serving plate. This whole procedure takes 2–3 minutes. The low-heat technique produces a light omelet that just barely begins to brown. High heat can make the omelet leathery. This omelet will serve 1 or 2.

*An omelet pan is a specific type of frypan with a gently curving interior that allows foods to slide around the surface easily and even be flipped up into the air with a flick of the wrist. When you see a chef on television or in a restaurant tossing sautéed foods to turn them, this is the type of pan he is using. For the best omelet and for easy cleanup, look for a 9- or 10-inch heavy-gauge aluminum omelet pan with a Silverstone or other nonstick interior; use a plastic pancake turner for its great flexibility and no-scratch quality. This pan also makes an excellent sauté pan for meats and vegetables.

POACHED EGGS

Bring about 4 inches of water to a gentle simmer in a saucepan; add 2–3 tablespoons distilled white vinegar. When water returns to a gentle simmer, tap egg on side of pan so shell cracks but does not break open. Bring the egg over the water and quickly pull open shell so egg drops into water in a mass. It will sink and, after a moment or two, rise to the surface. If it appears to stick to the bottom of the pan, loosen it very carefully by sliding a slotted spoon under it.

Cook large eggs 4 minutes. You can cook more than one egg at a time as long as the pan is not crowded. This may, however, increase cooking time slightly.

To test a poached egg for doneness, lift it from the water with a slotted spoon, allow to drain, then press yolk with finger. If yolk feels very soft, egg is probably undercooked. Return it to the water for 1–2 minutes. If yolk feels firm and appears to be solidifying, egg is probably overcooked. A properly poached egg will have a soft, hot, liquid yolk and a solid, tender white. After some practice, you will learn by touch to detect this.

When egg is done, dip in bowl of cold water to stop the cooking and to rinse off the vinegar. Immediately drain for a moment on paper toweling, then serve plain or with a sauce. If desired, use kitchen scissors to trim off dangly pieces of white and create an oval. An oval shape can also be achieved by using a French egg poacher (available in gourmet shops). Simply place it in the simmering water a few minutes before adding egg, then cook in the same manner.

HARD-COOKED EGGS

Cook as for soft-cooked eggs, preceding, increasing cooking time to 14–15 minutes for medium eggs and 16–17 minutes for large eggs. Adjust heat so water is at a "shimmer" (barely simmering) during cooking. This gentle cooking insures a tender egg without the dark green ring that can rim the yolk. Remove eggs to a bowl of cold water to stop the cooking. Crack each egg by tapping with a spoon and then let sit in cold water about 5 minutes.

To peel, crack each egg all over by tapping on a countertop or inside of sink, then rolling between the palms of your hands. The shell practically falls off at this point. Return peeled eggs to cold water and store in the refrigerator for up to 5 days. (Always peel hard-cooked eggs and place in water before storing in the refrigerator.)

To chop hard-cooked eggs, cut in half lengthwise, then into quarters. Cut crosswise into pieces and finish with chopping action for finer texture.

SOFT-COOKED EGGS

These instructions are based on using large eggs from the refrigerator. Reduce cooking time slightly if using smaller or room-temperature eggs.

In a saucepan over medium heat, bring 3 inches of water (or more) to a simmer. With a hat pin or needle, poke a tiny hole in the large end of each egg, penetrating the shell about 1/2 inch. (This simple step insures the cold egg will not crack when hitting the hot water and makes peeling of hard-cooked eggs, which follows, very easy.) With a slotted spoon, lower 1 or more eggs into simmering water and cook 4 minutes or to desired degree of doneness. (You will have to experiment to find the perfect time for your personal taste.) Remove eggs with slotted spoon and rinse under cold running water for a few seconds or until eggs are cool enough to handle. Tap large end of shell with a teaspoon to crack it and peel away top of shell. Eat directly from shell or spoon into a small bowl or cup. Add salt, pepper and butter, if desired.

MEATS

OVEN-FRIED BACON

This method eliminates the range-top mess and yields evenly brown bacon. Preheat oven to 375° or 400°F. Place bacon slices in a single layer on a jelly-roll pan. Bake in preheated oven about 10 minutes or to desired degree of crispness. Remove bacon to paper toweling to drain momentarily, then serve immediately.

To save bacon drippings, place funnel in clean wide-mouth jar and line funnel with coffee filter or paper toweling. Pour warm bacon drippings through funnel. Cover jar tightly and refrigerate or freeze.

MICROWAVE BACON TIP To save bacon drippings, which come in handy in a number of recipes, use a bacon cooking rack rather than the paper-towel method. In this way you can save the drippings to use for cooking. See your microwave care-and-use booklet for specific directions.

STEAM-FRIED HAM OR SAUSAGE

To cook up ham and other breakfast meats so they are moist and tender, use this combination of steaming and frying. Add enough water to frypan to produce a film on the bottom, set ham slices, sausage patties or sausage links in the frypan and place over medium-high heat until water comes to a simmer. Cover and steam 2–3 minutes for ham, 5–6 minutes for sausage. Remove cover and continue to cook until liquid evaporates and ham just begins to brown or sausages brown evenly, turning as needed. Serve immediately.

OTHER BREAKFAST DISHES

LOU MITCHELL'S FRENCH TOAST

Sometimes the easiest is the best. And that holds true for this french toast recipe based on Chicago restaurateur Lou Mitchell's famous breakfast special. Even Julia Child has praised this light and tasty treat.

Makes 4 servings
1/2–1 loaf unsliced french bread
 (fresh or day-old)
Peanut oil for frying
4 large eggs
1/2 teaspoon vanilla extract
Butter, maple syrup, powdered
 sugar, jam and/or fresh berries

Cut bread into 1-inch-thick slices.* If slices are large in diameter, cut in half. Pour peanut oil into a 10-inch frypan to a depth of 1/2 inch. Set over medium heat. With an electric mixer, beat together eggs and vanilla until light and fluffy. Add bread slices, turn to coat, and then let soak 1 minute. Test oil by adding a bit of dry bread crust; when it sizzles upon hitting the oil, add bread slices. Fry 2–3 minutes, or until golden brown; turn and fry 2–3 minutes more. Turn only once. Drain on paper toweling and serve immediately. Top toast with butter and other desired toppings.

*For an elegant version, trim crusts from bread slices before soaking.

T.J. KESMAN'S HAWAIIAN OATMEAL

At the tender age of two, T.J. discovered this trick to make his oatmeal more palatable. Now at the advanced age of four, T.J. still prefers his oatmeal with the added fruit.

Makes 1 serving
1 bowl plain cooked oatmeal
1 jar Hawaiian Delight "junior"
 baby food

Taste oatmeal, then stir in as much baby food as it takes to make it taste good, usually 2–3 spoonfuls. Save the rest of the baby food for another oatmeal day.

STICKY BREAKFAST BITES

A simple version of monkey bread made with refrigerated biscuit dough. Yummy for brunch.

Makes 8 servings
1/3 cup (5-1/3 tablespoons) unsalted butter
1/2 cup plus 2 tablespoons chopped pecans or walnuts
1/2 cup firmly packed brown sugar
1 tablespoon water
1 teaspoon ground cinnamon
Two tubes (10 ounces *each*) refrigerator biscuits

Preheat oven according to biscuit package directions. Melt butter in a small saucepan and stir in 1/2 cup of the chopped nuts, the brown sugar, water and cinnamon. Bring to a boil and remove from heat. Sprinkle remaining 2 tablespoons chopped nuts in the bottom of a greased 12-cup bundt pan. Cut each biscuit in half and roll into a ball. Place half the balls in the pan and pour half of the butter sauce over the biscuit balls. Repeat with remaining biscuits and sauce. Place in preheated oven and bake about 25 minutes or until golden brown. Immediately unmold by inverting a platter on the bundt pan, turning the pan over and then lifting off the pan. Serve warm. To eat, pull off sticky dough balls by hand, and butter, if desired.

QUICK QUESADILLA

For those who like a zesty breakfast.

Makes 2–4 servings
4 flour tortillas (Ronnie Bull's Flour Tortillas, page 119, or purchased)
1/4 pound bulk breakfast sausage (homemade, page 104, or purchased)
4 eggs
1/4 cup water
Bottled salsa of choice (optional)

Preheat oven to 300°F. Wrap tortillas in aluminum foil and place in oven 3–5 minutes, or until hot and pliable. In a 10-inch frypan, brown sausage over medium-high heat until crumbly but not dry. Beat eggs with water, pour over sausage and cook, stirring, until eggs are set and moist. Spoon onto hot tortillas and top with salsa, if desired. Fold tortilla in half, pick up and eat as you would a taco.

APPLES AND SAUSAGE HEIDELBERG

Makes 2–3 servings
2 tablespoons firmly packed brown sugar
1/4 teaspoon ground cinnamon
1–2 apples
6 breakfast sausage patties, each 1/2 inch thick (Bertie Selinger's Breakfast Sausage, page 104, or purchased)
1/2 cup shredded natural swiss or muenster cheese

Stir together brown sugar and cinnamon; set aside. Core apples and cut each into 6 slices 1/2–3/4 inch thick. In a large frypan, brown sausage patties on both sides over medium heat. Remove sausage and reserve; pour excess fat from pan. Add apple rings and sauté 1–2 minutes per side. Sprinkle brown sugar mixture over apples; top each ring with a sausage patty and a generous pinch of shredded cheese. Cover and cook until cheese melts, about 2 minutes. Serve with toast or English muffins.

SKILLET PANCAKE WITH SAUSAGE FILLING

This pancake is baked in the oven in a cast-iron frypan until it rises high and handsome, creating a "shell" for the filling. Great for company brunch.

Makes 8 servings
1-1/2 pounds sage-flavored bulk pork sausage
1 medium onion, peeled and finely chopped
1 tablespoon unsalted butter
1 tablespoon olive oil
2 medium zucchini (unpeeled), sliced 1/8 inch thick
1 large sweet red pepper, seeded and diced
Salt and freshly ground black pepper to taste
1/4 cup water

PANCAKE
3/4 cup unbleached flour
1/2 teaspoon salt
Dash of freshly ground black pepper
3 large eggs
3/4 cup milk
1 tablespoon unsalted butter

Cook sausage over medium-high heat in large frypan until it loses its pink color. Stir in onion and cook about 2 minutes or until sausage is crumbly. Pour off excess fat and set sausage mixture aside; keep warm.

In a separate frypan, melt butter with olive oil, add zucchini and red pepper and fry over high heat about 3 minutes. Season with salt

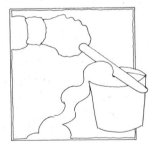

and pepper. Add water, cover and steam about 2 minutes or until vegetables are crisp-tender. Uncover and continue to cook until liquid evaporates. Set aside and keep warm. (Can be prepared in advance up to here and then reheated before spooning into pancake.)

Preheat oven to 450°F. To make pancake, combine flour, salt and pepper in a large mixing bowl. Stir together eggs and milk until blended and add to flour while beating with hand-held mixer. Beat at high speed until smooth. Melt butter in a 12-inch cast-iron frypan. Pour in pancake batter and place in preheated oven. Bake 10 minutes; reduce heat to 350°F and bake an additional 10 minutes. Pancake will rise and form a high edge. Remove from oven and fill with hot reserved fillings, spreading zucchini in the center and spooning sausage around it. Immediately cut into wedges and serve.

IX WHEN THE GUYS GET TOGETHER

When "the guys" get together, food doesn't have to be fancy, just handy. All the recipes in this chapter can be made either fully or partially in advance of serving, which makes them ideal for poker games, football-watching parties, after-bowling get-togethers or just plain ol' bull sessions.

CHEESE NACHOS WITH GUACAMOLE

Makes 4–6 servings
1 recipe Homemade Tortilla Chips, page 102, or purchased tortilla chips
6 ounces Monterey jack cheese with jalapeño peppers, shredded (about 1-1/2 cups)
6 ounces cheddar cheese, shredded (about 1-1/2 cups)
Bottled salsa of choice
Guacamole (following)

Preheat oven to 300°F. Spread chips on a jelly-roll pan; stir together shredded cheeses and sprinkle over chips. Bake in the preheated oven 5–7 minutes or until cheese melts. To serve, use pancake turner to dish out servings. Pass salsa and Guacamole.

GUACAMOLE

Makes about 1-1/2 cups
2 avocados, peeled, pitted and mashed
Juice of 1/2 lemon
1/4 teaspoon kosher salt
1 tablespoon minced onion (optional)
About 2 tablespoons bottled salsa of choice

Stir together all ingredients until well blended. Taste and adjust seasonings. To store leftovers, cover with plastic wrap pressed against its surface and refrigerate. This locks out air and keeps mixture from turning brown.

ANTIPASTO PLATTER

A good antipasto depends upon high-quality ingredients. Look for a good Italian deli, or a supermarket stocked with the following specialty items.

Makes 6–8 servings as snack or first course
1/2 pound genoa salami, thinly sliced
1/2 pound provolone cheese, thinly sliced
1/2 pound mortadella, very thinly sliced
1 tin sardines, well drained
About 1/2 cup hot or mild pepperoncini, well drained
About 1 cup Italian-style pickled sweet red peppers, well drained
About 1/2 cup Italian ripe olives
Best quality olive oil (optional)
1 loaf italian bread, sliced

Cut salami and cheese slices in half; roll or fold mortadella slices. Arrange meats and cheese on a large platter with all remaining ingredients, except oil and bread. Drizzle platter with oil and serve bread on the side.

SAUSAGE AND MUSHROOM PIZZA

A classic thin-crust Neapolitan pizza.

Makes one 13-inch pizza*
1/2 recipe Rapid Rising Pizza
    Dough (following)
Unbleached flour
Pinch of cornmeal
3/4–1 cup All-Purpose Tomato
    Sauce (page 82), or Prince
    brand all-natural pizza sauce
1-1/2–2 cups shredded mozza-
    rella cheese
1/2 pound Savory or Hot Italian
    Sausage (page 103), or pur-
    chased Italian sausage, free of
    casing
7–8 fresh mushrooms, sliced
1/2 sweet green pepper, seeded
    and thinly sliced (optional)
1 small onion, peeled and thinly
    sliced (optional)
1 tablespoon grated parmesan
    cheese

*Double this recipe for a large crowd.

Preheat oven to 450°F. Roll out pizza dough on a lightly floured board to 1/8-inch thickness. Dough can be any shape as long as it fits your no-sides baking sheet. Sprinkle cornmeal over baking sheet. Transfer dough to sheet by rolling dough onto rolling pin and then unrolling over sheet. Dip fingers in flour and pinch dough edge all around to form rim.

Spread tomato sauce over dough with back of a large spoon. Sprinkle with mozzarella, dot with chunks of sausage and distribute mushroom, pepper and onion slices between sausage pieces. Sprinkle with parmesan. Bake on lowest rack in the preheated oven about 15 minutes or until crust just begins to brown and cheese is bubbling. (Use preheated pizza stone under baking pan if de-sired.) Remove pizza from oven, slide off sheet onto cutting board and let cool 2–3 minutes. Cut into pieces with large chef's knife or pizza cutter. Serve immediately.

RAPID RISING PIZZA DOUGH

Due to the advent of rapid rising granular yeast, yeast doughs now take only half the time to make. This pizza crust takes about forty minutes from start to roll out.

*Makes 1-1/2 pounds dough;
enough for two 13-inch pizzas*
3-1/2 cups unbleached flour
1 package (scant 1 tablespoon)
    rapid rising dry yeast
1 teaspoon kosher salt
1 cup hot water (125°–130°F)*
1/4 cup olive oil
Additional 1/2 tablespoon olive oil

This dough can be made by hand with a bowl and wooden spoon, or in a heavy-duty electric mixer fit-ted with a dough hook. Place 2 cups of the flour, rapid rising yeast and salt in a mixing bowl and stir well. Add water and 1/4 cup olive oil and quickly stir into a batter.

*Use instant-read thermometer to test water. Add boiling water to hot tap water if needed to reach 125°–130°F.

Continue to stir while adding the remaining 1-1/2 cups flour. Form dough into a ball; it will be stiff and may appear dry after all the flour is added. Turn out onto a floured board and knead 10 minutes by hand, adding flour if needed; or knead 5–7 minutes with a dough hook in an electric mixer. Coat clean mixing bowl with 1/2 tablespoon olive oil, place dough ball in bowl and turn dough ball over to coat with oil. Cover top of bowl with clean kitchen towel and put bowl in a warm draft-free place for 25–30 minutes or until dough doubles in size.

Punch dough down, knead a few strokes and cut in half. Roll out dough to make 2 pizzas, or shape one or both dough portions into a 1-inch-thick slab, wrap slab in plastic wrap and freeze for future use. To thaw, place frozen dough on cooling rack at room temperature for about 2 hours or until dough is soft but still cold.

DAN ROBERTS'S CHOPPED LIVER

Dan, who heads up a public relations firm bearing his name, has a number of Chicago's finest restaurateurs as his clients. Some of that culinary talent must have rubbed off.

Makes 10–12 servings
About 6 tablespoons rendered
   chicken fat (available in
   delicatessens)
1 pound Spanish onions, peeled
   and finely chopped
Kosher salt
1/2 pound calf liver
Freshly ground black pepper
1/2 pound chicken livers
4 hard-cooked eggs, peeled and
   halved
Thinly sliced black bread
Snipped parsley

In a 10-inch frypan, melt about 4 tablespoons chicken fat. Set aside about one-eighth of the chopped onions; add remaining onions to pan and sprinkle with salt to taste. Cook over medium heat until soft and transparent, 4–5 minutes. With slotted spoon, remove cooked onions to mixing bowl; add reserved raw onions to bowl. Reserve drippings in pan.

Cut calf liver into chicken-liver-sized pieces. Add 1 tablespoon chicken fat to same frypan, if needed. Season calf liver with salt and freshly ground pepper, add to frypan, cover and cook over medium heat, stirring occasionally, until cooked medium well (about 6 minutes). Remove to a shallow bowl or dish. Season and cook chicken livers in same way, stirring occasionally, 8–10 minutes. Remove chicken livers to shallow bowl; reserve cooking juices. Refrigerate the calf and chicken livers and cooking juices 1-1/2–3 hours.

Grind together both livers and eggs using a hand grinder, the grinder attachment on your electric mixer or a food processor fitted with a steel blade. If using food processor, fill bowl only half full and use 6–7 on-off pulses per batch. Stir together liver-egg mixture and reserved cooking juices. Pack into a serving bowl, cover and refrigerate until set, about 3 hours. Serve in bowl or unmold by turning out onto serving platter. Surround with bread slices and garnish with parsley.

MUSHROOMS A LA ZWECKER

Bill Zwecker is a bright young retailer who entertains with great taste and great-tasting foods. His mushrooms can be set out for munching or used in a buffet menu, plus there is a salad dressing bonus.

Makes 8 servings
2 pounds fresh small mushrooms
1 cup olive oil
1/2 cup dry white wine or dry vermouth
Juice of 1 lemon
2 tablespoons minced onion
3 garlic cloves, peeled and minced
1 teaspoon dried oregano, crushed
1 tablespoon kosher salt
1/4 teaspoon freshly ground black pepper

Wipe mushrooms clean with damp paper toweling and place in a saucepan. Add all remaining ingredients to pan and simmer 20 minutes, stirring occasionally. Cool and refrigerate up to 2 days; the longer the mushrooms marinate, the better they will taste. Serve with toothpicks. Once the mushrooms have all been eaten, use the marinade as a salad dressing.

JIM KRIZ'S DYNAMITE FINGER FOOD

A spicy snack devised by a gentleman who's always looking for shortcuts in the kitchen.

Snacks for 6–8
1 pint cherry tomatoes, washed and dried
About 1/2 cup bottled pickled jalapeño pepper slices, drained

Make a slit in center of each tomato, being careful to cut only three-fourths of the way through. Slide 1 pepper slice into each slit tomato. Arrange tomatoes on a serving plate, or add to a platter of cold meats.

HE-MAN GRILLED CHEESE SANDWICHES

No namby-pamby cheese sandwiches here. Red pepper gives them zip.

Makes 1 or more sandwiches
Rye bread
Colby or cheddar cheese slices
Red pepper flakes
Melted unsalted butter

Make as many sandwiches at a time as will fit in your frypan. For each sandwich, place 1 cheese slice on a slice of bread, sprinkle with pinch of red pepper flakes and top with a second cheese slice and piece of bread. Heat frypan over low heat 2–3 minutes or until hot. Generously brush both sides of sandwich with melted butter. Place sandwich in hot pan, cover pan and cook until golden brown, 3–5 minutes. Turn sandwich over, cover and cook another 3–5 minutes or until golden and cheese melts.

BEST-EVER TURKEY SANDWICHES

Convenient oven-roasted turkey breasts can be found in the refrigerated-meat sections of supermarkets.

Makes 4 sandwiches
8 slices whole-wheat bread, lightly toasted
Mustard Sandwich Spread (following)
4 lettuce leaves
1/2–3/4 pound oven-roasted breast of turkey, thinly sliced*
8 tomato slices (only if in season)
1 small avocado, peeled, pitted and thinly sliced

Spread each slice of toast with Mustard Sandwich Spread. Top with lettuce, turkey, tomato and avocado. Place remaining toast slices on top and cut each sandwich in half.

*Substitute thinly sliced ham for turkey, if desired.

MUSTARD SANDWICH SPREAD

Use on turkey, ham, beef or tuna sandwiches.

Makes 1 cup
1/2 cup mayonnaise (homemade, page 100, or purchased)
1/2 cup Dijon-style mustard

Combine mayonnaise and mustard and stir to blend. Cover and store in refrigerator.

WHISKEYED BEEF BROTH

Makes 8 servings
4 cans (10-1/2 ounces *each*) condensed beef broth
2 bay leaves
2 tablespoons minced dehydrated onion
6 whole cloves
1/2 cup Canadian blended whiskey

Place beef broth in saucepan, add 4 canfuls of water, the bay leaves, onion and cloves. Bring to a boil, reduce heat and simmer 10 minutes. Remove from heat, stir in whiskey and pour into vacuum bottle for transport.

SUPER BOWL SNACK STICKS

These spicy sticks and Whiskeyed Beef Broth (preceding) make a tasty twosome to tote to football games or any outdoor cold weather event.

*Makes about 40 sticks**
2 packages (9 ounces *each*) pretzel sticks, 1/2 inch in diameter
1/4 pound (1 stick) butter
3 tablespoons Canadian blended whiskey
1 rounded tablespoon firmly packed brown sugar
1 teaspoon garlic powder
1/2 teaspoon cayenne pepper

Preheat oven to 250°F. Place pretzels in a single layer in an 11-by 17-inch jelly-roll pan. Melt butter in small saucepan, stir in all remaining ingredients and pour over pretzels. Turn each pretzel to coat on all sides. Bake in the preheated oven 20 minutes, turning pretzels to coat after 10 minutes. Cool completely, then pack into an airtight container.

*This recipe can be easily halved.

X COOKING & KITCHEN BASICS
Terms, Techniques, & Equipment

TOWEL

COOKING TERMS AND TECHNIQUES

Cooking, like every other field of expertise, has its own working language. Not understanding the terminology is to deprive one's self of ever mastering the recipes in this or any other volume. And preparing recipes successfully for the satisfaction of self, family and guests is the true joy of cooking. When a discriminating friend praises your presentation, when someone you love requests one of your special dishes, when a child gleefully asks for a second helping, cooking becomes more than sustenance—it becomes personal triumph!

But if you "boil" rather than "poach," or "chop" rather than "mince," you will never master recipe reading and duplication. The skills of cooking are simple, and they must be explained simply. The following is a straightforward glossary of cooking terms explained in everyday, easy-to-understand fashion. While reading through this list all at once will undoubtedly yield understanding of many a cooking nuance, it is not a necessary exercise. Use this section as a reference as you try the recipes in this book. Look to the Equipping the Kitchen section for a description of the equipment items mentioned in the listings here.

HANDLING INGREDIENTS

BEAT When done by hand, to combine ingredients vigorously using a large spoon in a fast circular motion. Today, beating that requires more than a few strokes is usually done by electric mixer, which is faster, more efficient and less tiring. (Anyone who remembers cake directions that read "beat 150 strokes" shouldn't confess his age.) Beating also incorporates air into batters and other products, such as whipping cream and egg whites, giving them lightness and volume.

To beat in the most efficient manner, hold the bowl firmly against the body and at an angle, and move the spoon in a circular clockwise motion. To beat with a hand-held mixer, move the beaters in a circular motion to increase efficiency.

CHOP To cut into pieces not necessarily uniform in shape. Coarsely chopped pieces are approximately 1/4 to 1/2 inch in size, while finely chopped pieces are usually less than 1/4 inch. Chopping by hand should be done with a chef's knife.

To chop by hand, cut item into chunks on a cutting board. Then hold point of knife on cutting board with left hand, grip handle with right hand (reverse if left-handed), and move handle up and down while moving knife blade toward you and away from you to cover more territory.

To chop in a food processor, cut item into large pieces with a knife, then process (with steel blade in place) using two or more on-off pulsing motions until you achieve desired size.

CREAM As a noun, cream is the dairy product we put in coffee and recipes. As a verb, it becomes a technique usually used in baking. To cream means to beat a softened substance—butter, shortening, cream cheese—until light and fluffy. Oftentimes sugar is added during creaming.

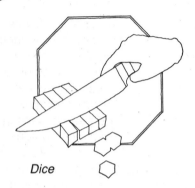

Dice

DICE No, not the ivory and ebony toys found on Las Vegas gambling tables. This dice means to cut foodstuffs into uniform cubes, most often cheese, potatoes and other large items. Dicing is more precise than chopping and cannot be performed in a food processor. It is also not used in recipes as much as other cutting methods. Recipes specify the size of the dice, generally 1/4- to 1-inch pieces.

To dice, cut foodstuff into strips. Align several of the strips and cut them into cubes simultaneously.

FOLD A specific way of combining ingredients so as to minimize loss of volume. Folding is commonly found in baking and dessert recipes and in those that include beaten egg whites. The technique is to pour or spoon one ingredient onto another, then use a rubber spatula as follows:

1. With blade of rubber spatula down, bring spatula straight down into center of bowl and toward you.
2. Turn blade edge upward (flatten it) as it approaches the side of the bowl to bring mixture from bottom gently up to the top.
3. Lift spatula from mixture; use free hand to turn bowl a quarter revolution counterclockwise. Bring spatula down through center of bowl again and repeat the folding stroke and bowl turn until ingredients are thoroughly combined.

GRATE See **SHRED**.

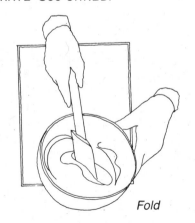

Fold

GRIND To force foodstuffs through the circular blades of a hand or electric grinder to achieve *fine* pieces. Commonly used in reference to meat, as in "ground" beef, and to nuts, as in "ground" almonds. A food processor fitted with a steel blade can chop food so finely as to resemble a grind. Some burger aficionados claim the best hamburgers are made from chopped rather than ground meat.

JULIENNE To cut into matchstick strips about 1/8 by 1/8 by 2 inches. Also the resulting product, e.g. a julienne of carrots.

KNEAD To work dough, usually a yeast dough, in a fold-push-turn manner to develop elasticity in a baked product. To knead, proceed as follows.

1. On a lightly floured surface, fold the mound of dough in half toward you.
2. With the heel of your hand, push the dough down and away from you.
3. Use the other hand to turn the dough a quarter revolution (clockwise if you are pushing right-handed, counterclockwise if you

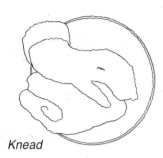

Knead

are pushing left-handed) and move it closer to you.
4. With that same hand, fold the dough in half as before and continue this push, turn and fold until dough is smooth and elastic. Recipes specify kneading times. Kneading can also be done in a heavy-duty electric mixer fitted with a dough hook; in that case, reduce kneading time by about one-third.

MINCE To chop extremely fine.

MIX See STIR.

PEEL Used interchangeably with pare; both words mean to remove the skin or outer surface of an item, such as the ingredient description "2 medium carrots, peeled" or "6 small potatoes, peeled." Peeling can be done with a paring knife or a vegetable peeler. A vegetable peeler is gen-

erally easier to use and peels more thinly than a knife, leaving more edible product behind.

PUREE As a verb, to render solid foods to a smooth consistency in a food processor or blender, or by pressing through a food mill or sieve. As a noun, a puréed food.

SHRED To force solid foodstuffs across the small curved blades of a shredder, which separates food into long, thin shavings. Commonly used in reference to cheese and certain vegetables, such as carrots and zucchini. The term grate is often used in place of shred, as in grated chocolate (actually shavings of chocolate). Grate can also refer to tiny particles of a solid food, as in "grated parmesan cheese," which can be achieved by using a shredder, or by processing to a fine texture in a food processor fitted with a steel blade. Certain shredded convenience products, like cheese and coconut, are available in supermarkets.

SLICE To cut through a food to create uniform slices. Often used in recipes as a noun along with "cut," as in "1/4 pound ham, cut

into 1/8-inch-thick slices." While most frequently used in reference to breads and meats, it is also used to describe the cutting of certain produce items, such as celery, zucchini, carrots and other long, obviously sliceable items, as well as apples and globe onions.

SNIPPED Used in reference to fresh herbs such as parsley and chives, it means to cut finely with kitchen scissors.

STIR To use a spoon or other utensil in a circular motion to combine ingredients. Often the word combine is used instead of stir, as in the direction "combine first 4 ingredients." Mix also means the same as stir and usually appears with "together," as in the direction

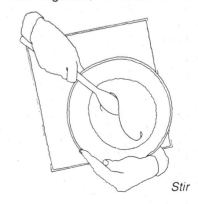

Stir

"mix together flour, baking powder and salt." If using an electric mixer, stirring (combining, mixing) is done at the low-speed setting.

WHIP To beat with a beater or whisk to add air and increase volume. Used principally in reference to whipping cream and egg whites. The term "beat" is often used in place of whip.

WHISK Until the American public discovered the eminently efficient French wire whisk, this direction was rarely seen. It simply means to use a whisk to combine two or more ingredients, such as whisking egg yolks into a sauce or whisking a thickening agent into a gravy. Whisking is done with a fast back-and-forth motion, followed

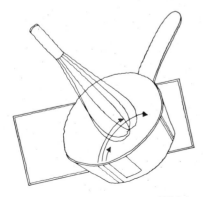

Whisk

by a circular motion to cover the entire bottom surface of the pan or bowl.

TEMPERATURE-RELATED TERMS

BARBECUE See GRILL OR BARBECUE.

BOIL To cook in liquid, usually water or stock, over high heat so that liquid bubbles. A "rolling boil" is so violent that the bubbles create a rolling up-and-down action in the pot. Boiling should be done in a deep saucepan or stockpot to eliminate messy overflow. This method is also used to reduce liquids.

BRAISE To cook solid foods in simmering liquid. A pot roast is meat and vegetables braised in stock. Chili and stew are also braised dishes. In America, braising usually refers to a number of foodstuffs cooked together in liquid, whereas in French cooking, braising often means just one item, such as braised lettuce. Braising is generally done in a large saucepan or dutch oven with a cover. For more on braising, see Chapter 3.

BROIL To cook food by intense direct heat in an oven broiler, convection oven, counter-top broiler or on an outdoor grill. When properly executed, it is a healthful and especially flavorful way to prepare meats, as the direct heat sears the surface, sealing in natural juices and eliminating the need for added fats. When improperly done, broiling results in a dry, tough and/or charred product. For more on broiling, see Chapter 1.

BROWN Not just the color of many cooked foods, but a technique used to give foods, especially meats, color and flavor. Browning is done in a small amount of fat or oil (or if a fatty product like ground beef is being cooked, with no oil at all) over medium to high heat. The food must be watched carefully and turned until all sides and edges are brown and seared (sealed). Many sautéed dishes begin with the browning of meat or poultry. Roasts can be browned in a very hot oven.

CHILL Usually appears in recipes as an instruction to refrigerate a dish at some point during preparation. "Chill" and "refrigerate" are interchangeable in recipes unless other specific directions are given, such as "chill over a bowl of ice water, stirring constantly."

CONVECTION A method of cooking with circulating hot air. "Convection oven" is the most common use in recipes. This technique, unlike conventional oven cooking that bathes food in heat, attacks food with fan-driven heat that sears the product, sealing in natural juices. Convection heat can bake, broil and roast, and is a major meat-cooking technique in many fine restaurants across the country. It is also a faster-cooking heat than radiant (standard) heat.

DEEP FRY See FRY.

DEGLAZE Deglazing a pan means to remove the essential flavoring agents from the bottom of a sauté or roasting pan so they can be used to make sauce or gravy. First, pour off or spoon off excess fat. Place pan over medium heat, bring contents to a simmer and immediately add liquid, usually stock or wine. Simmer while scraping up cooked-on bits and juices from the bottom of the pan. This mixture becomes the flavoring agent to

which additional liquid is added to make sauce or gravy.

FREEZE To place a foodstuff in the freezer until it is solid, or for the stated amount of time. For optimum efficiency, home freezers should be kept at 0°F. A specially designed freezer thermometer can be used to check freezer temperature.

FRY To cook in a shallow quantity of oil or fat at medium to high temperatures so as to achieve a brown and crispy product. This is usually done in a frypan, also known as a skillet. To deep fry, use a high-sided heavy-gauge saucepan or a deep-fat fryer and a greater quantity of oil so the product is totally submerged during cooking. For more on frying, see Chapter 2.

GRILL OR BARBECUE These terms, which have become interchangeable to many cooks across America, generally refer to cooking (broiling) foods outdoors. More specifically, to grill food is to broil it on a grilling rack over the heat source, while to barbecue is to flavor those foods with barbe-

cue sauce or seasonings. Backyard grills are available in portable and installed models and can be powered by gas, electricity or charcoal. Grilling can also refer to broiling food indoors.

HEAT A general term that means to heat on top of the range. "Heat" is often used in recipes with the addition of more specific directions; for example, "Add water, stir and heat to boiling. . . ."

MICROWAVE To cook foods quickly with radio waves in a microwave oven. Microwave cooking, the fastest method known, is very good for vegetables but not at all good for meats, except bacon. Two of the oven's best uses are thawing frozen foods and reheating cooked foods. Microwave ovens are often used in fast-food restaurants.

POACH Not just a technique for cooking eggs, poaching is the gentlest method of cooking in liquid. To poach means to cook an item or items over low heat in liquid that is barely rippling. The French like to say the liquid is "at a shimmer," and that really describes how it looks. Eggs, fish, poultry and other delicate foods that would be toughened by excessive heat are poached very successfully.

ROAST To cook foods, most often meats and poultry, in an oven on a rack set in a shallow pan. Almost any shallow pan fitted with a rack can be an efficient roasting pan, although the V-shaped rack seems to be most readily available. For more on roasting, see Chapters 1 and 2.

ROUX The French word for a thickening agent for sauces and gravies made by cooking together fat and flour. In the classic roux, the fat is butter, but it can be bacon or beef drippings or rendered pork or chicken fat, depending upon the flavor you wish to impart to the dish. The usual technique is to heat the fat, add an equal or slightly greater amount of flour, stir into a paste and cook, stirring constantly, until mixture boils for 2 minutes. Then liquid, usually stock, is added and the mixture is whisked until smooth and heated until thick.

When softened butter and flour are blended into a paste off the heat, the mixture is called a beurre manié. It can be used to thicken soups, stews and sauces by simply whisking bits of the beurre manié into the boiling liquid.

SAUTE To cook foods, usually meat, poultry, fish or vegetables, quickly and gently in a small amount of butter and/or oil over low or medium heat in a frypan. For more on sautéing, see Chapter 2.

SEAR To seal the surface of a food product with heat. Usually applied to meat and poultry, searing can be done on the range top by browning an item over high heat in a small amount of fat, in a convection oven, in a very hot standard oven, or in an oven broiler. Proper searing seals in the natural juices of the product and adds flavor by browning.

SIMMER Used both as a verb and a noun. As a verb, simmer means to heat a liquid (water, soup, sauce) just below the boiling point. Unlike boiling where consistent and definite bubbling action occurs, simmering is achieved when the surface of the liquid is gently and occasionally broken by small

bubbles around the edge of the pan. It is more gentle than boiling and is done at a lower temperature. As a noun, simmer most commonly appears as "bring to a simmer," or in a similar context.

STEAM To cook food on a rack or in a basket over gently boiling water in a tightly covered pan. Steaming is an excellent, low-calorie way to cook vegetables, and is handy for reheating foods. For more on steaming, see Chapter 5.

MEASURING INGREDIENTS

The proper measuring of ingredients is a key to recipe success, and should be learned by everyone, even those with the most experimental temperament. If you find conventional procedures boring and unfulfilling, then take the time to train your eye to measure by sight. This can be done for small amounts of dry ingredients by putting the ingredient in a measuring spoon and, before adding it to the recipe, pouring it into your hand and observing to what extent it fills your palm.

It is more difficult to "eyeball" larger amounts, but it can be done by pouring the properly measured amount into the recipe and taking a few seconds to note the quantity when out of the boundaries of the measuring cup. Soon, if you are conscientious, you will be able to add ingredients without measuring because your eye will judge the amount visually. This is not a good practice for baking recipes, however. Even the most experienced chefs will not take a chance on the delicate proportions required for pastries and cakes.

MEASURING LARGE AMOUNTS: DRY INGREDIENTS Dry-ingredient measuring cups are used to measure flour, sugar, cornstarch, oatmeal, etc. The proper technique is to fill the cup to slightly overflowing, then sweep off the excess with a flat-edged metal spatula to make the ingredients level with the top of the cup.

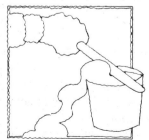

Sweep off excess with a flat-edge spatula.

Since the measurement of flour is often crucial, certain specific methods of measuring have evolved. The most popular is the dip-and-sweep method: simply dip the measuring cup into the flour and sweep off the excess with a metal spatula. For flour that is packed lightly, stir the flour, then scoop or spoon into the cup and level off. This method results in the use of a little less flour than with the dip-and-sweep style.

The most accurate and professional method of measuring dry ingredients for pastry and bread making is to weigh them on a kitchen scale. Most American cookbooks, including this one, give the amounts rather than the weights of flour and other dry ingredients. Should bread or pastry making become a passion, however, weighing dry ingredients will become necessary if European cookbooks are used.

MEASURING LARGE AMOUNTS: LIQUID INGREDIENTS Liquid measuring cups have lines to indicate amounts. Fill cup to desired amount so that top of liquid is even with line. In some cases, liquids need not be measured. For exam-

ple, when a recipe calls for one cup whipping cream, the entire half-pint (one cup) carton of cream can be added. Likewise, if a recipe calls for four cups or one quart milk, simply pour in a one-quart carton. See the equivalents chart that follows.

MEASURING SIFTED INGREDIENTS There was a time when sifting flour was a common step in recipes. Today, most flours are presifted and most recipes do not require additional sifting. However, there are still enough recipes that call for sifted ingredients that the technique should not be ignored. When a recipe calls for sifted flour or powdered sugar in the ingredient listing, use this method: place dry-measuring cup in the center of a large sheet of waxed paper. Position sifter or sieve over cup and spoon dry ingredient into sifter. Sift directly into the cup until it is heaping full, then sweep off excess with a metal spatula. Empty cup and repeat as needed. When sifting is done, pick up waxed paper and pour any excess flour back into its container. If a recipe calls for sifting various ingredients together, add all the measured ingredients to the sifter or sieve, and sift directly into the mixing bowl.

MEASURING SMALL AMOUNTS: DRY INGREDIENTS Dip a measuring spoon into the container, then level off. When measuring herbs and spices, dip spoon into jar or tin, position a metal spatula over the container mouth and draw spoon up and out against spatula edge, automatically leveling off. Baking powder cans and baking soda boxes have cardboard edges designed for leveling off in this manner.

MEASURING SMALL AMOUNTS: LIQUID INGREDIENTS Pour ingredient, such as vanilla extract, cream, water or Worcestershire sauce, into spoon until spoon is full. When viewed from the side, the liquid should be rising over the edge slightly.

MEASURING: EQUIVALENTS AND THE PROGRESSION Once the progression of measurements, i.e., how the various units interrelate, is understood, you will be able to double, triple, halve and otherwise multiply or divide recipes to fit your needs.

Since 1 cup (c.) = 16 tablespoons (T.):
3/4 c. = 12 T.
2/3 c. = 10 T. + 2 t. (10 2/3 T.)
1/2 c. = 8 T.
1/3 c. = 5 T. + 1 t. (5 1/3 T.)
1/4 c. = 4 T.
1/8 c. = 2 T.

Since 1 pound (lb.) = 16 ounces (oz.):
3/4 lb. = 12 oz.
1/2 lb. = 8 oz.
1/4 lb. = 4 oz.

The Progression

3 t. = 1 T. = 1/2 fl. oz.
2 T. = 1 fl. oz.
16 T. = 1 c. = 1/2 pt. = 8 fl. oz.
1 pt. = 2 c. = 16 fl. oz.
2 pts. = 1 qt. = 4 c. = 32 fl. oz.
4 qts. = 1 gal. = 16 c. = 128 fl. oz.

HANDLING FRESH FRUITS AND VEGETABLES

APPLES

So many apple varieties are available that it would be impossible to list all of them here. Each variety varies from the next in flavor, texture and recipe suitability. Many are found in only a single area, and then only during a certain season. In general, though, apples are most abundant and freshest in the fall, with good availability the remainder of the year.

Experiment to find your favorite apples for out-of-hand eating by tasting different varieties. For baking needs, Delicious, Golden Delicious and Jonathan are popular. If you want a tart-sweet eating apple that is also great in recipes, look for a Granny Smith, a crisp, green spring apple that must have been the prototype for the color apple-green. No matter which you choose, look for firm apples with good color and no soft or shriveled spots.

TO WEDGE To cut attractive wedges for cheese platters or fruit plates, cut apple in half along the stem, and then into wedges. With a paring knife, slice seeds off each wedge. To keep cut surfaces from turning brown, brush with or dip in fresh lemon juice.

TO SLICE FOR BAKING RECIPES Wash the apple, peel with vegetable peeler, then remove core with apple corer or paring knife by using circular cutting motion first from one end, then the other. Cut in half along the core, place cut side down on cutting board and slice crosswise through core to desired thickness.

AVOCADOS

Two basic types are available, one with a rough, pebbly skin and the other with a smooth, shiny skin. Generally, the meat of the rough-skinned type,often called a Haas avocado in supermarket ads, is firmer and richer in flavor than the smooth-skinned one,which tends to have watery meat.

Rough-skinned avocados will be green when underripe and turn brown or black as they ripen. To test an avocado for ripeness, cradle it in the palm of your hand, curl your fingers around it and gently squeeze. When the avocado yields to gentle pressure, it is ready for eating. There are different stages within the "eating range": A newly ripened avocado is easiest to handle when slicing for salads and fruit plates. An avocado that may feel overripe might be just right for guacamole. As you work with avocados you will begin to be able to tell the difference. Never buy an avocado that is "rock hard," for it may never ripen. To ripen fruit at home, leave at room temperature; to ripen more quickly, place in a paper bag at room temperature. Brush avocado pieces with lemon juice and add it to mashed avocado to keep the flesh from turning brown.

TO PIT
1. With the tip of a knife, flip stem from avocado end.
2. With a chef's knife and starting at stem end, cut in half lengthwise, bringing blade all the way around the pit and back to the starting point in a circular motion.
3. Gently grasp avocado with both hands, twist and pull apart to separate halves.
4. To remove pit, whack it with sharp edge of chef's knife blade so that blade is embedded in pit. Twist knife to loosen pit and then lift pit out.
5. Peel avocado halves by pulling skin from meat. Slice or cut into cubes as needed.

TO MASH Cut avocado in half and remove pit as described. Use a teaspoon to cut through the meat down to the skin lengthwise and crosswise.

Use the spoon to scoop avocado cubes into a bowl, then mash with a fork.

BANANAS

Don't be afraid to buy green bananas. In a day or two they will be yellow and ripe. (Bananas are gassed before they ever get to the supermarket to promote quick ripening.) They are good for out-of-hand eating when yellow or yellow speckled with brown, and best for baking from the speckled stage on, since they get sweeter as they ripen. Don't be alarmed if you find a completely brown banana in your fruit basket—one you undoubtedly overlooked. It will make great cookies or banana bread (see One-Bowl Banana Bread, page 120).

Never store bananas in the refrigerator as they are injured by temperatures below 55°F. Avoid bruised fruits and those with a grayish appearance, a sign of exposure to cold.

TO PEEL AND SLICE Cut off both ends of banana. Peel back skin with edge of knife or hand. Slice to desired thickness.

BROCCOLI

This member of the cabbage family should have compact, firm clusters of buds as heads and stems that are firm, but not woody or tough. Heads should be green or purplish-green; avoid those that have begun to yellow, an indication of aging. When steamed, boiled or stir fried to the crisp-tender stage, broccoli takes on a vibrant green color.

TO PREPARE FOR COOKING Cut off tough stem end of each bunch. Cut or separate bunch by hand into spears. If stems are tough, use vegetable peeler to remove outer layer, and make lengthwise incisions with paring knife to

speed stem cooking time. Heads will cook faster than stems, so if cooking in pieces rather than whole, you may want to add the stems to the pot first.

CABBAGES

Look for firm, heavy heads that are not discolored or bruised.

TO REMOVE CORE With a strong knife, cut core from head in a circular motion. Or cut head into halves or quarters, then cut away core. Do not use core in slaws, as it is tough and bitter. To keep cored cabbage crisp, use rinse-drain-and-bag method described in lettuce entry.

CANTALOUPES (MUSKMELONS)

Look for melons that are slightly soft to the touch. A good indication of ripeness is a softness at the stem end when pressed with the thumb. If a firm, unripe melon is selected, it may continue to ripen over the next few days. Once a melon is cut open, ripening stops and decay starts. This tells us two

things: never cut open an under-ripe melon and, once cut, eat a melon as quickly as possible for best flavor.

TO SEED AND CUT A MELON
1. With a chef's knife, cut melon in half through stem end.
2. Run a spoon between seeds and melon meat; scoop out and discard seeds.
3. Serve halves, or cut halves into wedges to be used on fruit platters or as breakfast fruit. To cut into chunks for fruit bowls, use procedure described in steps 4 and 5 of pineapple entry.

CAULIFLOWER

Most cauliflowers are sold wrapped in plastic and with their green jacket (outer) leaves removed. The white portion, called the curd, should be compact and clean. Avoid those heads that have begun to discolor and are soggy to the touch.

TO PREPARE FOR COOKING Cut away any outer leaves. Whole cauliflower can be steamed or simmered in water or stock. To cut into florets (small clusters) before cooking, turn head core side up and use narrow-bladed knife to cut small clusters from the core. These clusters can also be served raw with dip.

CELERY

Look for unblemished pale- to bright-green stalks that are rigid, and leaves, if present, that are crisp and fluffy.

TO KEEP CRISP AND STORE Cut a thin slice from the bottom of the celery bunch. Put the bunch, cut end down, in a tall container of cold water and place in the refrigerator. Use as needed and remove from water to a plastic bag after twenty-four to forty-eight hours. Keep bag in vegetable crisper.

TO MINCE Pull stalks off bunch, wash well and then cut each stalk into four or more lengthwise strips. Keeping strips aligned, thinly slice crosswise.

CUCUMBERS

Cucumbers should be firm, unblemished and dark green. Most supermarket cucumbers are coated with an edible wax to help maintain freshness. While it is not harmful or distasteful, it can be unpleasant and hard to digest, and it is best removed by peeling.

If you shun cucumbers except for the "burpless" (more expensive) variety because the others leave you in a gaseous state, you will be glad to learn that the following technique for removing the seeds will render any cucumber burpless.

TO SEED AND SLICE
1. Peel cucumber with a vegetable peeler and cut in half lengthwise.
2. Working with half of the cucumber at a time, run a teaspoon down one side of the seeds where they join the meat, then down the other side.
3. Beginning at the top, insert spoon tip and pull down sharply to strip seeds away. Discard seeds.
4. Slice hollowed-out cucumber to desired thickness, or use as is and fill with tuna or egg salad.

GARLIC

Look for firm, compact heads colored white or pinkish white. Avoid heads with soft spots. Do not buy too much fresh garlic at one time. It is wiser to buy one head at a time and replenish your supply as needed. Store garlic at room temperature in a jar with a hole punched in its lid, or in a small burlap bag.

TO PEEL AND MINCE
1. Cut off bud end of clove.
2. Place flat of a chef's-knife blade on garlic clove and hit with closed fist to burst clove.
3. Peel skin off clove—it will lift away easily. (The clove is now "bruised.") Use mincing technique as described in Handling Ingredients section of Cooking Terms and Techniques, flattening clove as needed by "smearing" it with flat of knife. If more than one garlic clove is needed, peel one at a time and mince all together.

TO MINCE IN A FOOD processor With steel blade in place and processor turned on, drop one or more peeled garlic cloves through feed tube into bowl. Remove minced garlic by running a plastic spatula around inside of bowl.

GRAPEFRUIT

One of the joys of winter is the constant availability of luscious grapefruit—white, pink and red! Pink- and red-meat varieties are generally sweeter than white. Look for fruit with a firm, unblemished rind. To obtain grapefruit's full flavor and nutritional goodness, section it (the way it is served in fancy hotels and restaurants!) as described here and forget that ridiculous "halve the grapefruit" saw. You can section an orange in the same manner.

TO SECTION
1. Cut off stem end, exposing grapefruit meat.
2. Hold the grapefruit in your left hand (if you are right-handed) and position it over a bowl to catch any juices. With a sharp, preferably narrow-bladed knife, start at the stem end and use a sawing motion to cut away the rind, including a thin layer of grapefruit meat. This removes the thick outer membrane and rind all at once. If you rotate the grapefruit as you work, the rind will come off in a single long curl.

3. Still holding the grapefruit over the bowl, remove the first section by cutting down along the membrane on one side of it; then bring the knife up and cut down along the other side, freeing it from the remaining sections. With the knife blade, ease the section out and let it drop into the bowl.
4. To remove the next section—and all remaining sections—cut down to center of grapefruit along other side of membrane, turn knife blade away from you and slide blade along next membrane, freeing section with a flip of the wrist.
5. When all sections are freed from the membrane, squeeze the membrane to release any remaining juices into the bowl. You now have all the goodness that a grapefruit has to offer.

KIWIS

These fruits are fuzzy on the outside and vibrant green on the inside. They have a delectable flavor and a spray of tiny black edible seeds that give the slices a most exotic appearance. The best kiwis come from New Zealand May through October, but the sizable California crop keeps these special fruits in the market year-round. Look for kiwis that yield to slight pressure when cradled in the palm of your hand.

Here are two ways to prepare kiwi, one sliced for serving guests and one for eating out of hand.

TO SLICE With a paring knife, cut around and discard the hard core at stem end. Remove the fuzzy skin with a vegetable peeler or paring knife. Slice crosswise to desired thickness.

TO EAT OUT OF HAND For a fast snack, do what they do in New Zealand: cut kiwi in half and scoop out and eat meat with a teaspoon, leaving nothing behind but the skin.

LEMONS

Lemons are used primarily for their juice and secondarily for their rind, which is grated into dessert recipes. Look for bright yellow fruit with a shiny, unblemished rind. Lemons should be slightly soft to the feel when squeezed; a very hard lemon can mean a thick skin and/or meat that is low in juice.

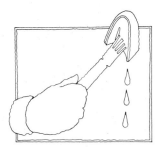

To squeeze lemon juice.

TO SQUEEZE A WEDGE To squeeze the juice from a lemon wedge into a beverage, over salad greens or onto seafood, always insert the tines of a fork into the pulp and hold it there while squeezing. This will eliminate the squirting of lemon juice into the eyes and will help release more juice. If substantial juice is needed, cut lemon in half and use this same technique, or squeeze on an electric or manual juicer.

TO GRATE RIND Run the lemon over a fine-hole grater, removing only the yellow portion and turning the lemon constantly so no pith is grated.

TO CUT ZEST When lemon zest is needed for drinks or cooking, use a vegetable peeler to remove a strip of rind, cutting away only the yellow portion. The white pith beneath the yellow is bitter to the taste. To release the essence of lemon zest, twist or rub along the edge of a glass.

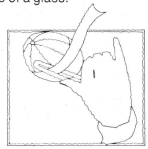

Remove a strip of rind.

LETTUCE (HEAD OR ICEBERG)

Look for a firm head with light- to bright-green color. Leaves should be free of brown spots and crisp to the feel. To maintain crispness, store as follows.

TO CORE, STORE AND WASH
1. With a paring knife, cut around core, or bang core end of head firmly down on counter top to "pop" core, then pull core from head.
2. Run cold water into core opening, allowing head to fill with water. Drain head for about 5 minutes by placing in a dish drainer or sink core end down. Place head in a plastic bag, close with a twist-tie and refrigerate in the vegetable crisper.
3. To wash lettuce leaves just prior to use, see directions under spinach entry. To dry lettuce leaves, use a salad spinner (available at gourmet shops) or pat dry between layers of paper toweling.

MUSHROOMS

Look for white or light-colored caps that are unblemished and as free of dirt as possible. One way to check for freshness is to look at the underside of the cap to see if it is still attached to the stem. The caps of the freshest mushrooms are closed around their stems or only slightly open, exposing light-tan gills. Never wash or soak mushrooms, as they will become waterlogged.

TO CLEAN Wet a paper towel with cool water, then squeeze so towel is barely damp. Wipe mushroom caps with the damp towel, folding over towel often to change surfaces.

ONIONS

Yellow globe onions are the most readily available and are used in a wide variety of recipes. Look for hard onions with dry paperlike outer skins that are free of soft spots. Avoid onions with fresh green sprouts. If your onions at home "sprout," remove green sprout completely when using, as it is bitter.

White globe onions, often called boiling onions, are generally small and can be used whole in stews and other braised dishes. Red onions are usually served raw in salads. Store onions in bins or burlap bags at cool room temperature.

TO PEEL To facilitate peeling, especially when you have several onions to prepare, place them in a bowl, cover with boiling water and let stand a minute or two. Drain, rinse in cold water and the skins will lift off easily. To begin the peel-ing, cut a thin piece off the root (hairy) end with a paring knife, then peel the thin brown skin away. If the first onion layer beneath this skin seems tough, or if it is brown or shriveled, peel it off.

TO CHOP

1. Peel onion, making sure not to cut off all of the root end, for it holds the onion layers together. Cut onion in half lengthwise through the root end.
2. Place each half cut side down on wooden board with root end away from knife. Cut down through length of onion at 1/8- to 1/2-inch intervals (depending on desired size of chop), leaving root end intact.
3. From the side, make one or more cuts almost all the way through the onion parallel to the board. Again, the number of cuts will depend on how fine you need to chop. Leave root end intact.
4. From the rounded top, cut down through the onion in the size intervals desired until you reach the root end. If onion becomes difficult to manage as you approach root end, turn it on its new cut side and continue cutting for a while before returning to original position. For a finer chop, continue cutting action on board as described in chop entry of Handling Ingredients in Cooking Terms and Techniques section.

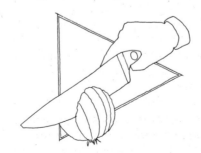

Cut down through onion.

ORANGES

Basically there are two kinds of oranges: eating and juice. Juice oranges tend to have thin skins and a softer feel than eating oranges. Supermarkets and produce markets should mark oranges as to type. If this hasn't been done, ask the produce manager to distinguish them. When selecting oranges for eating, look for firm but not hard fruit, with even orange color and unblemished rind.

TO SECTION Select a large eating orange and peel and section according to directions in grapefruit entry. Use sections in salads, fruit plates and bowls, desserts and for breakfast.

TO SLICE Smaller oranges can be sliced and used in the same way as sections. Peel as for sectioning, then slice in desired thickness.

PARSLEY

Fresh parsley, both curly and flat-leaf Italian varieties, are available in unwrapped bunches and in pre-packed trays. *Always* look for bunched parsley, as it is usually fresher. This is because its air and moisture supplies have not been cut off by plastic wrap.

Use the simple "refrigerator greenhouse" effect described here to keep parsley crisp; it can also be used to crisp and store fresh herbs, Romaine lettuce, endive, celery and any green that has its root end intact.

TO CRISP AND STORE Trim away parsley stems (or cut a thin slice from root end of greens like Romaine). This cut surface can now absorb water. If parsley is dirty, swish gently in a bowl or sinkful of cool water; shake off excess mois-

ture. Place parsley, stems down, in a large measuring cup or other high-sided vessel containing cold water. Place cup and parsley in a plastic bag and twist-tie bag closed. Store this miniature "greenhouse" in the refrigerator. Limp parsley should crisp up in two to four hours. If parsley is not used in three to five days, and leaves begin to turn yellow, remove from cup and water and store in plastic bag in the vegetable crisper.

PEA PODS, ORIENTAL (SNOW PEAS)

Look for bright-green color and a smooth unblemished surface that has a bit of a sheen. Select pods with small peas; large ones are a sign of maturity and potential toughness. If possible, buy pea pods at Oriental food markets as the turnover is fast and the product therefore is fresher than that sold prepacked at the supermarket.

TO DESTRING As soon as you get the pea pods home, place them in a bowl, cover with cold water and store in the refrigerator. This will

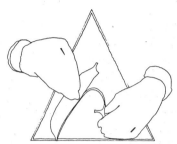

To remove string, pull down pod.

"crisp" even limp ones. To prepare pea pods for cooking, snap off stem end and pull down along pea side of pod to remove string. Flip pea pod over and repeat with other end. This can be done before storing in the refrigerator or just before using. Pea pods will keep in the vegetable crisper about 1 week.

PEPPERS, SWEET (GREEN AND RED)

Sweet green peppers should have smooth, shiny skins void of soft spots. Sweet red peppers, most readily available in the early fall, are green peppers that have matured on the vine and taken on a sweet flavor. Be especially careful in selecting red peppers as they are more prone to overripeness and decay. Check for firmness and bright red color.

TO SEED AND SLICE Cut pepper in half lengthwise through the stem end. Hold pepper half with open side away from you, and place thumb on stem and two fingers over the seed ball inside. Simply pull seeds out of pepper, pivoting on your thumb, and the seeds and stem will snap out in one motion. Pull out any white (bitter) ribs from inside and rinse pepper under cold water. Slice lengthwise into strips of desired width. To dice or chop, cut strips crosswise into pieces.

PINEAPPLES

One of the great treats of the fresh produce array available today is the pineapple. While a number of methods have been touted on how to tell if one is ripe, color seems to be the best indication. A dark green pineapple is usually mature but not ripe. As the pineapple ripens, the color turns to yellow, yellowish orange or reddish brown, depending upon the variety. Also, a ripe pineapple will be firm but not hard. If you wish to eat your pineapple the day you buy it, look for one that has turned an even yellow color. If you can wait, look for one just beginning to turn and

let it ripen at home at room temperature. Refrigerate a ripe pineapple and use it as soon as possible.

The following method of cutting a pineapple into chunks or spears has several steps, but they are easy to master and yield good results quickly.

TO CUT INTO CHUNKS OR SPEARS

1. With a large chef's knife, cut off the green top including about 1/2 inch of the fruit portion, then cut off stem end.
2. Cut pineapple in half lengthwise and then cut halves into wedges.
3. To remove the tough, stringy core, cut a small strip from the narrow edge of each wedge. You will be able to see the difference between the core and the adjacent sweet meat.

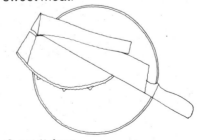

Cut strip from narrow edge of wedge.

4. Stand each wedge up on its rind and cut down through meat to rind at 1/2-inch intervals.
5. Cut chunks from rind by running knife horizontally along rind, but not so close as to cut through the eyes, which are spiny and tough. You should now have eye-free pineapple chunks. To cut spears, follow this same procedure but omit step 4.

SHALLOTS

Shallots are one of those fresh ingredients popularized in America by the rising interest in French cooking. They are smaller than onions, larger than garlic cloves and are lobed, which makes them tedious to peel.

Since the flavor of shallots is somewhere between onion and garlic, a little goes a long way. This is just as well as they can be quite expensive. If you adore shallots, grow them, if possible, or have a friend who gardens grow them for you.

TO PEEL For easiest peeling, break the shallot into lobes and cover with boiling water, as directed in the onion entry.

SPINACH

Available in curly and flat-leaf varieties, spinach should be bright to deep green in color, and have crisp, blemish-free leaves. Avoid bunches with unusually coarse or stringy stems. The younger the leaves, the more tender and flavorful they will be.

Greens such as spinach often have sand, dirt or even insects clinging to their leaves. Follow this procedure for best cleaning results.

TO WASH AND DESTEM Place spinach in a bowl or sinkful of cold water and swish leaves in water gently. Remove the leaves by lifting them out in handfuls. This is the best way to clean delicate greens, as the sand and dirt particles are left behind in the water. All types of lettuce, fresh herbs and parsley can be washed by this method.

To remove the stems from the leaves, fold each leaf in half and hold in one hand, stem end up. With the other hand, pull the stem down along the back of the leaf to remove the stem and any stringiness. On very young, tender leaves, stems can be simply cut off at the leaf.

STRAWBERRIES

Look for plump, firm berries that are evenly red and have green seeds.

TO WASH AND HULL Gently swish berries in bowl or sinkful of cold water and immediately lift by handfuls from water, leaving sand and grit behind. To hull, use point of paring knife to cut around stem and lift stem off.

TOMATOES

Summer is really the only season to get truly delicious tomatoes. Those available at other times of the year are generally disappointing. Look for red, tender-firm tomatoes with a minimum of green around the stem, and unbroken, unbruised skin. Sometimes aroma is an indication of a tasty tomato, but not always.

TO PEEL
1. Lower the tomato into boiling water for fifteen to thirty seconds, depending upon ripeness. The riper the tomato, the shorter the boiling time. Remove with a slotted spoon to a bowl of cold tap or ice water to stop the cooking.
2. With a paring knife, cut around the stem in a circular motion to remove the core.
3. Still using the knife, peel back the skin. It will easily separate from the meat.

TO SEED
1. Cut peeled (or unpeeled, if you prefer) tomato in half crosswise through the core.
2. Squeeze the tomato so seeds pop out into the bowl or sink. If needed, use your finger to coax stubborn seeds from their cavities. Discard the seeds.

TO CHOP Chop seeded tomato by slicing into strips, then cutting strips crosswise.

Squeeze tomato so seeds pop out.

EQUIPPING THE KITCHEN

AN OVERVIEW

The selection of kitchen equipment for the home is the most neglected aspect of culinary art. There are a number of reasons for this unfortuante situation, but there are no excuses once a cook understands the importance of equipment. Yes, one can point to the confusion caused by the veritable smorgasbord of kitchen equipment available today. And one can lament the fact that most of the information about equipment comes from the manufacturers' advertising, certainly a less-than-reliable source. Anyone who ever bought the now-defunct hamburger cooker, and enthusiastically took it home only to learn it made the worst hamburgers in history, realizes how appalling the situation is. Knowing that the amount of advertising touting a product does not necessarily insure quality should give rise to a healthy skepticism that, along with this dissertation on equipment, will guide even once-a-month cooks to make wise decisions when purchasing equipment.

Can the type of equipment you use make you a better cook? Yes, provided you handle it properly. What good equipment can do is reduce a cook's margin of error. Your sauce is more likely to come out right when prepared in a heavy-gauge stainless-steel-lined saucepan. You are apt to be more efficient and less fatigued if you use a sharp high-carbon-steel knife rather than a stainless-steel one that is almost impossible to sharpen once it has lost its edge.

THE PROFESSIONAL CONNECTION

Peek into any professional kitchen and you will see knives that can be sharpened daily, heavy-gauge pots and pans that can be used in ovens or on range tops, stainless-steel bowls and wooden cutting boards rather than plastic ones, and convection ovens and gas-range burners. You will not see a single ticky-tacky gadget that looks like it was picked up at the check-out counter of the local supermarket.

That's because a professional chef has to rely on his equipment constantly. It must be the sturdiest (though not necessarily the fanciest) available. This way he can concentrate on being accurate and creative without having to worry about frequent equipment replacement.

It is with this steely eye that at-home cooks should survey their kitchen needs and make their decisions. That is not to say that a residential kitchen should be as finely tuned or as potentially impersonal as a restaurant, hotel or cafeteria kitchen. It simply means family cooks must think in terms of cost efficiency (spending money commensurate with the task fulfilled and only on equipment that lasts) and actual efficiency (selecting only equipment that does the job well).

What follows are lists of everything the well-equipped kitchen needs, plus a final section on items that can be added to these basics to satisfy certain cooking preferences, styles and idiosyncrasies. Hardly anyone will need to—or want to—own everything described here, unless he has an equipment fetish.

These recommendations are the result of years of equipment

usage, housewares-show attendance both as an exhibitor and observer, equipment testing and demonstrations, and of an experienced food consultant's common sense. When it comes to outfitting a kitchen, "glitzy" is not where it's at. Getting the job done (a) easily and efficiently, and (b) with quick, simple cleanup are the standards all equipment should meet before you spend your hard-earned cash on it.

PREPPING EQUIPMENT
For Preparing Foods to Be Cooked and/or Served

BLENDER, ELECTRIC See ELECTRIC BLENDER.

BUTCHER'S STEEL Also known simply as a steel. Good-quality steels are available individually and in some knife sets, but those in sets are often too short for efficient sharpening. Select one with a twelve-inch-long steel portion, as shorter ones are difficult to use on long-bladed knives. As a knife is used, the fine edge of the blade gets crinkled and bent out of shape. Though most crinkling is so fine it can only be seen through a microscope, it still hampers the

progress of a blade through foodstuffs. Drawing the blade across the steel straightens out the crimped edge, thereby sharpening the knife.

One proper technique for sharpening knives on a steel is as follows: if you are right-handed, hold the knife in your right hand and the steel in your left hand (left-handers do the opposite), with the steel out in front of you chest-high and horizontal. Starting from above the steel, draw the knife blade down in a firm, sweeping action along the steel so the blade is at about a twenty-degree angle to the steel. (A greater angle might actually dull the blade rather than sharpen it.) Bring the blade back above the steel and repeat the sweeping stroke along the back of

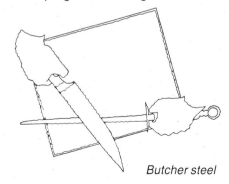

Butcher steel

the steel. This double stroke sharpens the blade from both sides. Repeat the cycle several times, or until the knife is the desired sharpness, always completing both strokes so as not to create a cock-eyed edge. Speed and agility will increase with practice.

CAN OPENER Forget the electric ones. They simply clutter the kitchen counter and wear out or break in a short time. Buy a good hand-operated model with a magnet for lifting and holding can lids.

CUTTING BOARD Wooden boards are best because they are the easiest on knives and do not melt when exposed to heat, a problem encountered with plastic ones. Seek one of sufficient size to make a practical work surface when set on a counter top. Or look for a butcher-block table or counter top when revamping your kitchen; thirty-six by thirty inches is a good size. A large cutting board, sometimes called a noodle board, can also be used as a pastry board; it is best to use one side for cutting, and the other for pastry and bread work. To clean any wooden board, simply wipe with a damp sponge or plastic pad, rinsing with cool water, if necessary, and then dry with a cloth. Use a wood preservative of 92 percent prorex oil and 8 percent paragon 128/30 wax (available in gourmet shops and hardware stores) to maintain the beauty and usability of all wooden kitchen equipment. Follow application directions on the package.

ELECTRIC BLENDER Do not select a blender for the number of buttons it has. Look for one with a metal rather than a plastic housing, as it will wear better and have greater stability. A blender and a food processor can coexist nicely in a kitchen. Use the blender principally for liquids, such as making frothy exotic drinks, and for purée-ing soft solids like bananas, strawberries and cooked vegetables. In contrast, the food processor performs slicing and chopping tasks admirably on solids like meat and raw vegetables.

ELECTRIC MIXER, HAND HELD
The quickest and most mobile way to stir and beat is with a hand-held, or portable, electric mixer. Cleanup is easy due to pop-out beaters, and arm fatigue is no problem because the machine is

lightweight. A portable mixer can be used in mixing bowls and in pots on the range. The proper technique is to move the mixer in a circular motion as you beat; this increases efficiency and speeds up the beating process. Some models are equipped with a dough hook, though this addition is not particularly useful since only small quantities of dough can be kneaded with a mixer of this size. The serious baker should consider a heavy-duty, freestanding electric mixer as well.

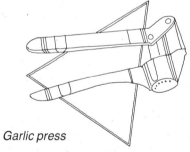

Garlic press

GARLIC PRESS A handy gadget that "presses" or "crushes" a peeled clove of garlic. It rices the clove, pushing its meat through little holes in a perforated face. The crushed garlic is then scraped

from the press face with a knife. The holes can be a bother to clean; keep a wooden pick handy. Or look for a self-cleaning garlic press, which can be found in some gourmet shops. Purists would say there is a difference between minced and crushed garlic, but for practical purposes you can substitute one for the other.

GRATER Many styles in a variety of materials are available, but in this item's case, the simplest design is still the best. Look for a paddle-shaped stainless-steel grater that is sturdy, easy to clean and so slim it can be stored in a drawer. Primary uses include shredding cheese and grating citrus rind.

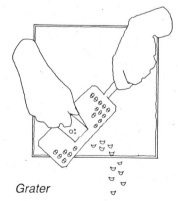

Grater

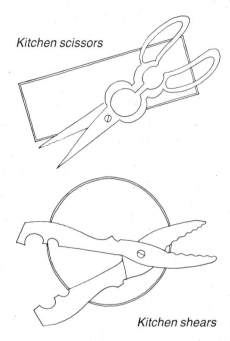

Kitchen scissors

Kitchen shears

KITCHEN SCISSORS AND SHEARS

Not a necessity, but kitchen scissors are quite handy for opening potato chip and pretzel bags, cutting twine and snipping parsley and other herbs. Wall-mounted models are particularly nice.

KNIVES

Four knives are needed: a nine- or ten-inch chef's knife for chopping, mincing and slicing; a paring knife for peeling and for small cutting jobs; a five- or six-inch utility knife to do any number of jobs where a larger, more-difficult-to handle knife simply isn't necessary; and a serrated knife for slicing bread, rolls, cake and buns. High-carbon-steel knives are best because they can be kept sharp with a butcher's steel (see entry for butcher's steel). Good knives are costly, but they are a wise investment because, if properly cared for, they will last for decades. Proper care includes always storing the knives on a rack or in a block, not in a drawer; washing and drying them promptly after use; and never placing them point down in a dish drainer.

MECHANICAL MEAT TENDERIZER

A rarely seen, but very effective item that tenderizes meat without having to resort to chemical-laden, sprinkle-on products. This invaluable aid to meat lovers tenderizes the less expensive cuts, giving them the qualities of pricier cuts, plus it reduces cooking time and minimizes shrinkage. The tenderizer is not a gadget, but a sturdy, well-designed piece of equipment with forty-eight needle-like blades that puncture the long striated muscles that make meat tough. To order, see Mail-Order Sources.

Mechanical meat tenderizer

MIXING BOWLS

Stainless-steel bowls are best because they are lightweight, unbreakable and will not pick up odors from pungent foods as plastic ones will. Another advantage is that they conduct heat and cold. They can, for example, be used to melt butter in the oven or on the range top, or to whip cream, which should always be done in a chilled bowl for best results. (A chilled stainless-steel bowl will remain cold throughout the whipping process.) Consider a "nest" of bowls, ranging in size from two cups to two quarts.

PEPPER MILL True pepper flavor is released when pepper is ground, and that flavor wanes as time goes by. So for full pepper flavor, use a pepper mill for recipes and at the table. Select a mill of wood or metal with adjustable grind and a metal rather than plastic grinding mechanism. This is simple to spot: just pick up the mill and look at the mechanism on its underside.

RUBBER SPATULA Also known as a rubber scraper. Two types are needed: one standard size for removing all of a foodstuff from a bowl or pan, and one slender version (known as a bottle scraper) for reaching into narrow bottles and other similar containers. Rubber spatulas are also used for folding ingredients together (see Cooking Terms and Techniques section). An institutional-size spatula (seventeen inches) is a good tool for any cook who likes to bake or to make dishes that require large quantities of beaten egg whites to be incorporated with other ingredients. Be careful, as most rubber spatulas are not heat resistant.

SCISSORS AND SHEARS. See KITCHEN SCISSORS AND SHEARS.

TRUSSING TOOLS Long trussing needles are available for use with kitchen twine or heavy string, but are not mandatory for trussing chicken and other fowl. In the technique described in Chapter 2, bamboo picks and string are used.

VEGETABLE PEELER The old-fashioned swivel-blade peeler, often called a potato peeler, is still the best. It removes thin strips of peel, a task even experienced cooks have difficulty duplicating with a paring knife. This is the item to use when making lemon and orange zests for recipes or drinks. Simply draw the blade across the fruit, shearing off only the colored portion of the rind. Twist or chop this strip to release the essence, the aromatic citrus oil. The white pith beneath the color is bitter, and generally not used in cooking except in a highly sugared state.

WIRE WHISKS Indispensable for beating small to medium quantities and for incorporating ingredients quickly. Each kitchen should have at least two, one about twelve inches long, and a six-inch one for small jobs like beating one egg or stirring melted chocolate. There is also a balloon whisk, a large, bulbous tool, for whipping air into substances such as whipping cream.

WOODEN SPOONS Despite all the technology of the plastics industry, wooden spoons are still the best for hand stirring and beating. They can be exposed to heat (some plastics cannot), are easy to clean and, like men, age gracefully.

MEASURING EQUIPMENT
For Measuring Ingredients and Foodstuffs

DRY MEASURING CUPS Available in metal and plastic; copper ones are an extravagance and strictly for "show." The usual sizes in a set are 1/4 cup, 1/3 cup, 1/2 cup and 1 cup. Laugh as you may at the in-home Tupperware parties, but they are the source of the handiest measuring-cup set ever designed: it includes all of the standard sizes, plus 2/3-cup and 3/4-cup measures. And they nest for easy storage.

LIQUID MEASURING CUPS
Available in glass and plastic.
They come in a standard cup
shape, and in the new 2-cup
beaker shape in high-impact plastic, which has a particularly good
pouring spout. A good assortment
includes 1-cup, 2-cup and 4-cup
measures, all sold separately. The
larger sizes can double as mixing
bowls.

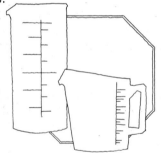

Measuring cups

MEASURING SPOONS Stainless-
steel spoons with an oblong shape
are best because they are heat resistant and will fit into narrow
spice containers. When selecting
measuring spoons, try out the 1
teaspoon measure on a spice-
rack bottle; if it doesn't fit, look for
a different set of spoons. A standard set includes five spoons: 1/8
teaspoon, 1/4 teaspoon, 1/2 teaspoon, 1 teaspoon and 1 tablespoon. Some sets also have the

handy 1/2-tablespoon measure
(1-1/2 teaspoons).

RULER Twelve or eighteen inches
long, and preferably made of a
rigid material, such as wood or
metal. A ruler comes in handy for
measuring a number of things: the
size of a rolled pizza dough, the
thickness of a piece of fish or
meat, the diameter of a pan.

SCOOPS Keep metal scoops
(available at gourmet shops) in
flour and sugar canisters for filling
measuring cups and sifters. Otherwise, use a large spoon.

COOKING EQUIPMENT
A Good Beginning

Read the following information on
pots and pans and frypans, and
then select these basic sizes, with
their lids, to begin your cookware
collection. Add more items as they
are needed.
- 1-1/2-quart saucepan
- 3-quart saucepan
- 5-quart double-handled saucepan, usually called a dutch oven
- 8-inch frypan
- 10-inch frypan

Dutch oven

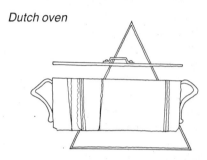

POTS AND PANS

Efficient, even-heating, easy-
cleanup cookware is a boon to
cooks on every skill level. To dis-
cuss all the pros and cons of the
myriad of cookware available
would fill a book. Instead, recommendations are in order.

A lot of nonsense can be found
on the cookware shelves of de-
partment stores and gourmet
shops, including:
- Plastic or wooden handles and
knobs that are heat resistant only
to certain temperature levels.
- The dreaded "hot-spot syndrome": uneven heating usually
due to thin pan materials.
- Fancy exteriors that require pol-
ishing to maintain their attractive-
ness. There is a world of better
things to do with your time than
polish copper.

• Interior finishes that are easily scratched by metal. Good for only two types of cooks: those who wish to prepare low-fat meals, and those fussy cooks in the mold of "Odd Couple" housefrau Felix Unger.

To cut through the nonsense, look for these types of cookware:

ANODIZED ALUMINUM Also called aluminum alloy. This cookware is made of heavy-gauge, but not heavy-weight, aluminum that has gone through an electrochemical process in manufacturing. The result is a smooth, sealed dark-gray surface that has many advantageous properties. The aluminum makes the pans good heat conductors. The surface, while not as nonstick as Silverstone, Teflon or T-Fal finishes, does possess certain nonstick qualities; at the same time it offers optimum sturdiness. No special utensils are needed, no seasoning is required and the surface will not discolor or pit (corrode) even when cooking acid foods, such as tomato- and vinegar-based sauces. Because this type of cookware is all-metal construction, saucepans can dou-

ble as oven casseroles. If you do casserole and oven cookery, purchase saucepans with two short handles rather than one long one that might not fit in your oven. Double-handled pans also store in less space and, in any size over three quarts, are easier to handle when hot and full. Calphalon, a popular anodized-aluminum product line, is handsome high-tech cookware well suited to a man or any no-nonsense cook.

ENAMELED CAST IRON
Honorable mention goes to enamel-coated cast-iron ware, which is a good heat conductor and easy to clean, but tends to chip if banged about a bit.

STAINLESS-STEEL-CLAD ALUMINUM This is costly (but by no means the *most* costly) cookware, well worth every cent for its heat efficiency and endurance. While some lines are imported from Europe at premium prices, the Master Chef line is American made and of excellent quality. This type of cookware has thick walls and is quite heavy when full, so it is not a wise selection for weak-armed cooks. A core of pure aluminum is sandwiched between an alumi-

num-alloy exterior and a highly polished stainless-steel cooking surface. The stainless interior will not chemically react with any foods, and the aluminum core makes for extremely efficient heat transfer. Iron handles are fastened to the pans with stainless-steel rivets. Under the All-Clad LTD name, this same cookware comes with an anodized-aluminum exterior surface for scratch resistance and easy cleanup.

FRYPANS

The frypan, also called a skillet, is a breed unto itself: in no other piece of cookware is a nonstick quality so important. While frypans that match your saucepans may make for an attractive appearance, a frypan should be purchased for its heavy gauge (thickness) and nonstick surface. The factor to consider when selecting a coated frypan is the pan under the coating; that is what will determine heat efficiency and evenness. But a pan with a manufacturer-applied coating is not the only choice, as the first recommendation illustrates.

CAST IRON Almost as old as the hills, cast iron, when properly seasoned, cannot be beat for frying. Never allow food to sit in the pan after cooking and never scrub a seasoned pan, even with the mildest of abrasives. Wash it in hot lightly soapy water using nothing harsher than a plastic pad, and then only on stubborn spots. Rinse in running water and place in a 300°F oven about 20 minutes to dry. Do not let water stand in the pan and do not towel-dry it. Any or all of these "do nots" can ruin the seasoning, which is the natural nonstick finish that builds up from cooked-on oil residues. If your grandmother is giving away her seasoned cast-iron skillet, you see one in a garage sale, or you find one, as I did, that was left behind by a previous tenant, run to it and make it your own. A cast-iron frypan is a treasure!

HEAVY-GAUGE ALUMINUM WITH SILVERSTONE LINING A marvelous frypan with excellent performance but inappropriate for careless cooks: one must be careful not to cut or scratch the Silverstone lining. A good selection for the cook who is meticulous about never letting metal come in con-tact with the pan surface during cooking, cleaning and storage. That means using wooden or plastic spoons and spatulas, not placing the pan in the dishwasher and never stacking pots and pans inside your Silverstone-coated frypan. (Ignore that television commercial showing nuts and bolts being stirred in this type of skillet. That's strictly hype.) Clean with a sponge or plastic pad in hot soapy water. Use a mild abrasive like Softscrub on stubborn spots. If possible, hang to store.

ADDITIONAL COOKING EQUIPMENT

BARBECUE GRILL Even though other cultures of the world practice the art of barbecuing, there is nothing quite so American and male as the love of cooking outdoors. Where once only charcoal grills were available, today we can select from charcoal, gas and electric models, in both portable and permanently installed versions. When shopping for a grill, take the following into consideration: How large is the cooking surface? The more people you cook for, the more room you will need. Is the grill versatile? Does it have a cover that allows use as an oven, as well as use in inclement weather? Is cleanup fast and easy, or will precious leisure time be wasted scrubbing the grill? Is the grill potentially costly to maintain? In the case of installed models, will money be spent on on-site repair calls?

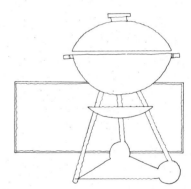

Barbecue grill

CASSEROLE DISHES Both shallow and deep casserole dishes, with and without lids, are used for baking casseroles, depending upon the recipe. Ovenproof pots from 1- to 5-quart sizes, like the anodized aluminum and stainless-steel-clad aluminum described earlier under Pots and Pans, make

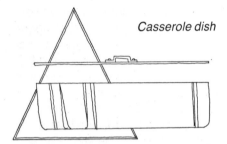

Casserole dish

excellent deep casseroles. Pyrex baking dishes, available in 1-1/2-, 2- and 2-1/2-quart sizes, make good and inexpensive shallow casseroles that can also double as baking dishes. Pyrostyrene, the white freezer-to-oven-to-table ware, is available in a variety of shallow and deep sizes.

COLANDER A bowl-shaped vessel with short legs and lots of holes, used for draining pasta and just about anything you wish to free of excess liquid. Look for a five-quart or larger size in stainless steel rather than plastic.

INSTANT-READ THERMOME-TER Also known as a microwave thermometer. This invaluable tool that lets you know the internal temperature of just about any cooked food was originally designed to measure the tempera-tures of meats cooked in a micro-wave oven. While testing meat and poultry temperatures is still its most frequent use, it can also be used for casseroles and reheated foods and for water for proofing yeast. Simply insert probe and watch needle for instant reading. To test thermometer's accuracy, plunge it in boiling water and look for 212°F reading.

JELLY-ROLL PAN Large, shallow (usually one inch deep) rectangu-lar pan that is, as the name im-plies, designed to bake jelly-roll cakes. Thank goodness it has more useful applications! It is the pan to use when making Cheese Nachos with Guacamole (page 143), Caroline's Homemade Crou-tons (page 101) or anything that requires a large surface and a slightly raised edge. It can be slipped under frozen dinners and similar items that would otherwise drip onto the oven floor. A jelly-roll pan topped with a V-shaped rack is good for roasting meats, as the pan's shallow sides allow heat to surround the roast and brown it more fully. Those same sides, however, do hamper cookie bak-ing. Look for heavy-gauge alumi-num or stainless steel to avoid buckling when exposed to high oven temperatures. Nonstick sur-faces are available but will require plastic or wooden utensils. Best sizes are fifteen by ten inches and eleven by seventeen inches.

LONG-HANDLED TONGS Long handles on metal tongs keep fin-gers away from heat when turning fried chicken and removing ears of corn from hot water and steaks from the broiler. Available in su-permarkets and housewares departments.

OVEN MITTS Have at least two and make sure they are thick but still pliable. A mitt that protects you from heat but doesn't give you flexibility is doing only half the job.

OVEN THERMOMETER Many a recipe has been ruined because the actual temperature of the oven did not match the temperature in-dicated by the dial setting. A verti-cal mercury thermometer in a stainless steel case is the most accurate and easy to read on the market. Place the thermometer in the oven and leave it there. Refer to it after preheating and before adding foods. If you find your oven off by 25 degrees or less, you can adjust your dial accordingly. If off by more, call your oven manufacturer, retail dealer or gas company for an adjustment.

PASTRY BRUSH Also known as a basting brush. Uses include brushing items to be baked with egg wash (a solution that produces a sheen), basting meats and poultry, applying barbecue sauce and brushing air-sensitive fruits like apples and avocados with lemon juice to retard browning. Natural bristles are preferable for their suppleness, but synthetic bristles retain their color and shape better. Having more than one brush is a good idea: use one for barbecue sauce, soy sauce and other dark liquids, another for butter and pastry tasks. Wash brushes by hand in hot soapy water, rinse in hot running water, squeeze out excess water and allow to air dry. If a brush has been used for applying beaten egg, rinse in cold water before washing. Never put a pastry brush in the dishwasher.

ROASTING PAN AND RACK Forget the old-fashioned high-sided roasters; they shield the lower portion of the roast from the searing heat. Select a shallow roasting pan of heavy metal and a roasting rack that will hold the roast up out of the pan drippings. Adjustable V-shaped racks are the most common, but are a little flimsy. A recently introduced stationary rack of heavy-gauge Teflon-coated steel has good stability in addition to its nonstick quality.

SIEVE Also known as a strainer. An item that comes in a myriad of sizes, from three inches on up. It can be used to drain canned goods, sift flour, strain apricot jam, purée soft foods, or strain used frying oil when lined with a coffee filter or paper towel. A sieve six inches in diameter is a good versatile size. When recipes call for an ingredient to be "drained, liquid reserved," be sure to place sieve over bowl to catch the liquid.

TIMER Many ranges have a timer built in; learn to operate it. Otherwise, small portable timers, including some you can wear on a string around your neck, are available at gourmet shops and hard-ware stores. Look for one with an easy to read face that does not require a lot of handling, as it could become very greasy and be difficult to clean. Each kitchen should have at least one timer.

TOASTER Look for one that is heavy enough to be stable on a counter top, and consider the number of people usually served at one time, since models come in 2- and 4-slice versions. Toaster ovens will toast bread and do small cooking tasks, like melting cheese on sandwiches and baking individual-serving pies.

UTENSIL SET Most frequently seen as the handle-matched set of utensils hanging on a bar-shaped holder, basic kitchen utensils can also be purchased individually. The items that belong in every kitchen include a ladle, pancake turner (also called a spatula), large spoon, large slotted spoon and a meat fork (also called a pot fork). Also try to include a long narrow spatula for spreading soft mixtures and leveling off measuring cups. Bypass pieces with plastic or wooden handles and opt for all stainless steel. Wood and heat-resistant plastic spoons and spatulas should be used exclusively in cookware lined with nonstick materials like Teflon, Silverstone and T-Fal.

BAKING EQUIPMENT

If baking becomes a passion, an assortment of baking pans will be necessary. Remember certain generalities when selecting bakeware: Metal is the best conductor of heat. Black steel bakeware will brown foods more than aluminum, sometimes too much unless heat is lowered. Bakeware is available with nonstick coatings like Silverstone, Teflon and T-Fal, but metal knives and spatulas cannot be used with these.

BAKING SHEET Also called a cookie sheet. A flat rectangular sheet with no sides used for baking cookies and other treats, as well as pizza. Preferable for pizza because the dough doesn't have to be rolled perfectly round to fit, the absence of pan sides makes for a crunchy crust, and the baked pizza can be easily slid onto a cutting board and quickly and neatly cut with a chef's knife, a simpler

technique than using a pizza cutting wheel.

COOLING RACK Square or rectangular metal-wire footed racks that elevate baked foods about 1/2 inch off counter top or table. This permits air to circulate around foods and cool them quickly. Used mainly for cookies and pastries. Typical size is 10-1/2 inches square; buy two.

JELLY-ROLL PAN Used for jelly-roll cakes and bar cookies. (See jelly-roll pan entry in Additional Cooking Equipment section for more uses.)

METAL LOAF PANS For yeast and quick breads. Standard sizes include 9 by 5, 8-1/2 by 4, and 7 by 3-1/2 inches. Buy loaf pans in pairs, since many recipes are for two loaves.

MUFFIN TINS For muffins and cupcakes; 2-3/4-inch wells with six wells per tin is standard. Smaller sizes are available, but are usually reserved for sweet-pastry baking.

PIE PLATE Available in metal and glass, with metal giving deeper browns and crispier bottoms. Glass pie plates are most readily available; you may want to reduce temperature settings slightly when using metal. Most common size called for in recipes is nine inch, but eight- and ten-inch plates are also available.

ROLLING PIN For rolling out pie dough, pizza dough and Ronnie Bull's Flour Tortillas (page 119). Select one with a straight rather than curved surface. Handles on ball bearings make for easy rolling. Don't skimp on size; look for an eighteen-inch pin.

ROUND CAKE PANS Available in a variety of sizes, with those eight and nine inches in diameter being the most popular. The best are heavy-gauge aluminum with perfectly straight sides. They result in the highest rise. When buying cake pans, remember that those that nest (fit into one another) do not have straight sides.

SIFTER For sifting flour and powdered sugar. Buy a triple sifter, which means the ingredients will pass through three screens. For-

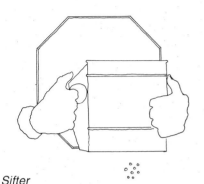

Sifter

get electric sifters; you can actually do it faster by hand. If a sifter isn't handy, push dry ingredients through a sieve with a spoon.

SPRING-FORM PAN The favorite pan for making cheesecake. Available sizes include eight-, nine- and ten-inch diameters, with nine inches being the most common. The pan is called a spring form because the sides spring away and can be lifted off from the completed cake.

SQUARE BAKING PAN Used for brownies, bar cookies and cakes. Eight- and nine-inch sizes are the most popular.

TUBE PAN A round, deep cake pan with a tube sticking up in the center of it. When the sides are straight, it's an angel-food cake pan; when the sides and bottom are fluted, it's a bundt pan. Ten to twelve-cup sizes are most readily available. Use to make Sticky Breakfast Bites, page 139.

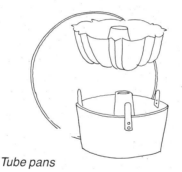

Tube pans

STORAGE AND CLEANUP EQUIPMENT

Intelligent food and equipment storage and easy cleanup are not incidental to a cook's talents. They are essential to good cooking habits. A kitchen stocked with the following items will have a heightened sense of organization and neatness, making it a more pleasant and productive place to work.

ALUMINUM FOIL Heavy-duty foil holds up the best for all uses, but is particularly necessary for lining broiler pans or barbecue grills for easy cleanup. Foil also comes in handy for heating and reheating certain items. Leftover biscuits, for example, can be wrapped in foil, stored in the refrigerator and then reheated in the foil in a 300°F oven for about five minutes.

CANISTERS For storing flour and sugar on a counter top or in a cupboard. There are many impractical designs on the market. The most important feature to look for is a wide mouth, so scoops and measuring cups can get in and out easily. If you cook Chinese food often, you might keep cornstarch in a third canister.

CLEANSER, KITCHEN The old-fashioned gritty kind has little use in the modern kitchen, but might come in handy on the outdoor grill. Many grill manufacturers, however, recommend not scouring the grill so that a natural seasoning will build up for nonstick cooking.

CLEANSER, MILD ABRASIVE A lightly abrasive liquid like Soft-scrub is an all-purpose cleanser ideal for cutting grease on pots, pans, bakeware, even glass items like casseroles and oven doors. It also works on broiler grids and pans; soak item in hot water about five minutes before scouring.

CROCK Look in gourmet shops for a fired-clay crock. Put it on the counter and fill it with spoons, tongs, rubber spatulas and all those utensils you need to grab at a moment's notice while cooking.

CUTLERY TRAY Some very nice high-tech ones are available. They keep the forks, spoons and knives that make up a place setting separated and easy to find.

DISHWASHING DETERGENT All of the brand-name ones are about the same in performance, so go for the best price. But don't count on generics to save you money; you'll need to use more and won't really save.

DRAWER DIVIDERS Available in hardware stores and housewares departments, these adjustable plastic dividers are fitted with self-sticking ends to hold firmly in place. An inexpensive way to turn that junk-drawer liability into an organized asset.

KNIFE BLOCK Proper storage of knives is essential to maintain their sharpness. Knives that are thrown into a drawer get nicked and crinkled blades, resulting in dullness. Look for a counter-top wooden block or a wall-mounted magnetic bar.

PAPER CLIPS It may sound strange, but this usually desk-bound item can be handy in the kitchen. Use paper clips to fasten closed half-finished bags of pretzels and potato chips.

PLASTIC BAGS Forget the zipper-closing style and stick with a twist-tie bag that you can mold to the shape of the stored item with your hands. Push out as much air as possible before fastening. To use bags for freezer storage of saucy ingredients, place open bag in glass measuring cup, fill to desired level, fasten with twist-tie, leaving some head space for expansion, and remove from cup. Place the bag in the freezer as is,

To freeze sauces, place plastic bag in glass measuring cup.

or place several on a baking sheet in the freezer until solid before removing sheet and stacking bags. Both sandwich size and 11-1/2- by 13-inch size are good to keep on hand.

PLASTIC CONTAINERS Made by a number of companies, they now come in a number of designs. The ones that "burp" out air when closing seem to have the best seal. Plastic containers, because they are reusable, save money in the long run because you will use less plastic wrap. Have a variety of sizes, including at least one small (one cup) container for storing small bits of leftovers like one scoop of mashed potatoes or a half cup of tuna salad.

PLASTIC WRAP All on the market claim to stick, but only the heavier ones do. Always wrap items snugly to lock out air, which draws moisture from foodstuffs and leaves them dry and shriveled. When topping a bowl, do not stretch the wrap over the top of the bowl, as the plastic wrap manufacturers have been showing us on packaging and television for the past three decades. This creates a pocket of air between food and the wrap that can dry out the foodstuff or nurture bacteria, depending upon conditions. Instead, place the plastic wrap right down against the food and press it up along the inside of the bowl to lock out air.

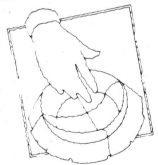

POT RACK A wall- or ceiling-mounted pot rack keeps pots and pans easily accessible and frees cupboard space for additional equipment and foodstuffs. Pot racks can also be positive decorating elements. Select a rack that looks attractive in your kitchen, fits in the space you have allotted, and has metal hooks that are movable and easy to use.

SCREW-TOP JARS Containers left over from peanut butter, mustard, mayonnaise, olives, jam, etc. are good for storage and as mini hand blenders for shaking up salad dressings and slurs (flour-water mixtures) for thickening sauces. Look for jars that need several turns of the lid to close (they seal out air the best) and have a rubber ring around the inside of the lid. Wash well in hot soapy water and drain until dry. If jar or lid retains any odors from original foodstuff, discard. This often happens with pickle and hot-pepper jars.

SCRUBBING PADS Metal is too harsh; plastic mesh cleans without scratching. Used with a mild abrasive, these pads are powerful grease busters.

SPICE RACK There are basically two kinds: racks that hold existing spice bottles and those that come with their own clear glass bottles. Wall-mounted styles free cupboard and counter space as well as make nice decorative touches. If you don't use up herbs quickly, look for a rack that shields bottles from light, which robs herbs of color and potency.

STACKER SHELVES Ingeniously simple and effective. Increase storage space in cupboards with footed shelves that create a second layer above the first. Available in different sizes to fit different needs at hardware stores and housewares departments.

SERVING EQUIPMENT

While this is not a book on dining etiquette, it does seem only right to continue equipment recommendations into the service area.

BASKETS Great for serving chips and munchies at parties. Always line with one or two paper napkins for style and to keep basket clean. Do the same for bread service.

CARVING SET If you carve for your guests, a carving set consisting of slicing knife and meat fork is a worthwhile purchase. If you carve in the kitchen, use a regular slicing knife and the fork from your utensil set.

CHEESE BOARD It could be the board you use for chopping in the kitchen: use one side for chopping, the other for serving cheese and crackers. Otherwise, there are some very handsome cheese boards in gourmet shops. Fruit, as long as it is well drained, can be served on boards, too. Remember to use wood preservative (page 168) on all wooden pieces to maintain their beauty.

CHOPSTICKS You'll want these if you prepare Asian food. The square-shaped bamboo ones are the easiest to use; next comes the round type, then the pointed Japanese variety. All are available in Oriental markets. Wash by hand and drain to dry.

DINNERWARE Plastic is tacky and doesn't wear well; china is expensive. Stoneware is your best bet. Select a basic design, preferably solid or banded, that can be mixed with serving pieces of other simple designs for an eclectic, yet pulled-together look. If you entertain, service for eight is not extravagant. If you live alone and rarely entertain, service for four is sufficient.

FLATWARE Buy a set with the same number of place settings as your dinnerware. Many stores are now carrying a style called "picnic" flatware, sold by the piece so you can buy just what you want. This attractive flatware has a masculine look due to rivets in the handles.

MEAT BOARD It really is the only way to carve meat at the table. Knives can't hurt the wood and the trough catches juices that can be spooned over servings. Use for beef, pork and poultry roasts.

PLATTERS Even for infrequent entertaining, a couple of platters are necessary. They come in handy for serving fruit, hors d'oeuvres, pasta, not to mention how beautiful a platter presentation can be at the table even with only simple garnishes like parsley sprigs, lemon wedges or small bunches of grapes. Available in glass, stainless steel, ceramic and, for an extravagant touch, silver.

SALAD TOSSERS While a salad can be tossed in any large bowl with two wooden spoons or a tablespoon and fork, it is nice to have long-handled tossers specially for the purpose. They are available in wood and in stainless steel, and are often part of a set that includes an attractive bowl.

SERVING BOWLS One or two large bowls to match or contrast with the dinnerware are enough to start.

WINEGLASSES What suave host would be without stemmed wineglasses? Purchase several eight-to ten-ounce red-wine glasses in the basic tulip shape and you can serve just about anything in them—orange juice, milk, mixed drinks, even wine!

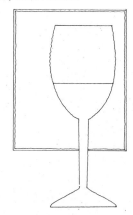

ADDING FOR STYLE

These are just some of the many items that can be added to the basic kitchen. They are not necessary, but are nice to have to satisfy the requirements of a particular cooking style.

BAKING STONE For cooks who like to bake pizza and bread. This stone, also called a pizza stone, is usually round or rectangular, but is sometimes found in tile form. Pizza and bread baked on it will have firm, crunchy bottom crusts. While directions advise putting foods directly on the stone, you can get good results by baking the product in a metal pan set directly on the stone. You'll never have a soggy bottom!

COFFEE MAKER For the avid coffee drinker. Electric coffee makers have come a long way since the plug-in percolator. Now some coffee machines not only make coffee, but also have clocks built in. Since coffee is an extremely personal beverage, with preference depending upon method of brewing (drip, percolate, instant, espresso), each coffee aficionado already has a favorite cup of coffee, whether it's served at some grand restaurant or the corner greasy spoon. Find out what method of brewing that establishment uses and survey gourmet shops and coffee shops before buying your coffee-making equipment.

CONVECTION OVEN For cooks who love to roast and broil meats and poultry. Convection ovens can be installed or counter-top models. If you are building a house or remodeling a kitchen, look into installing a convection oven. It cooks foods with circulating hot air, cutting cooking time 30 to 40 percent and maintaining natural juices. While baking and braising can also be done in a convection oven, its true strength is in its juicy roasting and delicate broiling. Gas- or electric-powered models are available.

DEEP-FAT FRYER For cooks who do a lot of deep frying and want all of the specially designed gadgetry. A deep-fat thermometer for checking oil temperature is also nice if you want to forgo the simple bread-chunk test. See Chapter 2 for more information on deep frying.

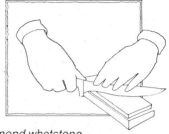

Diamond whetstone

DIAMOND WHETSTONE For cooks who take the investment in their knives seriously. This 8- by 2-5/8-inch knife-sharpening "stone" is actually made of plastic and perforated steel coated with diamond particles. It will quickly and easily give a keen edge to blades dulled by kitchen use. No oil is needed as with old-fashioned sharpening stones; simply sprinkle with a few drops of water. Use about once a month on frequently used knives. Available in hardware stores and gourmet shops.

ELECTRIC MIXER, HEAVY DUTY For cooks who love to bake and make desserts. Heavy-duty mixers are in the $200 to $300 price range and usually include a dough-hook attachment for kneading yeast doughs by machine instead of by hand. The wire-whisk attachment beats egg whites and whipping cream beautifully and in large quantities, if desired. Patterned after institutional mixers, their efficiency is much greater than standard counter-top mixers.

FISH POACHER For cooks who want to poach or steam whole fish. This long, narrow, deep pot, specially shaped for cooking fish, fits over two range-top burners. It has a perforated rack to hold the fish during cooking that can be easily lifted for removing the cooked fish. Poachers are usually stainless steel and costly, but worth it to a fish devotee.

FOOD MILL For cooks who like to get the seeds out of foods. A blender or food processor will purée foods, but only the simple food mill will purée *and* remove

Food mill

the seeds or other impurities. Depending upon the blade used, a food mill can leave some texture in foods that is often eradicated in a blender or processor. The food mill is excellent for making jelly, ice cream, and purées of vegetables to be used as side dishes or thickening agents.

FOOD PROCESSOR The exotica of the 1970s has evolved into the *objet de rigueur* of the 1980s. The food processor can save a cook innumerable hours of preparation but is best understood and utilized by someone who understands how to slice, chop, mince, etc. by hand. This versatile machine slices and shreds vegetables, chops meats and nuts, slices meats and fruits, shreds cheese, minces garlic, makes peanut butter, pastry and yeast doughs. Some models even make soft bread crumbs and mince fresh herbs. Food processors can also make blended drinks, but not with as foamy a result as a blender, which isn't necessarily bad. In day-to-day cooking, the processor shows its greatest strength in dealing with solid foods like onions, carrots, nuts, etc.

With so many models on the market, a food processor is not an easy product for which to shop. Look for a direct drive motor and a model that can expand its versatility with attachments like a pasta maker. Size will depend upon the number of people in your family and the nature of your cooking. If you entertain a great deal or bake processor breads frequently, a large-capacity model that can chop 3 pounds of meat and make up to 5 pounds of bread dough at a time is worthwhile. For the small family or the infrequent entertainer, a smaller model will do nicely; they are available in two meat-chopping capacities: 3/4 pound and 1-1/4 pound. Make sure to see at least one demonstration of the machine before buying so you can ask questions and make the best selection.

In the recipes that follow, it should be understood that simple tasks like mincing garlic, chopping onions and slicing zucchini can be done in a food processor even though recipes may not so stipulate. The real benefit of a processor is tested by analyzing how it fits into an already-existing cooking style. A cook should not feel compelled to change his style upon purchasing a food processor. He should simply ask "How can this help me?" Expanded processor use will follow naturally.

GRIDDLE For cooks who love to prepare breakfast. Electric counter-top models are available, as are round and rectangular griddles that fit on range-top burners. Nonstick surfaces are often found on griddles, which make them especially easy to use.

ICE CREAM MAKER For the ice-cream fiend and those who taste commercially made ice cream and say "This isn't as good as it used to be." Models range broadly in price from those under $50 utilizing table salt and ice cubes, to those over $400 that make ice cream and sorbets (sherbets) without salt and ice cubes. These models are trim, compact and make a great adult toy for anyone who loves to cook and to eat ice cream.

INDOOR ELECTRIC GRILL For indoor cooking that tastes like the outdoors. Compact counter-top models are available in grill and rotisserie styles and are especially appealing to apartment dwellers

who like grilled foods but have no backyard.

MICROWAVE OVEN For cooks whose main consideration is speed. Portable and built-in models are available. Glass or other non-metallic cookware must be used in microwave ovens; several lines of plastic cookware designed specially for microwave use are presently on the market. The fastest method of cooking available, microwaves are most popular for cooking bacon and vegetables, defrosting frozen foods and reheating already cooked foods. These ovens do not do a satisfactory job of cooking meats and poultry.

MORTAR AND PESTLE For cooks who enjoy using herbs and spices. Similar to the pharmacy mortar

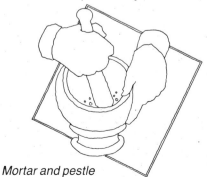

Mortar and pestle

and pestle, culinary versions are usually made of marble or ceramic, with the former preferred. They are used to crush and blend spices, and make a very attractive kitchen accessory as well.

OYSTER KNIFE For cooks who like to eat oysters on the half shell and to use freshly opened ones in recipes. Oysters cannot efficiently be opened with just any knife. The best oyster knife available has a short stainless-steel blade that is slightly curved and rises at the tip. The handle should be rubberized.

PASTA MACHINE For cooks who love to make pasta. There are machines that roll out and cut the pasta dough into various shapes, and there are machines that mix up the dough and extrude it into various shapes. Needless to say, the latter has the higher price tag. Cooks with food processors should check to see if their unit will accommodate a pasta-making attachment.

SALAD SPINNER For cooks who make salads regularly. A plastic basket that fits inside a plastic housing with a lid that spins the basket, forcing water from the greens inside. The only other way to get greens this dry is to blot them with paper towels, which uses far too many towels to be practical.

WOK For cooks who love to prepare Chinese and other Asian cuisines. The wok is most frequently used to stir fry, but is also good for deep frying and steaming. The best woks at the best prices are available in Oriental markets. Traditionally they are made of steel and are round bottomed, and must be seasoned before using. A good retailer will give you directions on how to properly season your wok, or may even offer to do it for a minimal fee. You will also need a lid, the ring that fits over your gas burner and holds the wok erect, and a long-handled spatula especially designed for stir frying. Add a perforated metal rack or bamboo stacking steamer for steaming and a Chinese-style skimmer for deep frying to complete this item's versatility. (There are also flat-bottomed woks designed for use on electric ranges, though a round-bottomed one will work on a very efficient electric stove.) Never buy an electric wok; if you get one as a present, take it back. The thermo-

static control prevents the pan from maintaining a constant high heat, the essence of stir frying. For proper care of your wok, see Chapter 1.

SCALE For cooks who like to bake and those who use European cookbooks where ingredient quantities are often listed by weight. Look for a wall-mounted model with increments in ounces and grams. Scales also come in handy when multiplying and dividing recipes.

STEAMER For cooks who opt for low-fat cooking. An inexpensive, collapsible steaming basket can turn any deep saucepan or dutch oven into a steamer. More sophisticated steaming sets include a pot, steaming basket and tight-fitting lid. Look for one in stainless steel.

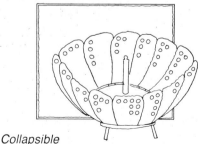

Collapsible steaming basket

KITCHEN STAPLES

A well-equipped kitchen must also be well stocked to be effective. Staples are those foods that make up the basic stockpile of cooking ingredients to which a continuing supply of fresh produce, meats and dairy products are added.

Because staples are the backbone of a kitchen, they will vary from one household to the next with the cook's style. These recommendations are designed (1) to make sure there is always a meal in the kitchen ready to be prepared in short order, and (2) to help execute the recipes that follow.

IN THE CUPBOARD

Aromatic bitters
Barbecue sauce
Breakfast cereal of choice
Catsup*
Cornstarch
Crackers (preferably with unsalted tops)
Croutons
Dijon-style mustard*
Dry vermouth
Flour
Garlic

Herbs and spices: basil, bay leaves, cayenne pepper, chili powder (preferably unadulterated), dry mustard, peppercorns (black and white), pickling spice, red pepper flakes, rosemary, tarragon, white pepper powder**
Olive oil
Onions
Pasta (dry), in your favorite shapes
Pork and beans
Potatoes
Red wine or sherry vinegar
Rice
Salt (preferably kosher)
Soy sauce
Spaghetti sauce (prepared, in jar)
Steak sauce*
Sugar
Tuna (preferably water packed)
Vegetable oil
White vinegar (distilled)
Worcestershire sauce
Yellow mustard*

IN THE REFRIGERATOR

Butter (preferably unsalted)
Cheese of your choice (for snacking)
Chicken and beef bases***
Eggs
Lemons
Lettuce (iceberg or Romaine)****
Milk or half-and-half cream
Oranges (in season)
Parsley****
Parmesan cheese
Tomatoes (in season)

IN THE FREEZER

Chicken breasts (individually wrapped)
Bread dough (purchased frozen)
Vegetable of choice (purchased frozen)
Hamburger patties (individually wrapped)
Raw nuts of choice
Steaks (individually wrapped)

*Store in the refrigerator once opened. For fullest flavor, bring to room temperature before using.

**Available in Oriental markets, a *very finely* ground white pepper. To order by mail, see Oriental Food Market listing in Mail-Order Sources.

***Available in pint-size tubs, Minor's brand beef and chicken bases (and other flavors) can be found in the refrigerator section of selected gourmet shops. These products are superior to bouillon cubes because they are lower in salt and have full flavor.

****See Handling Fresh Fruits and Vegetables.

THE WELL-DRESSED COOK

There is a special way to wear your apron that not only makes you look serious about cooking, but will also help you *be* a serious cook.

Select a bib apron (one with a top) that has clean, simple lines. The "skirt" should be broad enough to wrap at least part way around your hips, and the apron strings long enough to reach around your waist and be tied in front.

Once the apron is in place, slide a kitchen towel onto the apron string on your left side if you are right-handed, and on the opposite side if you are left-handed. This way a towel is always handy for wiping your hands, for using as a pot holder or for cushioning a surface from the heat of a pot.

MAIL-ORDER SOURCES

CHOCOLATE

MADAME CHOCOLATE
Dept. M
1940–C Lehigh Avenue
Glenview, IL 60025
Write for free catalog; includes a variety of chocolates, cocoas and candy-making supplies.

COOKING EQUIPMENT

THE CHEF'S CATALOG
Dept. M
3915 Commercial Avenue
Northbrook, IL 60062
(312) 480–9400
Professional-style cooking equipment for the home chef. To get one year of catalogs (five issues), send $1 with name and address.

STEAKS

PRIME TIME BEEF, INC.
Johnson Fine Meats and Foods
241–D Burlington Road
Write for free brochure, including price list.

ORIENTAL FOODSTUFFS

ORIENTAL FOOD MARKET
Dept CK
2801 West Howard Street
Chicago, IL 60645
(312) 274–2826
Dried and canned vegetables, sauces, seasonings, spices and other specialty foods of Asia are available by mail. Chicken and beef bases are available during cold weather months. Write for a free price list.

MECHANICAL MEAT TENDERIZER

MALE ORDER KITCHEN
RMSI/Suite 330
222 West Ontario
Chicago IL 60610
Send name and address for free brochure and order form.

INDEX

CAROLINE KRIZ

Caroline Kriz is a food consultant, food stylist, and writer who is equally at home in her kitchen, behind her typewriter, and in front of a radio or TV microphone. Since graduating in home economics from Purdue University and earning her master's degree in journalism from Northwestern University, Caroline has been a food editor for *The Chicago American*, an editor for *Sphere* magazine, director of home economics for Sphere Marketing Services, and a contributing editor to *Cuisine* magazine, as well as a restaurant columnist for the Lerner Newspapers. She has also studied in Paris at La-Varenne Ecole de Cuisine and in the south of France with Simone Beck.

Kriz's work on *Cooking for Men Only* began in 1977 when she originated classes with that name and allowed only men to attend. She has also hosted her own weekly radio show in Chicago, known as "Caroline's Kitchen," of which one media observer commented: "Caroline brings her brand of commonsense consumer-oriented food features to the public with pride and panache." She frequently appears as a guest on Chicago TV talk shows and serves as a judge for cooking contests. Her first cookbook, *Convection Cookery*, was published in 1980.

VERONICA DI ROSA

A graduate of Vancouver School of Art, Veronica di Rosa later opened Canada's first kitchen shop. After coming to California's Napa Valley, where she now resides, she produced three unusual single-recipe books—*Chocolate Decadence*, *Sinful Strawberries* and *Virtuous Vanilla*—with chef Janice Feuer. She has also illustrated three other 101 cookbooks: *Sweets for Saints and Sinners*, *Flavors of Mexico* and *Entertaining in the Light Style*. Her paintings have been exhibited in a number of one-woman shows in the United States and Canada.